PARTNERSHIPS THE NONPROFIT WAY

PHILANTHROPIC AND NONPROFIT STUDIES

Dwight F. Burlingame and David C. Hammack, *Editors*

STUART C. MENDEL and **JEFFREY L. BRUDNEY**

PARTNERSHIPS
THE NONPROFIT WAY

What Matters, What Doesn't

Indiana University Press

This book is a publication of

Indiana University Press
Office of Scholarly Publishing
Herman B Wells Library 350
1320 East 10th Street
Bloomington, Indiana 47405 USA

iupress.indiana.edu

Library of Congress Cataloging-in-Publication Data

Names: Mendel, Stuart C., author. | Brudney, Jeffrey L., author.
Title: Partnerships the nonprofit way : what matters, what doesn't / Stuart
    C. Mendel and Jeffrey L. Brudney.
Description: Bloomington and Indianapolis : Indiana University Press, [2018]
    | Series: Philanthropic and nonprofit studies | Includes index.
Identifiers: LCCN 2017029272 | ISBN 9780253025654 (cl : alk. paper)
Subjects: LCSH: Nonprofit organizations—Management. | Partnership.
Classification: LCC HD62.6 .M46 2018 | DDC 658/.048—dc23 LC record available at
    https://lccn.loc.gov/2017029272

1 2 3 4 5   23 22 21 20 19 18

Contents

Contents

Acknowledgments

WHEN WE STARTED this project in the early 2010s, we held the view that the scholarship on partnership involving nonprofit organizations was extensive. Many research articles, monographs, and edited volumes existed. It seemed that any addition to the discourse would require an innovative approach to the material on partnership that spoke to and for nonprofit actors and would have to utilize as large a sampling of organizations as we might reasonably manage within the limits of time and funding available to us.

We then waded into the intellectual thicket of partnership, collaboration, and cross-sector interactions. We observed that much of the scholarly inquiry appeared as derivative theory—theory drawn from theory—grounded by small sample sizes of case studies illustrating the theoretical principles. We quickly determined that any innovation of partnership research would draw upon our experiences in providing advice, mentorship, and shared learning with nonprofit executives and board leaders gleaned through funded and volunteer engagements with the local community.

The inspiration for the book—and the subsequent design of the research, data collection methods, findings, analysis, narrative structure, and conclusions—were all driven by the questions and challenges posed to us by nonprofit executives seeking answers to real problems in the practice of nonprofit management, leadership, and governance. Our effort to answer these questions shaped four contributions this book makes to the field, which we describe in the Introduction and in the topics and structure of the following book chapters. The payoff for these stakeholders from our work can be found throughout this volume, but particularly in the nonprofit partnership principles and theory described in final chapter of this book.

A second important driver for the innovation of partnership research was the institutional imprimatur of Cleveland State University—not to mention funding to support the field research—granted by the dean of the Maxine Goodman Levin College of Urban Affairs at the time, Edward (Ned) W. Hill. We gratefully acknowledge Dean Hill's encouragement to follow our curiosity and desire to turn the community engagement, education, and applied research work we perform and for which our institution is well known into "thought leadership" for the field of nonprofit sector studies.

Among our closest collaborators in performing the labors of this book are the truly outstanding graduate assistants who performed the heavy labor and seamlessly handed off the work of project support over four academic seasons. These determined and able graduate assistants included Erin (Carek) Vokes, Julie Quinn, Anna K. Jones, Heather Lenz, Cynthia (Biro) Connolly, and Rachael Balanson. We also thank Allison M. Campbell for her good work and contributions to this book project in researching various side themes and in helping to produce charts and graphs, and in the follow up, to thank many of the named and unnamed contributors to the work.

Much appreciation to Alyse (Lapish) Neville, Stephanie Allen, Emily Hoban, Courtney Matthews, Michael R. Elliott Jr., and Amy Hatem and other students of our graduate courses UST 550 Fundamentals of Nonprofit Administration & Leadership and UST 656 Advanced Topics in Nonprofit Management Practice from 2012 to 2014, who conducted interviews, verified data, and served to comment on many of the ideas and conclusions of the authors.

We acknowledge Dr. Jung Eun Kim, who at the time was completing her doctorate from the Jack, Joseph and Morton Mandel School of Applied Social Sciences, Case Western Reserve University, for the early developmental research design work; and Dr. Jennifer R. Madden, assistant professor of management and marketing, Carthage College, for her work advising us in data coding design and for confirmation of our trend analysis in her field of expertise.

We also acknowledge staff of the Levin College and Cleveland State University who aided various aspects of this book and with field interviews. Many thanks to Kathyrn Hexter, Rachel Singer, Molly Schnoke, Melanie (Furey) Baur, Matt Starkey, and Jane McCrone.

A challenge in drafting our acknowledgments involves the nonprofit executives and leaders who contributed their time and cases to our endeavor. A condition of our data gathering to ensure confidentiality was that we would not attribute quotes to named individuals or identify participants in any way. This promise was made to encourage nonprofit executives to offer their most candid views while limiting the potential for pushback from their partners or third-party stakeholders.

Despite the promise and opportunity for anonymity, we did gain permission to acknowledge many of those among the study participants who explicitly responded to our post-survey request to be recognized in this book. Our thanks and appreciation to William Beckenbach, Daniel Blain, Lisa Bottoms, Patricia Groble, PhD, Merle Gordon, Alan D. Gross, Sarah Hackenbracht, Bernard P. Henri, PhD, Stephanie Hiedemann, Deborah Hoover, Bob Jaquay, Linda Johanek, Greg Johnson, Major Lurlene Johnson, Kathryn Kazol, Bernadette M. Kerrigan, LISW, SPHR, Ray Leach, Bill Leamon, Joseph A. Marinucci, Mark McDermott, Rev. Dr. Brian Moore, Stephanie Morrison-Hrbek, Molly Neider, Patricia W. Nobili, MSSA, Stacey O'Brien, Bobbi Reichtell, Carol Rivchun, Jill Rizika, Myron Robinson, Chris Ronayne, Natalie Ronayne, Jared Schnall, Thomas

B. Schorgl, Sandra R. Schwartz, Charles See, Judy Simpson, Ken Slenkovich, Ron Soeder, Tony Thomas, LISW-S, ACSW, John Visnauskas, Lorry Wagner, PhD, Kristin Warzocha, Eva Weisman, Steve Wertheim, Brad Whitehead, Elaine Woloshyn, Deb Yandala, and Denise Zeman.

We express our gratitude to Gary Dunham, director of Indiana University Press, and the helpful suggestions offered by Dwight Burlingame and David Hammack during the proposal stages of the manuscript. Their suggestions guided several important aspects of our writing, particularly in the chapter on partnership subsectors. Much appreciation to the blind reviewers for their help-ful suggestions that shaped the final tone of the book and to Alex C. Nielsen for his work editing and revising the narrative to increase reader accessibility. We also extend our appreciation to Jon Vokes for improving the design of the tables and diagrams throughout.

A Note on Quoted Material

Along with the recognition of people, a final note is made to attend to a challenge of the research methods we wish to acknowledge in the front matter of this book. The issue involves the quotes that appear throughout, drawn from nonprofit executive comments and responses to our interview questions. Frequently, respondents answered questions imprecisely, abruptly with little elaboration, expansively with supra-elaborations, or embedded their answers to some questions within their answers to other questions. Transcribing the exact phrasing without edits was not practical for our data collection or citation in the text of our manuscript. Consequently, our use of quotes in the final manuscript required paraphrasing in many instances and was performed as a best-faith effort to preserve the spirit or intent of the speaker.

PARTNERSHIPS THE NONPROFIT WAY

Introduction: Why This Book?

From our perspective, partners must have complementary missions, seek mutual gains, and engage in a willingness to enhance the effectiveness and reach of their programs. This condition is not usually the case with our friends in government.

   —Executive of a nonprofit social services organization devoted to community re-entry.

Overview

In this chapter, we introduce and consider the term "nonprofit-first" in some detail. This term describes an approach centered on the nonprofit sector's nature, role, and institutions. We explain how the nonprofit-first approach is crucial to our study of partnership. We show how this perspective is valuable for both students and current nonprofit actors and provide an outline of future chapters.

Making the Case for Nonprofit-First Partnerships

Collaboration and partnership are well-known characteristics of the nonprofit sector. They can occur for a variety of reasons and may take many forms.[1] They can also be an important tool of public policy and for creating public value. Particularly in cities, collaborations and partnerships involving nonprofit organizations are frequently used to implement public policy through program planning and assessment, managing public sector initiatives, and solving problems in the community.[2] Nonprofits are also the central facilitating agents in many public-private partnerships, where accomplishing large-scale endeavors often requires the financial resources and imprimatur of government and business.[3]

   For more than a decade, scholars have examined collaborations that involve at least one nonprofit organization.[4] Much of the scholarly inquiry on partnership arrangements over the past thirty years examines the ways in which public managers and sometimes private sector businesses administer public-private contracts involving large sums of money with nonprofit health and human service providers.[5] This trend increased with 1990s changes in federal policy to delegate human services work products to nonprofit organizations.[6] As these processes unfolded, public managers had to adapt to new priorities and procurement practices, which created an urgent demand for public managers to learn more about the nonprofits with which they interact. Four well-scrutinized areas include crafting requests for proposals so that funds and services might be amplified or "leveraged" to the greatest degree possible, insuring best practices for public oversight of these government-nonprofit contractual arrangements, devising evaluative measures for the quality of vendor performance, and maintaining fiscal accountability in the use of tax dollars.[7]

Public managers' growing need for knowledge in this domain has drawn attention from scholars of public administration, public management, and public policy. Unfortunately for practitioners and researchers concerned about best practices leading to a vibrant and resilient nonprofit sector, much of this scholarship examines the relationships between government and nonprofit organizations, and thus focuses mainly on the role of government as an authority in the relationship.[8] Other scholarship uses adaptive business principles and increases to market share as the lens through which to examine business-nonprofit partnership.[9] Considerably less attention has been devoted to collaboration and partnership from the perspective of nonprofit organizations involved in working relationships with government, business, or other nonprofits.

From the perspective of the nonprofit sector, the public management and private sector–focused scholarship tends to de-emphasize the important but typically subtle distinctions of collaboration and partnership drivers. Partnership is more characterized by the heightened role of a key executive (passion for collaboration and experience in recognition and reciprocity) and by the way that the nonprofit partner must often align its operational culture to its partner's. Because of these differences, models framed by theories of the public and private sectors often lack sufficient appreciation for the exigent circumstances of nonprofit partnerships. A more suitable model would recognize the importance of cultural alignments between the partnering organizations and the way that a nonprofit partner must prioritize mission fulfillment. Similarly, an ideal model would acknowledge that "just-right balance" of organizational self-interests that tends to move collaboration or partnership to successful outcomes.[10] One nonprofit executive for a business development incubator organization expressed these sentiments quite succinctly: "Make sure that you have a clear understanding of the strengths and capabilities of the partnering organization. Build the program around the strengths and opportunities. Establish a commitment from the senior management from each partnering organization to make the partnership work, solve problems by intervening to iron out the problems that might arise from the partnership, and avoid miscommunications."

Ideally, all parties volunteer to enter nonprofit collaboration and partnership arrangements without third-party prompting.[11] This type of arrangement is often made for the organizations' own purposes and may increase program and operation efficiency, maximize cost savings and economies of scale, and adapt to market changes or to approach similar organizational missions. The nonprofit executive director of a health-care organization that merged five regional affiliates with independent boards of directors explained,

> The overall partnership rated an 8 out of 10 because the partnership met most of its goals but not all of them. The best part of the partnership was that five emotionally intelligent organizations each put the partnership mission before their personal agendas for the betterment of all the organizations. Everyone agreed that none of the organization participants would get stronger without some sort of collaboration and consolidation. The boards were all supportive and took the direction from the CEOs. The CEOs were driven, and the partnership thrived because of this. The partnership also minimized the differences in cultures of each organization, and this was a helpful part of creating a new system from partnership.

Although collaboration and partnership are common practices, many nonprofit leaders believe that the conditions are seldom ideal: more often, the conditions of a partnership or collaboration are far from perfect. Forced or rushed partnerships arise, for example, where policy makers, public managers, grant makers, and others require collaboration and partnership as application criteria for grants or for contract or project work. From the perspective of the nonprofit actor, the practice of mandated collaboration may appear to have more to do with political expedience or the funder's desire to model partnership than with the performance capacity of an applicant organization. For nonprofits weighing expected outcomes, benefits, and responsibilities in these required instances of partnership, the process can result in confusion, consternation, and worse. In such arrangements, nonprofit organizations may be disinclined to embrace their partners beyond the mechanistic, transactional, and arm's-length aspects of the relationship.[12] The nonprofit executive director of a large social services agency engaged in collaboration partnership, and merger explained, "We recommend that anyone should make careful consideration of who their partner might be. A good organization can be impacted by a bad partner. With this in mind, it is essential to take the time necessary to develop relationships with your partner on all levels of the organization. It is more important to the well-being and health of an organization than money. And, finally, to have a structure and plan in place to work under."

The View from the Field

In our experience interacting with hundreds of nonprofit executives through our scholarly research, contracted work, and community service over the past two decades, we observe that the more enduring points of tension raised by nonprofit executives engaged in collaboration and partnership are that the nonprofits charged with delivering services face the frequently uncompensated and difficult tasks of creating and managing them. These tensions are exacerbated in mandated partnerships. Nonprofit executives have also told us that best practice strategies for partnership projects often come from experience, rather than from scholarly writing or the classroom.[13] For example, one nonprofit leader in a central business district community development corporation shared, "As the project progressed, there was a steady improvement of perspective by each partner as we learned to trust each other.... Our organizations gained increased confidence."

Another nonprofit executive in a federated institution that provides resources to a network of autonomous agencies, sets policies for operations, and values fiscal transparency, noted, "There are inherent tensions in any partnership based on a natural condition where service providers want to provide more services while being asked for less in terms of compliance and administrative reporting by funders. An agency's desire to exercise independence creates tensions with those from which it seeks support."

We also understand from nonprofit leaders that policy makers, public managers, business executives, and philanthropic civic leaders often overlay their own views and expectations of collaboration in ways that add complexity, costs, and risks for the nonprofit participants. For many smaller nonprofits, this tendency by those holding the purse strings can have a chilling effect on their autonomy and capabilities. Repeatedly, the differences in perspective between the nonprofits and the other parties contribute to unfulfilled expectations, negative experiences, and increased barriers to forming lasting, resilient, and meaningful partnerships. Many times, these circumstances of partnership jeopardize not only the collaboration and its objectives, but also the vitality of the nonprofit organization itself. As the nonprofit executive director of an after-school youth program explained, "The primary factor that worked against our meeting the goals of the partnership was the timing of the public funds and the limited nature of government resources.... For example, [the] State of Ohio['s] need for consistency for all of the program sites they fund creates extra complications for us, such as getting licensure that is not legally required by law but by administrative practice."

Forming and sustaining partnerships that are important and meaningful to the nonprofit participants also hold special significance for nonprofit organization leaders. In the experiences reported to us by nonprofit executives, important and meaningful partnerships are desirable achievements that support the fulfillment of both organizations' missions. Meaningful partnerships are described as those which produce value resonating beyond the mechanistic transactions of a "contract-for-hire."[14] Nonprofit executives credited such partnerships as worth the hard work, risk, sacrifice, and commitment required of them—behind-the-scenes obligations that are often overlooked by public managers and grant makers, as well as many researchers. One nonprofit executive leading a local food bank noted, "The survival of our organization depends on collaboration, and thus it's important to cast individual egos aside ... to look for ways to partner or collaborate with like institutions that would be impacted by your goals and objectives."

Moreover, our experience indicates that the challenge to understand the best ways to create productive, valuable nonprofit partnership also presents a problem for educators offering theoretical knowledge and practical examples for students pursuing undergraduate, graduate, and advanced certificates in nonprofit studies, management, and leadership. Too often, academic pedagogy lacks the detailed learning that can instill among our students and graduates the preparation and applied methods necessary to craft durable, productive, and successful partnerships.[15] Even if some bias exists in self-attribution by our respondents, in our conversations with nonprofit leaders, we noted repeatedly that many senior nonprofit executives credited their own on-the-job experiential learning as the source of their success in collaboration, as opposed to their exposure to concepts presented in higher education coursework. The applied learning presented in this book can help to overcome this lacuna in the curriculum.[16]

The Principle of "Nonprofit-First" as a Catalyst for This Inquiry

Even a cursory perusal of the literature reveals scores, if not hundreds or even thousands of studies of collaboration, so why add one more? In short, why this book?

> We find that the difference between partnering with nonprofit, government, or business organizations is that nonprofits like us are usually a contractor of government funds and we do not see this as a "true" partnership with the government. This is due to our being at the mercy of the priorities of the government. Within the private sector, the relationship is very contractual. Most of our rewarding partnerships are with other nonprofits where we feel there is a level playing field.
>
> —Executive of a nonprofit organization devoted to technology transfer for small business development.

Our overview of the literature suggests that the nonprofit audience for the existing collaboration and partnership research literature is not served sufficiently well by the extant scholarship focused on contractual performance and accountability to public sector agents and business social entrepreneurship. We conceive our audience as primarily students, executives, volunteer practitioners, scholars, and organizations in the nonprofit sector. Given its adherents, the public management focus and guiding questions of much extant scholarship does little to inform nonprofit executives contemplating interorganizational cooperation, collaboration, networks, partnership, and even merger, who face a bewildering array of challenges, each with its own complexity. For nonprofit organizations and leaders, the options, advantages, and costs for decision makers are not always clear or obvious; key leaders may not readily recognize when the opportunity for a mutually beneficial partnership arises, or what can reasonably be expected from each partner.[17]

Nonprofits' challenges entering into collaboration or working to sustain a durable partnership are further complicated by the jumble of subtle, yet distinct labels attributed to the phenomenon by thought leaders, researchers, and practitioners in the public, private, and nonprofit sectors. Many examples of intricately parsed terminology are found in the writings on human services organizations, public administration and management, and business.[18] These terms further cloud nonprofit leaders' and organizations' understanding and conduct of meaningful partnership.

In conducting our primary research and analysis for this study, we seek to inform nonprofit practice concerning collaboration with other organizations. We collected rich case studies to inform our thinking about nonprofit partnerships. The foundation of our primary research for this book rests on fifty-two highly detailed, structured interviews of nonprofit organizations in which senior executives answered primarily open-ended and some closed-ended questions concerned with partnership relationships involving their organizations. A total of eighty-two cases recounted by these executives describing nonprofit-nonprofit, nonprofit-government, and nonprofit-business partnerships were collected and examined to inform the analysis, findings, and conclusions of this book. More specifically, we introduce a nonprofit-first perspective in great detail that is new to the literature.

Contributions of This Book to the Field of Scholarship and Practice

This book embraces a nonprofit-first philosophy and perspective, and our goal in writing it is to focus, shape, and refine theories and practices of collaboration and partnership where at least one member of the arrangement is a nonprofit organization. This goal emanates from our belief that too few nonprofit-first voices leaven the scholarship on collaboration and partnership involving nonprofit organizations. To our knowledge, the literature largely overlooks the nonprofit-first partnership paradigm in the context of a three-sector application of nonprofit, government, and business sector collaboration.

A nonprofit-first approach refers to research centered on the unique role and nature of the nonprofit sector and its institutions in American society. As this book demonstrates, nonprofit-first opens the way to pursuing research on under-studied aspects of nonprofit life. This perspective includes the importance of emotional intelligence for professionals who work regularly with volunteers, the role that nonprofits play as intermediaries and facilitators in public-private partnerships, and the challenges associated with public advocacy, to name just a few key points. This approach incorporates the professional conventions and behavioral nuances common to the nonprofit sector.[19]

Using a nonprofit-first framework for our research inquiry and data collection has oriented the findings and conclusions of this book for both researchers and practitioners in the nonprofit sector. We study the concept of nonprofits engaged in important partnerships, which are particular kinds of arrangements with distinctive qualities and characteristics, because our view is that scholars have done little to improve understanding of partnership from the perspective of nonprofit organization actors and the variables they consider before, during, and after their involvement in such endeavors. For the purposes of this discussion, important partnerships are those in which at least one party recognizes the efficacy of his or her collaboration and is using the social, economic, and/or political capital of their counterpart to take benefits of its own away from the collaboration.[20]

We feel that the existing scholarship on collaboration and partnership does not contribute as much as we might like to our understanding of the contrast between longer-term, transformative partnership outcomes and those relationships that by contrast produce less-enduring, more "shallow" transactional outcomes. Based on our primary research for this book, we observe and argue that important partnerships are typically transformative beyond the transactional work of the tasks carried out by the participating organizations. Further, important partnerships have notable impacts that generate public value. The linkage between these concepts—partnership derived from voluntary association for public good, purposes, and values—is well established in the scholarship and popular American literature on civil society, traceable to the writings of Alexis de Tocqueville and Americans' tendency to "associate" to accomplish endeavors that would otherwise not be possible in either the public or private sphere.[21]

Our focus on "important" and "meaningful" partnerships offers lessons to nonprofit organizations engaged in and considering collaboration. We believe that the findings and conclusions will resonate with policy makers and philanthropic institutions seeking the best return on their investments for economic, social, and political change.

This book rests on four central framing concepts. The first is to use case examples of partnership to identify partnership characteristics. We also use quotations drawn from the cases to amplify our research findings and analysis. The second is to cast partnership arrangements in terms of dyads involving a nonprofit organization and another actor. The partner actor can be an individual nonprofit, a government or business entity, or a network of entities with a single point of contact that may act on behalf of all members of that network. Examples might be a federated fundraising agency or a nonprofit mutual benefits intermediary organization with a defined membership. The third is a

Table 0.1. Partnership Cases by Sector Pairings.

Partner Dyad Relationship	Number of Cases	Percentage of Cases
Nonprofit-Nonprofit	46	56
Nonprofit-Government	28	34
Nonprofit-Business	8	10
Total	82	100

nonprofit-first perspective in the examination of the partnership. We focus on the perspective of the nonprofit organization participant for the reasons already mentioned. Fourth, we consider our primary data as derived from the experiential learning of nonprofit executives as a key source for deriving partnership best practices. The point for us of experiential learning as a driver for partnership best practices is that it makes use of evidence-based learning from the field. These concepts are explained in greater detail below.

Why Dyadic Sector Partnerships and the Nonprofit-First Perspective?

Each of the partnership cases informing this book involves a nonprofit organization as the central actor engaged in collaboration with another nonprofit organization (or identifiable consortium of nonprofits), a government agency, or a private for-profit business entity. The partner relationships are cast as dyads to identify and emphasize the role that nonprofit organizations play in collaboration with other nonprofit, public, and private sector actors.

We collected the dyadic partnership cases from nonprofit executives who had responded to our call for participation. The call was issued to a cumulative listing of 800 nonprofit organizations maintained by the Center for Nonprofit Policy & Practice at Cleveland State University. The large, heterogeneous listing consisted of nonprofit organization participants in public-policy forum events or technical service projects between 2001 and 2012. The case study narratives provided by the nonprofit executives in the interviews describe sector pairings, or dyadic partnerships centering on a nonprofit organization and a partnering organization (nonprofit-nonprofit, nonprofit-government, and nonprofit-business). Table 0.1 presents the distribution of partnership cases by sector pairings.

As explicated in the chapters following, our research confirms that each of the three dyadic collaboration pairings held distinctive features. For example, characteristics we found heavily emphasized in nonprofit-nonprofit partnerships were mutual authority and risks between partners and reciprocity of financial and nonfinancial contributions by both participants. In nonprofit-government partnerships, examples of salient characteristics included clarity in the roles and expectations of each member, emphasis on performance accountability, and the presence of a formal contract for services. In nonprofit-business partnerships, distinguishing features emphasized the principles of profitability, such as enhanced market share and reduced costs.

Although many studies focus on collaboration between nonprofit organizations, government-nonprofit contracting, and business-nonprofit collaboration, for the most part the tri-sector differences reflected in these illustrative observations have not received great coverage in the literature of nonprofit organizations.[22] The purpose of this book is to analyze the different partnerships, and from this foundation provide insight to nonprofit organizations for forming durable, effective, and replicable partnerships with nonprofit, government, and business organizations.

Nonprofit-First Partnerships and the Five Subsectors: Human and Social Services, Public and Social Benefit, Health, Arts and Culture, and Education

Clustering partnerships by subsector organization type is an important contribution of our research for several reasons. First, scrutiny of nonprofit-first partnership by subsector enables us to identify key characteristics consistent with the nuances of a particular field of service or mission fulfillment. In our view, understanding field-specific partnership organizational behaviors and expectations can help increase the likelihood that nonprofit executives and decision makers, public policy makers in particular areas, action-oriented advocates, and other stakeholders engaged in partnership will have the tools to make good choices and improve the prospects of success of their partnerships.

Second, a change in the lens through which we examine the partnerships from sectors to nonprofit subsectors helps to cluster the cases thematically. In addition to our focus on the larger dyadic pairings, we look for trends associated with, for example, social services, education, economic and community development, health, and arts and culture that might otherwise have been overlooked by the concentration on cross-sector pairings. This approach was particularly helpful in identifying patterns followed by nonprofit grant makers, whose partnership characteristics merited a separate treatment of their own.

Devising a classification nomenclature to group the partnership cases was complicated. In many instances across the fifty-two nonprofit organizations contributing cases in our sample of eighty-two partnership cases, nonprofit executives suggested multiple partnership purposes, missions, and outcomes that fit into more than one subsector classification; for example, social services organizations engaged in partnership with arts organizations, or nonprofits devoted to community and economic development. We also came to realize that a "third mission principle," which arises from partnership purpose and mission fulfillment, was operative in many partnership cases. The third mission principle refers to the motive of each partner to fulfill their own individual missions while simultaneously fulfilling the third mission of the partnership. An example of the third mission (which we discuss in chapters 3, 4, 5, and 6 in greater detail) is a partnership case wherein a social services organization dedicated to treating people with mental health needs works with another organization dedicated to job readiness and creating training, education, and employment placements. The third mission is derived through the partnership, which specifically targets formerly incarcerated adults who comprise a new and partnership-specific category of clients with special needs previously not targeted by either partner.

Because we utilized aspects of three existing classification systems to assign nonprofit organizations to subsectors, we devote significant space in our narrative to explaining the methodology we applied to address these challenges. Using three complementary systems of classification, we were able to categorize the nonprofit organizations by subsector and to cluster the partnership cases according to their stated purpose and outcomes of the partnership. The subsector clusters we identify reflect a concentration of cases in categories that would remain hidden, were we to apply a single classification. In the end, we were able to identify five subsectors of partnership categories.

Nonprofit-First

The third and perhaps most salient contribution of this book is our nonprofit-centric or nonprofit-first approach. We both collect and analyze the data explicitly from the perspective of nonprofit organizations and their leaders.[23] The following observation by the nonprofit executive director of an intermediary organization devoted to housing redevelopment provides an illustration:

> We attribute our satisfaction with the partnership to the alignment that exists between our pursuit of mission and that of our partners on the strategies of the initiative and our shared interest to address vacant land reuse. The partnership isn't perfect, but the problems aren't anything that we feel are harmful to the initiative—sometimes things take longer than we would like—but there is genuine trust and goodwill between us and our partners along with an equal commitment to the initiative. We share a mutual respect and collegial relationship with our partners, who we believe contribute to the success. We also all have a little humor.

In this book, the nonprofit-first viewpoint is applied to nonprofit organizations engaged in partnership with another nonprofit organization, government agency, or private business. The nonprofit-first approach frames our research to examine the partnership characteristics of nonprofit case examples. We mine and develop the experiential knowledge of the nonprofit leaders interviewed in our best effort to bridge theory and practice in a novel way that we believe and assert is new to the scholarly literature of the nonprofit sector.

The interview narratives shared by experienced nonprofit executives offer key insights into partnership arrangements both successful and unsuccessful.

Using the nonprofit executives' rich practical experience, we looked for common themes among partnership types and illustrated them with the case narratives.[24]

As a basis for data collection and analysis, the nonprofit-first perspective is significant for several reasons. First, nonprofit-first focuses on the mission fulfillment motivations of nonprofit leaders and managers to engage in partnership. Second, from the nonprofit point of view, nonprofit-first allows us to account for best practices, administrative procedures, and financial and human capital necessary from nonprofit-centered partnership to yield successful collaboration outcomes. And third, a nonprofit-first framework differentiates this book from those in public management, public administration, and business administration, which often use the lens of contractual "principal agent" relationships (or other framework) as a primary analytical tool.

Principal agent theory has been both helpful and limiting to nonprofit sector scholarship. On the positive side of the ledger, principal agent theory has driven scholarly inquiry toward the performance and accountability measurement of nonprofits, especially as studied in public administration. This approach has raised public sector managers' awareness that nonprofit organizations are worthy of their attention, and books on the nonprofit sector have taken advantage of this scholarship to increase understanding of the involvement of nonprofit organizations to achieve both public and private sector purposes.[25]

On the other side of the ledger, principal agent theory has not provided a suitable frame for nonprofit leaders and managers themselves to hone their craft. The nonprofit executives interviewed for our study noted that contractual obligations rarely, if ever, account for nonprofit mission fulfillment outcomes of their organization. In their view, public management scholarship taking a principal agent view focused on nonprofit accountability and performance does not address the practical matters of partnership from the nonprofit-first vantage point. Hence, it has contributed relatively little to the understanding of collaboration or partnership by nonprofit executives.

Experiential Learning

A partnership is hard to define. It can be … anything from an emotional connection with loose cooperation … [to] a more fully integrated collaboration.… It is a vague term.

—Executive of a grant-making institution promoting healthy communities

It is the partners themselves who most consider the relationship as a partnership. Outsiders cannot attest to a partnership.

—Executive of a federated fundraising and grant-making institution

A fourth feature of this book is the use of nonprofit executives' practical experiences. Since these executives are the ones who most carry out the work of partnership, their experience is a valid and rich source of data for analysis. In our experience consulting and working with nonprofit organization partnerships, we find that nonprofit executives validate the usefulness of experiential learning more than academic learning as among the more important frames for advancing the understanding of partnership. For example, the nonprofit executive of a private family foundation observed, "The partnership had an impact on our organization by the lessons we learned in how to prioritize types of capacity-building; on our target foundation peer population, who learned to support nonprofits and collaborate with one another; [and] on services delivered by requiring consultants to collaborate, which increased their sensitivity and understanding of what the nonprofits were going through."

The use of narrative and experiential learning to create replicable models of thriving nonprofit partnerships is an innovation for the broader field of nonprofit sector studies. In this book, we employ a qualitative strategy to make sense of the case data generated by the experiences related by fifty-two nonprofit executives. Our approach is to share the collective wisdom of the executives, informed by scholarly sources on a subject that bedevils many. In our view, this approach is essential because collaboration takes place among a bewildering array of variables that may change from situation to situation. Typically, nonprofit executives seeking to stimulate or engage in partnership are left to their own devices, and consequently rely on their own experiences. Because individual situational learning offers too small a sample for replicable practices, a book that emulates many experiences leads readers toward inductive theory and the practical tools necessary to craft effective outcomes.

Structure of the Book

In this introduction, we have presented the justification for the topic of nonprofit partnership and the reasons to parse the dyadic differences between nonprofit-nonprofit, nonprofit-government, and nonprofit-business partnerships. The chapter poses and answers the questions: why undertake this study, and what is its value to the field? What is different about this study, and what are its data sources?

In chapter 1, "Summing Up, Summing Down: A Review of the Literature on Partnership," we review extant literature on nonprofit-based partnerships with government, business, and other nonprofit organizations. The chapter shows that although this literature is useful for some audiences, particularly academic researchers and public managers, it does not offer sufficient or compelling guidance to executives and leaders of nonprofit organizations. Consistent with our nonprofit-first perspective, we document gaps in the field and explain how this book will offer a research-based foundation as well as help to guide effective and sustainable partnerships between nonprofit organizations and government agencies, private businesses, and other nonprofit organizations. The chapter elaborates our methodology for filling this research gap as well as its advantages and limitations.

In chapter 2, "Nonprofit Partnerships: The Gold Standard," we synthesize the primary data collected from nonprofit executive leaders through their descriptions of "partnership" and "important partnerships." The viewpoints of nonprofit-first executives are bound within our research premise that important partnerships are essential to the ability of a nonprofit organization to meet its core mission. We are guided by the proposition that sustainable partnerships involve sharing and an exchange of some type between the partner organizations. In our view, these exchanges may include funding, personnel, facilities and equipment, expertise, information, knowledge, capacity, and access to other opportunities, or any combination of these resources. This analysis adopts our "nonprofit-first" approach, which has not characterized previous literature. This chapter sets the stage for a more detailed comparison of each dyadic partnership type in the chapters to follow.

In chapter 3, "The Point of Partnering," we discuss each partnership type, that is, a nonprofit organization partnering with another nonprofit, a government agency, or private business, and the reasons why nonprofits engage in partnership, as well as the conditions under which partnership is likely to be more or less beneficial. Although previous scholarship on partnership may have identified possible benefits to the participants, rarely has the research confirmed those benefits with nonprofit practitioners. This chapter examines the realization of benefits from the nonprofit's point of view, and whether perceived benefits vary across sector dyads or subsector categories. Based on our analysis of the nonprofit respondent viewpoints, this chapter explains the factors which are likely to lead to more positive results for nonprofits engaged in partnership.

In chapter 4, "Good to Great: Recognizing the Signs of High-Quality Partnerships," we discuss the satisfaction factors of partnership that worked for or against achieving its goals. Our findings are based on the respondents' views of reasons why partnerships do or do not meet their potential for success and sustainability. The chapter rests not only on the case narratives comprising the primary data for this book, but also on the ratings that we asked the nonprofit executives to provide regarding the partnerships. We also discuss the conditions for partnership that respondents described.

In chapter 5, "Nonprofit Partnerships by Subsector," we discuss distinctive aspects of nonprofit mission orientation that cast our cases into nonprofit subsectors, such as social services, education, economic and community development, health, and arts and culture. Five subsector categories are addressed in detail in this chapter based upon elements of three existing subsector classification systems recognized in the scholarly literature of nonprofit studies. The qualitative narratives shared by experienced nonprofit executives comprise key insights into whether or not partnership arrangements and outcomes vary across subsectors.

Chapter 6, "Grant Makers' Partnership Practices," presents a stand-alone, supplemental subsector cluster of cases arising from the classification systems devised in chapter 5. Grant makers comprise an important subclass of organizations not only because of their role as funders of nonprofit organizations, but also as institutions who must fulfill their missions through collaborative ventures. The cases described in this chapter offer important insights into the promises and challenges of nonprofit partnerships involving nonprofit grant-making actors. Conceptual fuzziness on whether or not a grant maker constitutes a "partner" raises barriers to successful and effective partnership outcomes as grant makers frequently cast even the most superficial relationships in which they engage as "partnerships." Many of these partnership endeavors are perceived by nonprofit executives as "something other than partnership." Consequently, a theme of this chapter is that many grant maker–induced partnerships differ in important ways from nonprofit-first partnerships and those differences are neither well known or well understood by nonprofit organization executives or leaders.

In chapter 7, "Toward Nonprofit Partnership Theory: Collaboration as a Way of (Work) Life," we discuss the advice and recommendations of the nonprofit executive and decision maker respondents to questions we asked about best practices for partnership. Using the research data drawn from the partnership cases, we devise valuable principles of nonprofit first partnership and use the broad knowledge documented in the pages of this book to craft a nonprofit-first-derived partnership dashboard for nonprofit executives, grant makers, and others to use in devising and measuring the performance and value of their partnerships. This chapter offers insights regarding important characteristics and practices of effective partnership. It describes the role of experiential learning in crafting sustainable partnerships and how nonprofit executives structure and carry them out. It analyzes the respondents' statements within the framework of different types of nonprofit-centric partnerships with government, business, or another nonprofit organization.

In Review

> Because nonprofits are not like government or businesses with no inherent means of accruing funding through taxpayers or profit-making, forming a partnership in a nonprofit setting requires a clarity of serving the core mission of each organization and aligning the values of both organizations.
>
> —Executive director of a fast-growing nonprofit residential social services facility

> Our organization ... engaged in a partnership with high stakes ... must be fully committed to making the partnership successful, because the risks of failing are too high to not do whatever is necessary to reach the goals of the partnership.
>
> —Executive director of a nonprofit arts organization serving special community populations

In this introduction, we formalized the idea that partnership is driven by the culture and mission of the nonprofit sector and asserted that partnership can offer transformative benefits for the actors involved, even with the dyadic characteristics that differentiate nonprofit-nonprofit, nonprofit-government, and nonprofit-business partnerships. We also outlined the four central features of this text: case examples, dyadic partnership arrangements, the nonprofit-first perspective, and a focus on analyzing and reproducing real-world experience. We introduced the nonprofit-first perspective, which we explore further in chapter 1.

Notes

1. Mendel, Stuart C. "Are Private Government, the Nonprofit Sector, and Civil Society the Same Thing?." *Nonprofit & Voluntary Sector Quarterly* 39, no. 4 (2010): 717–733, doi:10.1177/0899764009337897; Mendel, Stuart C. "The Ecology of Games Between Public Policy and Private Action: Nonprofit Community Organizations as Bridging and Mediating Institutions." *Nonprofit Management and Leadership* 13, no. 3 (2003): 229–236, doi:10.1002/nml.12.

2. Keating, W. Dennis, Norman Krumholz, and David C. Perry. *Cleveland: A Metropolitan Reader* (Kent, OH: Kent State University Press, 1995).

3. Mendel, Stuart C., and Jeff L. Brudney. "Putting the NP in PPP: The Role of Nonprofit Organizations in Public-Private Partnerships." *Public Performance & Management Review* 35, no. 4 (2012): 617–642, doi:10.2307/23484758.

4. Gazley, Beth. "Why Not Partner with Local Government? Nonprofit Managerial Perceptions of Collaborative Disadvantage." *Nonprofit and Voluntary Sector Quarterly* 39, no. 1 (2010): 51–76, doi:10.1177/0899764008327196; Alexander, Jennifer, and Renee Nank. "Public-Nonprofit Partnership Realizing the New Public Service." *Administration & Society* 41, no. 3 (2009): 364–386, doi:10.1177/0095399709332296; Gazley, Beth, and Jeffrey L. Brudney. "The Purpose (and Perils) of Government-Nonprofit Partnership." *Nonprofit and Voluntary Sector Quarterly* 36, no. 3 (2007): 389–415, doi:10.1177/0899764006295997; Selden, Sally Coleman, Jessica E. Sowa, and Jodi Sandfort. "The Impact of Nonprofit Collaboration in Early Child Care and Education on Management and Program Outcomes." *Public Administration Review* 66, no. 3 (2006): 412–425, doi:10.1111/j.1540-6210.2006.00598.x; Guo, Chao, and Muhittin Acar. "Understanding Collaboration among Nonprofit Organizations: Combining Resource Dependency, Institutional, and Network Perspectives." *Nonprofit and Voluntary Sector Quarterly* 34, no. 3 (2005): 340–361, doi:10.1177/0899764005275411; Mulroy, Elizabeth A. "Community as a Factor in Implementing Interorganizational Partnerships: Issues, Constraints, and Adaptations." *Nonprofit Management and Leadership* 14, no. 1

(2003): 47–66, doi:10.1002/nml.20; Austin, James E. "Strategic Collaboration Between Nonprofits and Business." *Nonprofit and Voluntary Sector Quarterly* 29, no. suppl. 1 (2000): 69–97, doi:10.1177/089976400773746346

5. Smith, Steven Rathgeb, and Michael Lipsky, *Nonprofits for Hire: The Welfare State in the Age of Contracting* (Cambridge, MA: Harvard University Press, 2009).

6. Alexander, Jennifer, Renee Nank, and Camilla Stivers. "Implications of Welfare Reform: Do Nonprofit Survival Strategies Threaten Civil Society?." *Nonprofit and Voluntary Sector Quarterly* 28, no. 4 (1999): 452–475, doi:10.1177/0899764099284005.

7. Forrer, John, James Jed Kee, and Eric Boyer, *Governing Cross-Sector Collaboration* (Hoboken, NJ: John Wiley and Sons, 2014).

8. Forrer, John, James Jed Kee, and Eric Boyer. *Governing Cross-Sector Collaboration* (Hoboken, NJ: John Wiley and Sons, 2014); Salamon, Lester M. "The Nonprofit Sector and Government: The American Experience in Theory and Practice." *The Third Sector. Comparative Studies of Nonprofit Organization,* Berlin and New York, Walter de Gruyter (1990): 210–240.

9. Seitanidi, Maria May. *The Politics of Partnerships: A Critical Examination of Nonprofit-Business Partnerships* (New York: Springer Science and Business Media, 2010).

10. Bromley, Patricia, and John W. Meyer. ""They Are All Organizations" The Cultural Roots of Blurring Between the Nonprofit, Business, and Government Sectors." *Administration & Society* (2014) doi:10.1177/0095399714548268; Brinkerhoff, Jennifer M. "Government-Nonprofit Partnership: A Defining Framework." *Public Administration and Development* 22, no. 1 (2002): 19–30, doi:10.1002/pad.203.

11. Snavely, Keith, and Martin B. Tracy. "Collaboration among Rural Nonprofit Organizations." *Nonprofit Management and Leadership* 11, no. 2 (2000): 145–165, doi:10.1002 /nml.11202; Wood, Donna J., and Barbara Gray. "Toward a Comprehensive Theory of Collaboration." *The Journal of Applied Behavioral Science* 27, no. 2 (1991): 139–162, doi:10.1177/0021886391272001.

12. Mendel, Stuart C. "Achieving Meaningful Partnerships with Nonprofit Organizations: A View from the Field." *The Journal of Nonprofit Education and Leadership* 3, no. 2 (2013). ISSN 2157-0604. Available at: <http://js.sagamorepub.com/jnel/article/view/4968>.

13. Kearns, Kevin P. "Management-Capacity Building in the Pittsburgh Region." *Nonprofit Management and Leadership* 14, no. 4 (2004): 437–452, doi:10.1002/nml.45.

14. Mendel, Stuart C., and Jeffrey L. Brudney. "Cross-Sector Collaboration and Public-Private Partnerships: A Perspective on How Nonprofit Organizations Create Public Value in an Archetypical City in the United States," in *Creating Public Value in Practice: Advancing the Common Good in a Multi-Sector, Shared-Power, No-One-Wholly-in-Charge World,* ed. John M. Bryson, Barbara C. Crosby, and Laura Bloomberg (Boca Raton, FL: CRC Press, 2015), 225–244.

15. Mendel, Stuart. "A field of Its Own." *Stanford Social Innovation Review* 12, no.1 (2014): 61–62.

16. Racine, David. "Dissolving Dualities: The Case for Commonsense Replication." *Nonprofit and Voluntary Sector Quarterly* 32, no. 2 (2003): 307–314, doi:10.1177/0899764003032002009.

17. Mendel, Stuart C. "Achieving Meaningful Partnerships with Nonprofit Organizations: A View from the Field." *The Journal of Nonprofit Education and Leadership* 3, no. 2 (2013). ISSN 2157-0604. Available at: <https://js.sagamorepub.com/jnel/article/view/4968>.

18. McDonald, Mary B. "Understanding Social Capital, Civic Engagement, and Community Building," in *Leadership in Nonprofit Organizations: A Reference Book,* ed.

Kathryn Agard (Thousand Oaks, CA: Sage Publications, 2011), 46–55; Yankey, John, and Carol Willen. "Collaboration and Strategic Alliances," in *The Jossey-Bass Handbook of Nonprofit Leadership and Management*, 3rd ed., ed. David O. Renz and R. D. Hermans (San Francisco, CA: Wiley and Sons, 2010), 375–400; Bedsworth, William, Ann Goggins Gregory, and Don Howard. *Non-Profit Overhead Costs: Breaking the Vicious Cycle of Misleading Reporting, Unrealistic Expectations, and Pressure to conform* (Boston, MA: Bridgespan Group, 2008), URL: <https://www.bridgespan.org/insights/library /pay-what-it-takes/nonprofit-overhead-costs-break-the-vicious-cycle>; Seitanidi, Maria May. *The Politics of Partnerships: A Critical Examination of Nonprofit-Business Partnerships* (New York: Springer Science and Business Media, 2010); Bovaird, Tony. "Public-Private Partnerships: From Contested Concepts to Prevalent Practice." *International Review of Administrative Sciences* 70, no. 2 (2004): 199–215, doi:10.1177/0020852304044250; Brinkerhoff, Jennifer M. "Government-Nonprofit Partnership: A Defining Framework." *Public Administration and Development* 22, no. 1 (2002): 19–30, doi:10.1002/pad.203; Austin, James E. "Strategic Collaboration Between Nonprofits and Business." *Nonprofit and Voluntary Sector Quarterly* 29, no. suppl. 1 (2000): 69–97, doi:10.1177/089976400773746346; Linder, Stephen H. "Coming to Terms with the Public-Private Partnership: A Grammar of Multiple Meanings." *American Behavioral Scientist* 43, no. 1 (1999): 35–51, doi:10.1177/00027649921955146.

19. Mendel, Stuart. "A Field of Its Own." *Stanford Social Innovation Review* 12, no. 1 (2014): 61–62.

20. McDonald, Mary B. "Philanthropic Leadership at the Community Level," in *Leadership in Nonprofit Organizations: A Reference Book*, ed. Kathryn Agard (Thousand Oaks, CA: Sage Publications, 2011), 522–529; Yankey, John, and Carol Willen. "Collaboration and Strategic Alliances," in *The Jossey-Bass Handbook of Nonprofit Leadership and Management*, 3rd ed., ed. David O. Renz and R. D. Hermans (San Francisco, CA: Wiley and Sons, 2010), 375–400.

21. Hammack, David C. *Making the Nonprofit Sector in the United States: A Reader* (Bloomington: Indiana University Press, 2000).

22. Guo, Chao, and Muhittin Acar. "Understanding Collaboration among Nonprofit Organizations: Combining Resource Dependency, Institutional, and Network Perspectives." *Nonprofit and Voluntary Sector Quarterly* 34, no. 3 (2005): 340–361, doi:10.1177/0899764005275411; Snavely, Keith, and Martin B. Tracy. "Collaboration among Rural Nonprofit Organizations." *Nonprofit Management and Leadership* 11, no. 2 (2000): 145–165, doi:10.1002/nml.11202; Linder, Stephen H. "Coming to Terms with the Public-Private Partnership: A Grammar of Multiple Meanings." *American Behavioral Scientist* 43, no. 1 (1999): 35–51, doi:10.1177/00027649921955146; Kearns, Kevin P. "Management Capacity-Building in the Pittsburgh Region." *Nonprofit Management and Leadership* 14, no. 4 (2004): 437–452, doi:10.1002/nml.45; Salamon, Lester M. "The Nonprofit Sector and Government: The American Experience in Theory and Practice," in *The Third Sector: Comparative Studies of Nonprofit Organization* (Berlin and New York: Walter de Gruyter, 1990), 210–240, doi: 10.1515/9783110868401.219; Seitanidi, Maria May. "Introduction" in *The Politics of Partnerships: A Critical Examination of Nonprofit-Business Partnerships* (New York: Springer Science and Business Media, 2010); Austin, James E. "Strategic Collaboration between Nonprofits and Business." *Nonprofit and Voluntary Sector Quarterly* 29, no. suppl. 1 (2000): 69–97, doi:10.1177/089976400773746346.

23. Mendel, Stuart. "A Field of Its Own." *Stanford Social Innovation Review* 12, no. 1 (2014): 61–62.

24. Gottschalk, Louis Reichenthal. *Understanding History: A Primer of Historical Method* (New York: Knopf, 1961); McNabb, David E. *Research Methods in Public Administration and Nonprofit Management* (London: ME Sharpe, 2002); Hancock, Dawson, and Bob Algozzine. "'Qualitative and Quantitative Research' and 'Setting the Stage,'" in *Doing Case Study Research: A Practical Guide for Beginning Researchers* (New York: Teachers College Press, 2006), 8–11, 15–27; Stemler, Steve. "An Overview of Content Analysis." *Practical Assessment, Research & Evaluation* 7, no. 17 (2001): 1–10, URL: <http://eric.ed.gov/?id=EJ638505>; McDonald, Robert E. "An Investigation of Innovation in Nonprofit Organizations: The Role of Organizational Mission." *Nonprofit and Voluntary Sector Quarterly* 36, no. 2 (2007): 256–281, doi:10.1177/0899764006295996; Thach, Elizabeth, and Karen J. Thompson. "Trading Places: Examining Leadership Competencies Between For-Profit vs. Public and Non-Profit Leaders." *Leadership & Organization Development Journal* 28, no. 4 (2007): 356–375, doi:10.1108/01437730710752229; Dart, Raymond. "Being 'Business-Like' in a Nonprofit Organization: A Grounded and Inductive Typology." *Nonprofit and Voluntary Sector Quarterly* 33, no. 2 (2004): 290–310, doi:10.1177/0899764004263522; Wodak, Ruth, and Michael Meyer, eds. "Introduction," in *Methods for Critical Discourse Analysis* (Thousand Oaks, CA: Sage, 2009).

25. Salamon, Lester M. *Partners in Public Service: Government-Nonprofit Relations in the Modern Welfare State* (Baltimore, MD: Johns Hopkins University Press, 1995); Boris, Elizabeth T., and C. Eugene Steuerle. *Nonprofits & Government: Collaboration & Conflict*, 1st and 2nd eds. (Washington, DC: The Urban Institute, 1996, 2006); Forrer, John, James Jed Kee, and Eric Boyer. "Introduction," in *Governing Cross-Sector Collaboration* (Hoboken, NJ: John Wiley and Sons, 2014).

1 Summing Up, Summing Down: A Review of the Literature on Partnership

> Partnerships are hard work to create, hard to fund at their outset, and hard to maintain.... Organizations must understand why they are partnering and how they support the core mission of partnership.
>
> —Executive director of a nonprofit community development organization

Overview

In this chapter, we consider how the most common approaches to collaboration in scholarly literature are not particularly useful to nonprofit actors seeking to maximize their chances of partnership success. Building from the overview of the nonprofit-first approach presented in the introduction, we begin to synthesize useful theory with interviewees' practical experience. We hope both to fill a gap in the literature and to begin providing nonprofit actors with tested, replicable models of successful nonprofit-first partnerships.

Introduction

The nonprofit sector has long been the subject of sustained scholarly inquiry, but most critical insight into partnership and partnership engagement can be traced to the last three to four decades. Since the 1980s, scholars have begun to outline the broad principles of partnership, drawing these principles from theory as well as the practice of their own disciplines (e.g., Barbara Gray; Beth Gazley and Jeffrey Brudney; John Forrer, James Kee, and Eric Boyer; John Yankey and Carol Willen; Darlene Bailey and Kelly Koney; Chao Guo and Muhittin Acar; James Austin and Mary Seitanidi; and John Bryson).[1]

For the most part, the scholarly literature on nonprofit partnership adheres to frameworks characterized by interorganization or cross-sector collaboration intended for public, private, and nonprofit actors. Select examples of this literature also consider relationships between public and private organizations, or between individual or autonomous nonprofits on one side and institutional networks and associations on the other.[2] Other examples of the scholarly literature on nonprofit partnership cast interactions between two or more actors as a linear progression differentiated by varying levels of relationship formalization and integration.[3]

Despite the volume and value of scholarly inquiry into partnership, this literature does not adequately discuss or consider the nonprofit-first perspective; indeed, we still have much to learn about the best conditions for forming partnerships, overcoming barriers to partnership operations, and understanding the views of the officials doing the "hard work" of collaboration.

In this chapter, we elaborate the nonprofit-first point of view by bringing together the literature and interview information. We correlate the descriptions offered by nonprofit executives as they engage in partnerships with other nonprofits, governments, and businesses and weave them together with the most relevant scholarly literature. Each of the two—the executives' experiences as a primary source, and the research literature as a secondary counterpart—adds to the discussion by compensating for what the other lacks. For instance, we are able to illustrate real-life examples of the theories that the literature hypothesizes, and at the same time extrapolate what the literature underemphasizes or even lacks from examples in the executives' experiences.

Gaps in the Literature

Our interest in a nonprofit-first perspective on partnership is twofold.

First, we seek to fill a gap in the scholarly literature by providing answers to certain practical problems of partnership as experienced by nonprofit sector leaders.[4] Second, we offer governments, businesses, and nonprofits ways to understand and engage in partnership differently, so that actors desiring to stimulate nonprofit partnerships do not establish unfamiliar ground rules for the nonprofit participant.[5] For example, one nonprofit executive in a social services organization devoted to strengthening fatherhood skills shared that his past experience in working with the government is that it cast his organization as a "not equal member" of the partnership. In his view, the nonprofit did not participate in setting the rules or norms governing the partnership; rather, the nonprofit played a subordinate role. Over the course of the partnership, this subordination ultimately threatened the fiscal health of his organization. The executive attributed the poor performance of the partnership to the small size and grassroots origin of his nonprofit organization—and also to the larger partner not crediting his smaller organization with competency or professionalism or equal status.

A second example of a gap in the scholarly literature in providing answers to practical problems of partnership stems from the paucity of replicable nonprofit-first theory-tested-in-practice partnership models. Because few grounded theories in the scholarly literature on partnership adopt a nonprofit perspective, nonprofit executives entering a partnership must rely on others' past experiences when weighing the costs and benefits of partnership endeavors, information that is often not readily available or relevant.[6]

A third example of a gap in the scholarly literature is that partnership theories centered on public sector or private market motives do not speak to the ways in which mission fulfillment is often the principal reason for a nonprofit's engagement in partnership. Of all sectors, nonprofits most often use mission alignment as a criterion for partnership, which means that a public or business-induced partnership can be out of sync with the nonprofit actor's intents and purposes. In public sector endeavors, the nonprofit actor is often seen as an agent to a government principal, suggesting that these arrangements are not "partnerships" but something else. Steven Smith and Michael Lipsky have notably labeled this phenomenon as "nonprofits for hire."[7] In such interactions, nonprofit leaders encounter government actors whose interest in the relationship is limited to contractually dictated performance outcomes, regardless of changing circumstance or unplanned, exigent conditions that may require resources beyond the partnership's or the nonprofit's expectations and capacities.[8]

Practice Informs Theory

Consistent with the scholarly literature on partnership and collaboration, most of the fifty-two nonprofit executives interviewed for this book expressed the opinion that their decision to enter into a partnership involved a practical and careful weighing of the ways in which a partnership would benefit their organization against the costs.[9] Several described the need for what is essentially a cost-benefit analysis, since the time, dollars, opportunity cost, and effort required in collaboration raised the stakes and heightened the risks for their involvement in partnerships. The executive director of an organization devoted to serving developmentally disabled adults explained that, despite his organization's due diligence and care before entering into a partnership, this partnership induced unanticipated changes in his operations that were necessary to keep up with the partner organization's practices.

In describing their partnerships, nonprofit executives offered a range of return-on-investment (ROI) value judgments used to assess the degree to which a partnership was/is important and/or meaningful. These judgments are described in greater detail in the following chapters. In summary, they are frequently bound up in links between ROI and planning steps that set decision makers' performance expectations and their ability to overcome problems. A specific example offered by one executive was expressed in their "advice to others" through the following list:

- Think carefully about your partner and the dynamics of the relationship.
- Anticipate as many issues in advance as you can and look for signals that engender trust.

- Create a deliberate agreement as to how you will handle issues.
- Decide how will you meet the goals that enable you to work together.
- Expect the unexpected through flexibility and compromise at times.
- Accept that time delays will be a problem.

Other examples of ROI outcomes arising from careful planning and hard-to-anticipate partnership performance included ways their organization benefits from the social, economic, and/or political capital of their counterpart.[10] Although the degree of formality of ROI as might be determined through cost-benefit analysis differed, many of the fifty-two nonprofit executives interviewed expressed interest in and pointed to use of predictive indicators and progressive benchmarks against which they might measure partnership success. The scholarly literature often indicates a similar desire for tools to predict the likelihood of success in partnership.[11] Scholars attribute the importance of partnership process indicators and performance to the premise that, in the earliest stages of collaboration, participants seek confirmation that the partnership will succeed in at least some limited way, if not completely. Evidence or intuition that the partnership mission, external factors, stakeholders, and participant capabilities are all in sync can significantly raise participants' confidence that the partnership is worth the risk.[12] An example offered by a nonprofit executive described the factors that work toward meeting the goals of the partnership as an historical connection between the two partner institutions, an organizations track record for successful partnership, and the alignment of goals between institutions.

In the absence of a nonprofit-first perspective in scholarly literature to guide them, nonprofit executives engaged in partnership endeavors have little to inform their work other than their own experiences and anecdotal learning from the experiences of more seasoned peers.[13] The executives interviewed echoed another theme from the existing literature here when maintaining that their own past experiences usually offered the best source of predictive knowledge for achieving successful, important partnerships.[14] As one executive noted, "My perspective on partnership was not changed by the project, it was confirmed. Our organization had a prior relationship with our government partner and that relationship was reinforced by the potential of a successful project of this collaboration. My past experience with this organization allowed for problem solving to go around the system the agency resided in so that we figured out how to deal with problems before they occurred and before we initiated the partnership. We also understood our partner's limits and sold them on our ability to produce benefits for them."

Other insights from this school of thought included the idea that important and meaningful partnerships occurred when both parties viewed themselves as approximate equals in participation, decision-making, risk, and accountability. By contrast, in several cases the executives interviewed shared that not all partnerships—and especially those imposed by public policy or private grant makers—rose to the level of meaningful partnership or even qualified as "partnerships."[15] For example,

> Yes, there is a difference between partnering with different industries such as government, business, or other nonprofits. When it is a nonprofit and another nonprofit or a nonprofit and a foundation, the relationship can feel competitive, especially if they are compelled to work together by some third organization. This is not a true partnership. You don't want to acquiesce to do things you might have not wanted. So, the agreements in advance are really important and what you get in the end is not really a partnership but a project. There are huge problems with other nonprofits as well. Barriers to enduring relationships are the limitations to the designated organization willing to take an interest in the partner. An organization can be aware of this within five minutes based on the tone of the partnerships. Mutual interests or a desire to have a return of benefits at the same time is important. In partnerships between a nonprofit and business or government, the participants don't care about competition, and there is no power struggle and issues of visibility. Sometimes this is a transactional quid pro quo relationship.

Help Wanted: Nonprofit-First Guidelines for Forming Partnerships

As discussed earlier, nonprofit executives seeking theory to inform best practices typically lack a nonprofit-first viewpoint on which they can draw to design and undertake partnerships. Here, we propose an additional reason to understand the nonprofit-first perspective to help nonprofit actors gain a sense of the differences that a nonprofit can expect in the practice of partnership across all three sectors.

In order to garner a sense of these working differences, we interviewed fifty-two nonprofit executives through the administration of a semi-structured questionnaire. Each executive was asked about dyadic partnership experiences between their organization and a partner from one of three sectors: another nonprofit, a government agency, or a business organization. Questions were mostly open-ended to facilitate description and discussion. The fifty-two executives described eighty-two cases of partnership by their organizations. Before we analyze the features of partnership as described by these nonprofit executives, we draw on the vast cross-disciplinary literature of collaboration and partnership.

What the Scholarly Literature Tells Us about Stimulating Nonprofit Partnerships and Cross-Sector Expectations

Public and private sector policies that encourage the formation of partnerships are consistent with the nature and function of nonprofit institutions.[16] Scholarly writing and practical experience have established that collaboration and partnership are important characteristics of the nonprofit sector in the United States,[17] and scholars note that partnership between nonprofits can arise for a variety of reasons.[18] Rationales for partnership include purposes related to the participant organizations' missions, external incentives that encourage collaboration, the self-interest and motivation of key stakeholders,[19] and large-scale community processes that can build trust and social capital in a system of service providers.[20]

In the best circumstances, nonprofits' partnership arrangements with businesses, government actors, or other nonprofits are entered into voluntarily.[21] Partnerships can take place without third-party prompting and may be entered for purposes such as program and operations efficiency, cost savings and economies of scale, changes in the marketplace, and mission convergence, among others.[22]

Despite the nonprofit sector's fertile conditions for forming partnerships voluntarily, public managers can also require nonprofits to form partnerships as a criterion for funding by using the influence of requests for proposals (RFPs) and grant application processes.[23] Frequently, public and elected officials raise confusion when they promote awarded contracts for services with nonprofits as "partnerships."[24] Private philanthropy is not immune from this phenomenon, either, as evidenced by the way the Bill and Melinda Gates Foundation makes collaboration a requisite for grant-making. This requirement came into play with the Gates Foundation's much-lauded award of $4 million to the National League of Cities in the early 2000s, an initiative that targeted seven cities to boost college graduation rates by better coordinating the services that colleges, schools, and communities provide to students.[25]

The rationale for requiring partnerships and other collaborative ventures seems apparent: public contracting funds and philanthropic grant-making dollars are limited. To obtain the best return on investment, policy makers and funders use their dollars to stimulate and oblige partnership from nonprofit contract and grant seekers. In their view, compelling nonprofits to work together results in higher efficiencies, service delivery capacity, and public value—which in turn amplify the reach of public-serving programs.[26] Moreover, these actors and contractors hold that by requiring collaboration from nonprofit respondents public dollars can be used as an instrument of policy to control the behavior of nonprofit service providers.[27] This trend was illustrated in Ohio in 2009 when Cuyahoga County public officials required two nonprofits, the Cleveland Food Bank and the Hunger Network of Greater Cleveland, to share public funding resources and submit joint proposals.[28]

One reason for scholars' emphasis on public sector, contract-inspired partnerships is the plethora of real-world examples arising from increased public-contracted work performed by nonprofits since the end of the Reagan administration.[29] As a result of the rise in public sector principal agent work with nonprofit service providers, the scholarly literature on nonprofit partnership has covered the impact and efficacy of cross-sector collaboration and public-private partnership much more heavily since the mid-1990s.[30]

An important feature of funder-mandated partnership is that public managers, policy makers, and private grant makers expect nonprofit organizations to form and manage the partnership relationships both prior to and during the contract or grant project. However, placing the burden of the partnership on the nonprofit participants brings unassigned costs that they must absorb. In effect, the nonprofit partner subsidizes the public sector funder or private grant maker by fulfilling an unfunded project performance requirement.[31] One nonprofit executive in our sample explained that a nonprofit that has a partnership with a government or business funder is cast as the manager or agent and its public funding partner as the "owner" or principal that has the authority to make demands that the nonprofit must satisfy.

The scholarly literature concurs on this point. Some scholars observe that public and private funder expectations overlook the complexity and costs incurred by nonprofit organizations in forming and managing partnerships.[32] Others have noted that it is the nonprofit participants who assume the risks and expenses incurred to one or both partners during the partnership's formative stages: these risks include the indirect costs of opportunity lost in drafting a response to an RFP, the direct costs of time and effort committed to diverting staff to a partnership endeavor, and the infrastructure costs required to administer and liaise with the partnership actors.[33]

It is not surprising that scholars have also noted that a top-down, policy-driven practice of required partnership between nonprofit players involved in a partnership with any organization seldom results in enduring partnerships.[34] Nonprofit executives shared similar observations, noting that many organizations do not recognize that one of the pitfalls of partnership involves leadership: the skills required of forming a partnership differ considerably from the skills required to manage one, and it is rare to find both skill sets in a single person.[35] One executive observed that a "nightmare scenario" for joint ventures is the risk of entrusting the organization's intellectual and human capital, credibility, and reputation to a partner who is unable to deliver on stated commitments, offering little benefit, or even harm, in return.[36] For example, one executive described their partnership with a small grassroots social services organization

> We do not believe that given the circumstances now the partnership can reach its full potential of success. Both our organization and our partner have different goals. We believe the main difference in these goals is that our partner is limited to the best interest of its business reputation in mind, while our goals are for the best interest of the client we are referring them to (and maintain our

funding). We don't believe the partnership will be ongoing, and is limited in its ability to be successful in meeting primary goals because our partner has modified the terms of its program to which we refer which sets us back from the purpose of the partnership and damages our credibility with our other sponsors and institutional relationships.

A second example: "Among the greatest risks to the agency of entering into a partnership with government or others is that either partner will not be able to live up to its commitments or that the partners will not be able to deliver on its responsibilities."

Poor conception, funding uncertainties, and community-level factors can all complicate the odds of successful partnership still further because they are beyond the nonprofit's control, yet affect partnership outcomes.[37] For example, as one executive noted, "Both organizations are publicly and privately funded, so limits imposed by internal fiscal controls complicate things that then don't always work out as smoothly as they might have if there was a less restrictive, more reliable funding source.... One example involved a funding hitch that happened just this year; we opened a new programming site at Central Middle School in Euclid, and, due to a number of restrictions, the site was not able to receive food right away."

In addition, because forming a partnership is so complex and demands so much from the nonprofit, involved actors may become distracted by the appeal of celebrating shallow collaborations formed only to meet the funding prerogatives of organized philanthropy and government.[38] The executives we interviewed recognized similar examples of "partnership hyperbole," or over-celebrating interactions that are functional but do not reach the level of what they feel are legitimate collaborative endeavors. This hyperbole might include items such as annual giving to federated campaigns between nonprofits and corporations, service referrals by the government to local residents consisting of little more than a passive listing of vetted providers, successful grant applications between two or more participants for the purpose of fulfilling a checklist, or transaction-based cause-related marketing. As one executive shared, "An important factor is that the nonprofit develops a truth and understanding in the partnership. Some partnerships don't rate as others.... If the partnership is a result of funding, the goals for its success should be commitment toward the impact of the work rather than simply signing a contract that aims to meet the funding requirements.... This takes flexibility, perspective, and insight on behalf of each partner to determine how they can really impact the community.... Partnerships based on funding alone are not partnerships and have less impact than partnerships that passionately share a concern for accomplishing a goal."

Explaining Partnership Terminology Across Sectors

According to the executives we interviewed, the burdens of required or contrived partnerships often prevent nonprofit organizations from forming meaningful partnerships. The rote nature and necessity required by a funding or other outside requirement may result in the partnering organization leaving the nonprofit with additional unsought responsibilities beyond the burden of initiating and maintaining the relationship itself. This result may not be intentional but instead emanate from differing definitions of partnership and its elements among the partners.

The scholarly literature upholds this conviction, documenting notable differences in the ways that government, business, and nonprofit organization actors describe collaboration and partnership. As a consequence, understanding differences in the use of the terms "partnership" and "collaboration" across sectors is important both for policy makers seeking to kindle cooperative arrangements and for nonprofit leaders engaged in making them work.[39] For instance, nonprofit literature has noted the understated differences in the definitions and meanings of the terms "collaboration" and "partnership" across the three sectors.[40] These not-so-subtle differences can influence the decisions that organization across sectors make about the nature of collaboration and their expectations for the outcomes of collaborative endeavors. The manner in which the leaders of the partnership conceive of its meaning to their organization weighs strongly in any assessment of whether or not those relationships can be seen as successful.[41] Just as the interviewed executives articulated in the field of practice, so the literature also more subtly confirms that sector differences in the depiction and expectations of actor collaboration are often the greatest challenges to realizing important and meaningful partnerships, or even to setting expectations for nonprofit participants.[42]

Although the relevant literature reflects the nuanced differences in the ways that governments, businesses, and nonprofits may view partnership and collaboration, scant published research has parsed the jargon that leaders in public policy and private philanthropy use to describe such endeavors. Still less has it examined the subtle and somewhat mixed messages that such jargon often conveys to the nonprofit sector and other sector actors. Scholars' failure to address this issue of language has serious consequences. For example, terminology such as *strategic alliances, affiliations, consolidations,*[43] *interorganizational collaboration,*[44] *organizational networks,*[45] and *nonprofit collaboration*[46] are commonly used when describing the working relationship between two or more organizational participants, one of whom represents a nonprofit. By comparison, the phrase "public-private partnership" and the term "alliance" are more common in the scholarly literature of public management and business,[47] despite nonprofit actors' frequent involvement and performance expectations in such endeavors.[48]

In table 1.1, we illustrate differences reflected in the literature of partnership and collaboration.[49]

Table 1.1 contrasts partnership sector pairings, different sectors' notions of partnership motivation and purposes, summary explanations for the mix of partnership characteristics, and nonprofit-specific concepts that could support a dedicated field of nonprofit management theory. The first column refers to the dominant sector partnership character in a manner that allows for comparison between conceptual dyads. The second column of the table lists the dominant actor as driver for the partnership endeavor based on the sector pairings in column 1. The third column depicts the characteristics of the partnership types drawing on existing scholarly literature and our partnership cases. The comparison framework constructed in table 1.1 provides important insights for the development of nonprofit-first theories of partnership which we discuss here and in subsequent chapters of this book.

Sorting Through the Literature on Collaboration

Four major sector pair distinctions are evident in table 1.1. These distinctions in nomenclature and motivations are supported by both scholarly sources and nonprofit-first experiences.

First, the differences and variations of motive that drive collaborations where the scholarly literature describes government as the catalyst for a partnership and implied by the government-nonprofit partnerships category in the table, and the nonprofit-government partnerships described by our nonprofit-first partnership cases, contribute heavily to the contrast in partnership characteristics. By applying the theoretical work of scholars to public sector processes, for example, we can surmise that public policy makers seeking to generate high value at low cost through required collaboration would craft their relationships with a nonprofit actor around accountability for the delivery of services and the expenditure of tax dollars.[50] They might also require nonprofit service providers to engage in collaboration and partnership to affirm that the contract with multiple participants is leveraged or compounded in purchasing power beyond a dollar of funding for a dollar of services. "Leveraging" offers policy makers a way to measure return on investment, the potential of promoting changes in society, and the development of systemic capacity by stimulating a network of nonprofit service providers interacting with government as well as with one another.[51] Collaboration and leveraged funds can also be described to taxpayers as an investment that attracts private dollars brought to the endeavor by the nonprofit participants that act as service providers. As mentioned earlier, governments may have an interest in altering the behavior of private sector actors, both business and nonprofit, through incentives such as funded projects.

Second, government actors that initiate partnerships typically view their relationships with nonprofit service providers as hierarchical and legal contracts for services. By contrast, nonprofit actors typically employ a cost-benefit assessment

Table 1.1. Partnership Characteristics of Government, Business, and Nonprofits When Paired with a Nonprofit Member.

Sector Partner Pairing	Dominant Sector Partner	What Scholarly Literature Tells Us
Government-Nonprofit	Public	Services provided by contract organizations are more efficient and effective than government can perform alone. Emphasis where the sponsor (government) focuses on the services provision by the nonprofit through a political lens, and bureaucratic oversight, accountability, and contractual performance determine the success of the partnership.
Nonprofit-Government	Private Nonprofit	Emphasis on mission of the nonprofit as a reason to enter into the contract with government. Each actor can bargain on its own behalf. Partnerships are long-term and enduring (excludes relationships dependent on grants or competitive contracts). Each actor contributes to the partnership. All actors share responsibility for the outcomes. Relationships are a means for government to build trust with citizens.
Business-Nonprofit	Private Profit-Making	Access to markets, branding, and profits that business alone cannot achieve.
Nonprofit-Business	Private Nonprofit	Strategic advantage from access to expertise; financial support for purposes of sustainability. Philanthropic—where the nature of the relationship is that of charitable donor and recipient. Transactional—where there is an explicit exchange of resources focused on specific activities such as in-cause related marketing, event sponsorships, and contracts for services; integration—where the partners' mission, and activity begin to merge into more collective action and organizational integration.
Nonprofit-Nonprofit	Private Nonprofit	Mission achievement, organizational sustainability, and valued-added features of collaboration. Two organizations work together with parity of authority, investment, and commitment to address problems through joint effort, resources, and decision-making, and share ownership of the final product or service. Social capital; equity between partners; political, social, and economic engagement.

(Alexander and Nank 2009; Austin 2010; Bailey and Koney 2000; Brody 2005; Selden, Sowa, and Sandfort 2006; Gazley and Brudney 2007; Guo and Acar 2005; Linder 1999; Mulroy 2003; Seitanidi 2010; Yankey and Willen 2010.)

when deciding whether to enter a partnership. The cost-benefit framework includes measures that account for mission fulfillment, financial resources required of their organization, and overall merit of the endeavor.[52] Nonprofits may seek returns that include strategic advantages in a competitive marketplace for knowledge, power, prestige, and financial resources; opportunities to learn from one another; access to funding; benefits from the association with the partner organization; the ability to deliver services and expand their capacity to perform work; and political advantages for long-term sustainability.[53]

Third, other important findings emerge among the sector comparisons between nonprofit-government, nonprofit-business, and nonprofit-nonprofit partnerships. For example, the use of the term "alliance" in business-nonprofit ventures suggests separate institutions interacting for the convenience of both parties. Such an image conveys a temporary, transactional arrangement for a quick return on investment: this image trends toward brief interludes of connection of corporate philanthropy, cause-related marketing, or civic leadership. Few would argue that relationships aligning with these criteria are the same as important or meaningful nonprofit-first partnership endeavors.[54]

Finally, the nonprofit-nonprofit partnerships present insights into participants' shared motivations to try to maximize meaningful partnerships. Experienced nonprofit executives shared that the best outcomes and opportunities for enduring, effective, and mutually sustaining partnerships are those that offer a risk-reward return that each partner is likely to measure and value. In these situations, the nonprofits anticipate and recognize ways in which they can reduce the risks of collaboration if they view themselves not as powerless charities receiving alms from third-party funders, but as full negotiating partners among equal participants.[55] Several executives offered perspectives illustrating these principles. One executive shared, "We are responsible to send our partner a weekly report. The frequent reporting task requires us to up our game, and benefits both of us from the standpoints of performance statistics and the partnership communication. It also gives us a greater sense of team and cooperation." A second executive observed, "The partnership had an impact on the organization—the internal perspective was shifted because we did not have a history of engaging with other organizations as equals to solve community problems. It made us a participant and gave us an understanding of the value of mutuality in partnership. The partnership had an impact on services which significantly improve.... From a broad perspective, the partnership educated the board to a set of social issues that had not received resources in the past and increased awareness around a social issue."

Five Elements for Assessing Important and Meaningful Partnerships

Using both the scholarly literature and the partnership case data contributed by the fifty-two nonprofit executives interviewed, we note five ways of thinking

Table 1.2. Measures for Establishing Important and Meaningful Partnerships.

Relationship Measure	Description of Measure	Illustrative queries nonprofit executives may use to determine if the partnership was a "meaningful partnership"
I. Balance and equity in the partnership	Degree of authority, responsibility, and decision-making ability allocated to each participant as the partnership forms and operates.	Do nonprofit organizations perceive that they are equal partners?
II. Strength of a partnership bond	Reflected through the density of social interactions, buy-in, and participation of leadership in each partner organization, and the access to the partners' network of relationships outside the partnership. Change or influence of network behavior.	How well and in what ways do the partner organizations complement, supplement, and benefit from one another?
III. Longevity of a partnership	Duration of partnership. Short-term and temporary. Longer-term and renewable.	In what ways will the partnership endure beyond the project period?
IV. Formality of the bond between organizations	Whether or not the partnership has a written contractual agreement.	What is the commitment and enforcement of the leadership of the organization to the partnership?
V. Evidence of transformation	Observable changes that benefit the organization in some manner. Can include program deliverables, organizational culture and practices, or unanticipated developments. External evidence of changes to a "system" of service provision; the behavior of a "network of actions."	What did the organization learn from the counterpart organization? Have any changes occurred within the organization as a result of the bond with the partner?

(Carnwell and Carson 2005; Granovetter 1983; Knoke and Yang 2008; LeCompte, Schensul, et al. 1999; Linder 1999; Rasler 2007; Takahasi and Smutny 2002)

about and assessing meaningful partnership. These ways of observing and judging whether an endeavor rises to the level of partnership are listed in table 1.2.[56]

Column 1 lists meaningful partnership measurement elements drawn from scholarly sources, and column 2 offers a description of the element categories. Column 3 posits an illustrative set of queries that nonprofit executives may use to assess their organizations' performance on the designated element.

While considering the five elements elaborated in table 1.2, we observed a delicate balance and equity of power required in forming, maintaining, and utilizing bonds of connection effectively between nonprofit organizations.[57] We also discerned that the strength of a partnership bond is reflected through the density of social interactions and networks of the executives and leaders in each partner organization.[58] We further noted that the longevity of a partnership arises from the predictable actions of the participants, the perceived level of risk by each participant, and the return on investment or benefits that each participant realizes from the relationship.[59] The framework for collaboration may be marked by the formality of the bond between organizations and bonds that can be envisioned or demonstrated by social asset maps.[60] Finally, we noted that changes may occur in the way the partners carry out their work, or the way they or society benefit from the experience of the partnership.[61] The passage that follows by a nonprofit executive participant illustrates some of these conclusions:

> The two organizations realized they had a mutual problem and needed to work together to fix it. Shortly after the conversations began, the Department of Labor sought grant proposals for economic growth programs created and implemented by partnering organizations. The successful funding application started a partnership that took incumbent workers from one partner who had interest in being a nurse or radiology tech and set them up in a night and weekend certificate program. The local school district then referred students to the partners to fulfill the incumbent positions and participate in training. The other partner had to undergo some program changes to meet the goals of the partnership. They designed a new curriculum for people in this program, and moved the program to night and weekend courses to allow the students to continue working their positions for the first partner. The partners extended their project contract to fulfill the goal of providing training programs … after the grant was fulfilled and continued to work on this project together outside of the original contract.

Forming Important and Meaningful Partnerships

To stimulate the best circumstances for building important and meaningful partnerships, public and philanthropic actors might provide nonprofit partners with means to track the five elements listed in table 1.2. One method may be found in the adaptive use of evaluation logic models that are increasingly widespread in private and philanthropic grant-making with a significant caveat.[62] Typically, the heft of logic models trends toward the alignment of the project with the mission and purpose of the public funder or the mission of the philanthropic institution. Little provision is made for outcomes that include forming a meaningful partnership or other outcomes not directly aligned with the grant maker's priorities.

We find that this weighting tends to inhibit adaptation and flexibility in the realization of outcomes, despite circumstances that may require shifts by the partnering participants. For example, shifts might arise based on exigent circumstances or the need to deviate from a proposal and project work plan. These circumstances may be related to building trust and operational coordination in the partnership, unexpected external conditions, extended implementation timelines, and/or a host of other issues that may arise during the course of project work complicated by a partnership. Both scholars and the nonprofit executives interviewed for our study agree that following a strict logic model can hinder innovations that create opportunity between nonprofit organization partners while obstructing communications that nurture collaboration.[63] Therefore, if adopted, the logic model should include room for integrating emergent needs of partnership. One nonprofit executive participant illustrated these points: "As a contractor of government, we do not see ourselves in a legitimate or authentic partnership. This is due to being at the mercy of the priorities of the government and a strict performance regimen based on best practices and logic models for performance. In private sector relationships, our work tends to be contractual, where we have a distant and more quantifiable relationship that strengthens their business models. Most partnerships with other nonprofits are where we feel there is a level playing field and greater flexibility and opportunities to deepen the relationship."

Implications for Policy and Further Study

The benefits and costs experienced by nonprofit organizations involved in public and private sector-driven collaboration and partnership are important components to the realization of public policy. One of our main assertions is that policy-inspired collaborations and partnerships bear greater scrutiny by those encouraging them—and by those entering into them—than is typical of public managers and grant makers through requests for proposals (RFPs). Yet, interviewees informed us that meaningful partnerships have a return on investment (ROI) that can contribute to public value and offer the greatest potential to solve public problems with limited resources. So, parsing the subtle differences in the meaning of partnership that public, private, and nonprofit leaders and managers assign to their funding and RFPs is an important consideration for partner organizations committed to creating durable, high-performing, and meaningful partnerships.[64]

In Review

In this chapter, we found that the scholarly literature on partnership is typically lacking in terms of both nonprofit focus and potential for practical implementation. Although practice informs theory, we noted that most of the scholarly literature exhibits a cross-sector rather than nonprofit-first focus, and thus does not acknowledge that nonprofit actors' rationales and challenges in partnership differ from those of other sector actors. In some areas, the literature coincided with data from the executives we interviewed but could not provide workable models despite the overlap with actual nonprofit experience. We concluded this chapter by offering five initial means of assessing important and meaningful partnerships, a concept that we will revisit in later chapters to supplement this still-theoretical approach with workable practices.

Notes

1. Van Huijstee, Mariëtte M., Mara Francken, and Pieter Leroy. "Partnerships for Sustainable Development: A Review of Current Literature." *Environmental Sciences* 4, no. 2 (2007): 75–89, doi:10.1080/15693430701526336; Selsky, John W., and Barbara Parker. "Cross-Sector Partnerships to Address Social Issues: Challenges to Theory and Practice." *Journal of Management* 31 (2005): 849–873, doi:10.1177/0149206305279601; Wildridge, Valerie, Sue Childs, Lynette Cawthra, and Bruce Madge. "How to Create Successful Partnerships: A Review of the Literature." *Health Information and Libraries Journal* 21, no. suppl. 1 (2004): 3–19, doi:10.1111/j.1740-3324.2004.00497.x; Bryson, John M., Barbara C. Crosby, and Melissa Middleton Stone. "The Design and Implementation of Cross-Sector Collaborations: Propositions from the Literature." *Public Administration Review* 66, no. suppl. 1 (2006): 44–55, doi:10.1111/j.1540-6210.2006.00665.x.

2. Abramson, Alan, Benjamin Soskis, and Stefan Toepler. *Public-Philanthropic Partnerships in the US: A Literature Review of Recent Experiences* (Arlington, VA: Council on Foundations, 2012) <www.cof.org>; Chen, Bin. "Antecedents or Processes? Determinants of Perceived Effectiveness of Interorganizational Collaborations for Public Service Delivery." *International Public Management Journal* 13 (2010): 381–407, doi:10.1080/10967494.2010.524836; Babiak, Kathy, and Lucie Thibault. "Challenges in Multiple Cross-Sector Partnerships." *Nonprofit and Voluntary Sector Quarterly* 38, no. 1 (2009): 117–143, doi:10.1177/0899764008316054; Gazley, Beth, and Jeffrey L. Brudney. "The Purpose (and Perils) of Government-Nonprofit Partnership." *Nonprofit and Voluntary Sector Quarterly* 36, no. 3 (2007): 389–415, doi:10.1177/0899764006295997; Guo, Chao, and Muhittin Acar. "Understanding Collaboration among Nonprofit Organizations: Combining Resource Dependency, Institutional, and Network Perspectives." *Nonprofit and Voluntary Sector Quarterly* 34 (2005): 340–361, doi:10.1177/0899764005275411; Turrini, Alex, Daniela Cristofoli, Francesca Frosini, and Greta Nasi. "Networking Literature about Determinants of Network Effectiveness." *Public Administration* 88 (2010): 528–550, doi:10.1111/j.1467-9299.2009.01791.x.

3. Bailey, Darlyne, and Kelly Koney. *Strategic Alliance among Health and Human Services Organizations: From Affiliations to Consolidations* (Thousand Oaks, CA: Sage Publications, 2000), 9–10 and ch. 2; Cornwell, T. Bettina, and Leonard V. Coote. "Corporate Sponsorship of a Cause: The Role of Identification in Purchase Intent." *Journal of Business Research* 58 (2005): 268–276; Austin, James E. "Strategic Collaboration between Nonprofits and Business." *Nonprofit and Voluntary Sector Quarterly* 29, no. suppl. 1 (2000): 69–97, doi:10.1177/0899764400773746346.

4. Babiak, Kathy, and Lucie Thibault. "Challenges in Multiple Cross-Sector Partnerships." *Nonprofit and Voluntary Sector Quarterly* 38, no. 1 (2009): 117–143, doi:10.1177/0899764008316054; Racine, David. "Dissolving Dualities: The Case for Commonsense Replication." *Nonprofit and Voluntary Sector Quarterly* 32 (2003): 307–314, doi:10.1177/0899764003032002009; Robb, Colleen. *Social Ventures: The Development of the*

Theory of Sustainable Contributive Advantage and Initial Empirical Tests (Abo, Finland: Abo Akademi University Press, 2012).

5. Powell, Walter W., and Steinberg, Richard. *The Nonprofit Sector: A Research Handbook* (New Haven, CT: Yale University Press); Young, Dennis R. "Alternative Models of Government-Nonprofit Sector Relations: Theoretical and International Perspectives." *Nonprofit and Voluntary Sector Quarterly* 29 (2000): 149–172.

6. Bromley, Patricia, and John W. Meyer. "'They Are All Organizations': The Cultural Roots of Blurring between the Nonprofit, Business, and Government Sectors." *Administration and Society* (2014): 939–966, doi:10.1177/0095399714548268; Child, Curtis, Eva Witesman, and Robert Spencer. "The Blurring Hypothesis Reconsidered: How Sector Still Matters to Practitioners." *VOLUNTAS: International Journal of Voluntary and Nonprofit Organizations* (2015): 1–22, doi:10.1007/s11266-015-9564-4.

7. Smith, Steven Rathgeb, and Michael Lipsky. *Nonprofits for Hire: The Welfare State in the Age of Contracting* (Cambridge, MA: Harvard University Press, 2009).

8. Starling, Grover. *Managing the Public Sector* (Boston, MA: Cengage Learning, 2010).

9. Bovaird, Tony. "Public-Private Partnerships: From Contested Concepts to Prevalent Practice." *International Review of Administrative Sciences* 70, no. 2 (2004): 199–215, doi:10.1177/0020852304044250; Kanter, Rosabeth Moss. "Collaborative Advantage." *Harvard Business Review* 72, no. 4 (1994): 96–108.

10. McDonald, Mary B. "Understanding Social Capital, Civic Engagement, and Community Building," in *Leadership in Nonprofit Organizations: A Reference Book*, ed. Kathryn Agard (Thousand Oaks, CA: Sage Publications, 2011), 46–55; Yankey, John, and Carol Willen. "Collaboration and Strategic Alliances," in *The Jossey-Bass Handbook of Nonprofit Leadership and Management*, 3rd ed., ed. David O. Renz and R. D. Hermans (San Francisco, CA: Wiley and Sons, 2010), 375–400; Bedsworth, William, Ann Goggins-Gregory, and Don Howard. "Non-Profit Overhead Costs: Breaking the Vicious Cycle of Misleading Reporting, Unrealistic Expectations, and Pressure to Conform." Bridgespan Group (2008). <https://www.bridgespan.org/insights/library/pay-what-it-takes/nonprofit-overhead-costs-break-the-vicious-cycle>; Ralser, Tom. *ROI for Nonprofits: The New Key to Sustainability* (Hoboken, NJ: John Wiley and Sons, 2008); Gazley, Beth, and Jeffrey L. Brudney. "The Purpose (and Perils) of Government-Nonprofit Partnership." *Nonprofit and Voluntary Sector Quarterly* 36, no. 3 (2007): 389–415, doi:10.1177/0899764006295997; La Piana, David. *Beyond Collaboration: Strategic Restructuring of Nonprofit Organizations* (Washington, DC: National Center for Nonprofit Boards, 1998), <http://blueshieldcafoundation.org/sites/default/files/u11/Beyond_Collaboration.pdf>; Gray, Barbara. "Strong Opposition: Frame-Based Resistance to Collaboration." *Journal of Community and Applied Social Psychology* 14, no. 3 (2004): 166–176, doi:10.1002/casp.773.

11. Holmberg, Stevan R., and Jeffrey L. Cummings. "Building Successful Strategic Alliances: Strategic Process and Analytical Tool for Selecting Partner Industries and Firms." *Long Range Planning* 42, no. 2 (2009): 164–193, doi:10.1016/j.lrp.2009.01.004.

12. Maurrasse, David J. "Higher Education–Community Partnerships: Assessing Progress in the Field." *Nonprofit and Voluntary Sector Quarterly* 31, no. 1 (2002): 131–139, doi:10.1177/0899764002311006; Brinkerhoff, Jennifer M. "Assessing and Improving Partnership Relationships and Outcomes: A Proposed Framework." *Evaluation and Program Planning* 25, no. 3 (2002): 215–231, doi:10.1016/S0149-7189(02)00017-4.

13. Hackman, J. Richard. "Learning More from Crossing Levels: Evidence from Airplanes, Orchestras, and Hospitals." *Journal of Organizational Behavior* 24 (2003):

905–922, doi:10.1002/job.1774; Morton, Keith. "The Irony of Service: Charity, Project and Social Change in Service-Learning." *Michigan Journal of Community Service Learning* 2, no. 1 (1995): 19–32.

14. Kolb, David A. *Experiential Learning: Experience as the Source of Learning and Development* (Upper Saddle River, NJ: FT Press/Pearson Education, 2014); Mohr, Jakki, and Robert Spekman. "Characteristics of Partnership Success: Partnership Attributes, Communication Behavior, and Conflict Resolution Techniques." *Strategic Management Journal* 15, no. 2 (1994): 135–152. doi:10.1002/smj.4250150205.

15. Casey, John. "A New Era of Collaborative Government-Nonprofit Relations in the US?." *Nonprofit Policy Forum* 2, no. 1 (2011): 1–23; Amirkhanyan, Anna A. "Collaborative Performance Measurement: Examining and Explaining the Prevalence of Collaboration in State and Local Government Contracts." *Journal of Public Administration Research and Theory* 19 (2009): 523–554, doi:10.1093/jopart/mun022; Graddy, Elizabeth A. "Cross-Sectoral Governance and Performance in Service Delivery." *International Review of Public Administration* 13, no. suppl. 1 (2009): 61–73. <http://ssrn.com/abstract=1516845>; Linder, Stephen H. "Coming to Terms with the Public-Private Partnership: A Grammar of Multiple Meanings." *American Behavioral Scientist* 43, no. 1 (1999): 35–51, doi:10.1177/00027649921955146.

16. Mendel, Stuart. "Roles of Government, Nonprofit Sector, Business and Family and Their Interaction in Democracy," in *Leadership in Nonprofit Organizations: A Reference Handbook*, ed. Kathryn Agard (Thousand Oaks, CA: Sage Publications, 2011), 38–45; Drucker, Peter F. *Managing the Nonprofit Organization: Principles and Practices* (New York: Collins, 1992).

17. McDonald, Mary B. "Understanding Social Capital, Civic Engagement, and Community Building," in *Leadership in Nonprofit Organizations: A Reference Book*, ed. Kathryn Agard (Thousand Oaks, CA: Sage Publications, 2011), 46–55; Gazley, Beth. "Linking Collaborative Capacity to Performance Measurement in Government-Nonprofit Partnerships." *Nonprofit and Voluntary Sector Quarterly* 39 (2010): 653–673, doi:10.1177/0899764009360823; Alexander, Jennifer, and Renee Nank. "Public-Nonprofit Partnership Realizing the New Public Service." *Administration and Society* 41 (2009): 364–386, doi:10.1177/0095399709332296; Gazley, Beth, and Jeffrey L. Brudney. "The Purpose (and Perils) of Government-Nonprofit Partnership." *Nonprofit and Voluntary Sector Quarterly* 36, no. 3 (2007): 389–415, doi:10.1177/0899764006295997; Galaskiewicz, Joseph, and Michelle Colman. "Collaborations between Corporations and Nonprofits," in *The Nonprofit Sector: A Research Handbook*, 2nd ed., ed. Walter Powell and Richard Steinberg (New Haven, CT: Yale University Press, 2006), 180–206; Selden, Sally Coleman, Jessica E. Sowa, and Jodi Sandfort. "The Impact of Nonprofit Collaboration in Early Child Care and Education on Management and Program Outcomes." *Public Administration Review* 66 (2006): 412–425, doi:10.1111/j.1540-6210.2006.00598.x; Guo, Chao, and Muhittin Acar. "Understanding Collaboration among Nonprofit Organizations: Combining Resource Dependency, Institutional, and Network Perspectives." *Nonprofit and Voluntary Sector Quarterly* 34 (2005): 340–361, doi:10.1177/0899764005275411; Prychitko, David L., and Peter Boettke. "The New Theory of Government Nonprofit Partnership: A Hayekian Critique of the Salamon Paradigm." *The Philanthropic Enterprise* (2002): 1–32; Mulroy, Elizabeth A. "Community as a Factor in Implementing Interorganizational Partnerships: Issues, Constraints, and Adaptations." *Nonprofit Management and Leadership* 14, no. 1 (2003): 47–66, doi:10.1002/nml.20; Austin, James E. "Strategic Collaboration between Nonprofits and Business." *Nonprofit and Voluntary Sector Quarterly* 29, no. suppl. 1 (2000): 69–97, doi:10.1177/089976400773746346.

18. Shaefer, H. Luke, Mariam DeLand, and Theodore R. Jones. "Leading Collaboration: Creating Strategic Alliances and Restructuring with Mergers, Acquisitions, and Integration," in *Leadership in Nonprofit Organizations: A Reference Book*, vol. 2, ed. Kathryn Agard (Thousand Oaks, CA: Sage Publications, 2011), 559–567.

19. Singer, Mark I., and John A. Yankey. "Organizational Metamorphosis: A Study of Eighteen Nonprofit Mergers, Acquisitions, and Consolidations." *Nonprofit Management and Leadership* 1 (1991): 357–369, doi:10.1002/nml.4130010406.

20. Alexander, Jennifer, and Renee Nank. "Public-Nonprofit Partnership Realizing the New Public Service." *Administration and Society* 41 (2009): 364–386, doi:10.1177/0095399709332296; Kjaer, Louise, Peter Abrahamson, and Peter Raynard. *Local Partnerships in Europe: An Action Research Project: First Phase Summary Report* (Copenhagen, DK: Copenhagen Centre, 2001); Isaacs, Stephen L., and John H. Rogers. "Partnership among National Foundations: Between Rhetoric and Reality." *To Improve Health and Health Care* 4 (2001): 221–240; Bracht, Neil, and Agis Tsouros. "Principles and Strategies of Effective Community Participation." *Health Promotion International* 5, no. 3 (1990): 199–208, doi:10.1093/heapro/5.3.199.

21. McLaughlin, Thomas. "Secret Sauce of Backroom Collaborations" (2010), <http://www.nonprofitfinancefund.org/sites/default/files/docs/2010/1-25-10thenonprofittimes.pdf>; Snavely, Keith, and Martin B. Tracy. "Collaboration among Rural nonprofit Organizations." *Nonprofit Management and Leadership* 11, no. 2 (2000): 145–165, doi:10.1002/nml.11202; Wood, Donna J., and Barbara Gray. "Toward a Comprehensive Theory of Collaboration." *Journal of Applied Behavioral Science* 27, no. 2 (1991): 139–162, doi:10.1177/0021886391272001.

22. Takahashi, Lois M., and Gayla Smutny. "Collaborative Windows and Organizational Governance: Exploring the Formation and Demise of Social Service Partnerships." *Nonprofit and Voluntary Sector Quarterly* 31, no. 2 (2002): 165–185, doi:10.1177/0899764002312001.

23. Starling, Grover. *Managing the Public Sector* (Boston, MA: Cengage Learning, 2010); Smith, Steven Rathgeb, and Michael Lipsky. *Nonprofits for Hire: The Welfare State in the Age of Contracting* (Cambridge, MA: Harvard University Press, 2009).

24. Graddy, Elizabeth, and Bin Chen. "Partner Selection and the Effectiveness of Inter-Organizational Collaborations," in *The Collaborative Public Manager: New Ideas for the Twenty-First Century*, ed. Rosemary O'Leary and Lisa Bingham (Washington, DC: Georgetown University Press, 2009), 53–70; Chen, Bin. *When Collaboration Is Required by Public Funding Agencies: Formation and Performance of Nonprofit Social Service Networks* (Doctoral dissertation, 2006: WorldCat, UMI No. 3238314); Gray, Barbara. *Collaborating: Finding Common Ground for Multi-Party Problems* (San Francisco: Jossey-Bass, 1989).

25. Bill and Melinda Gates Foundation, *Seven Cities Launch Collaborative Efforts to Improve College Graduation Rates* (2009), http://www.gatesfoundation.org/Media-Center/Press-Releases/2009/11/Seven-Cities-Launch-Collaborative-Efforts-to-Improve-College-Graduation-Rates.

26. Brinkerhoff, Jennifer M. "Government-Nonprofit Partnership: A Defining Framework." *Public Administration and Development* 22, no. 1 (2002): 19–30; Alexander, Jennifer. "The Impact of Devolution on Nonprofits." *Nonprofit Management and Leadership* 10 (1999): 57–70; Moore, Mark H. "Introduction," in *Creating Public Value: Strategic Management in Government* (Cambridge, MA: Harvard University Press), 2–12.

27. Alexander, Jennifer. "The Impact of Devolution on Nonprofits." *Nonprofit Management and Leadership* 10 (1999): 57–70.

28. *Cleveland Plain Dealer*, Hunger Network of Greater Cleveland and Cleveland Foodbank must cooperate to put more food on the tables of the poor (2009, December 26), Editorial.

29. Fosler, R. Scott. *Working Better Together: How Government, Business, and Nonprofit Organizations Can Achieve Public Purposes through Cross-Sector Collaboration, Alliances, and Partnerships: Executive Summary* (Author, 2002); Smith, Steven Rathgeb, and Michael Lipsky. *Nonprofits for Hire: The Welfare State in the Age of Contracting* (Cambridge, MA: Harvard University Press, 2009).

30. Austin, James E. "Strategic Collaboration between Nonprofits and Business." *Nonprofit and Voluntary Sector Quarterly* 29, no. suppl. 1 (2000): 69–97, doi:10.1177/089976400773746346; Mulroy, Elizabeth A. "Community as a Factor in Implementing Interorganizational Partnerships: Issues, Constraints, and Adaptations." *Nonprofit Management and Leadership* 14, no. 1 (2003): 47–66, doi:10.1002/nml.20; Guo, Chao, and Muhittin Acar. "Understanding Collaboration among Nonprofit Organizations: Combining Resource Dependency, Institutional, and Network Perspectives." *Nonprofit and Voluntary Sector Quarterly* 34 (2005): 340–361, doi:10.1177/0899764005275411; Gazley, Beth, and Jeffrey L. Brudney. "The Purpose (and Perils) of Government-Nonprofit Partnership." *Nonprofit and Voluntary Sector Quarterly* 36, no. 3 (2007): 389–415, doi:10.1177/0899764006295997; Alexander, Jennifer, and Renee Nank. "Public-Nonprofit Partnership Realizing the New Public Service." *Administration and Society* 41 (2009): 364–386, doi:10.1177/0095399709332296.

31. Rose-Ackerman, Susan. "Altruism, Nonprofits, and Economic Theory." *Journal of Economic Literature* 34 (1996): 701–728, doi:10.1007/BF02354190; Steinberg, Richard, and Bradford H. Gray. "'The Role of Nonprofit Enterprise' in 1993: Hansmann Revisited." *Nonprofit and Voluntary Sector Quarterly* 22 (1993): 297–316, doi:10.1177/0899764093224004; Weisbrod, Burton. *The Nonprofit Economy* (Cambridge, MA: Harvard University Press, 1988); Hansmann, Henry B. "Economic Theories of Nonprofit Organization," in *The Nonprofit Sector: A Research Handbook*, ed. Walter W. Powell (New Haven, CT: Yale University Press, 1987), 27–42.

32. Gazley, Beth. "Beyond the Contract: The Scope and Nature of Informal Government-Nonprofit Partnerships." *Public Administration Review* 68, no. 1 (2008): 141–154, doi:10.1111/j.1540-6210.2007.00844.x; Mulroy, Elizabeth A. "Community as a Factor in Implementing Interorganizational Partnerships: Issues, Constraints, and Adaptations." *Nonprofit Management and Leadership* 14, no. 1 (2003): 47–66, doi:10.1002/nml.20

33. Norris-Tirrell, Dorothy. "Nonprofit Organization Lifecycles," in *Leadership in Nonprofit Organizations: A Reference Book*, vol. 2, ed. Kathryn Agard (Thousand Oaks, CA: Sage Publications, 2011).

34. Lounsbury, Michael, and David Strang. "Social Entrepreneurship: Success Stories and Logic Construction," in *Globalization, Philanthropy, and Civil Society: Projecting Institutional Logics*, ed. David Hammack and Steven Heidemann (Bloomington: Indiana University Press, 2009), 71–94; Organization for Economic Co-operation and Development (OECD). *Successful Partnerships: A Guide. Forum on Partnerships and Local Governance at ZSI* (Paris: Centre for Social Innovation, 2006), <www.oecd.org/cfe/leed/forum/partnerships>.

35. Mulroy, Elizabeth A. "Community as a Factor in Implementing Interorganizational Partnerships: Issues, Constraints, and Adaptations." *Nonprofit Management and Leadership* 14, no. 1 (2003): 47–66, doi:10.1002/nml.20; Takahashi, Lois M., and Gayla Smutny. "Collaborative Windows and Organizational Governance: Exploring the Formation and

Demise of Social Service Partnerships." *Nonprofit and Voluntary Sector Quarterly* 31, no. 2 (2002): 165–185, doi:10.1177/0899764002312001.

36. Mulroy, Elizabeth A. "Community as a Factor in Implementing Interorganizational Partnerships: Issues, Constraints, and Adaptations." *Nonprofit Management and Leadership* 14, no. 1 (2003): 47–66, doi:10.1002/nml.20; Foster-Fishman, Pennie G., Deborah A. Salem, Nicole A. Allen, and Kyle Fahrbach. "Facilitating Interorganizational Collaboration: The Contributions of Interorganizational Alliances." *American Journal of Community Psychology* 29 (2001): 875–905, doi:10.1023/A:1012915631956.

37. Mulroy, Elizabeth A. "Community as a Factor in Implementing Interorganizational Partnerships: Issues, Constraints, and Adaptations." *Nonprofit Management and Leadership* 14, no. 1 (2003): 47–66, doi:10.1002/nml.20

38. Witesman, Eva M., and Sergio Fernandez. "Government Contracts with Private Organizations: Are There Differences between Nonprofits and For-Profits?" *Nonprofit and Voluntary Sector Quarterly* 42 (2012): 689–715, doi:10.1177/0899764012442592.

39. Seitanidi, Maria May. *The Politics of Partnerships: A Critical Examination of Nonprofit-Business Partnerships* (New York: Springer, 2010).

40. Bielefeld, Wolfgang. "Social Entrepreneurship and Business Development," in *Leadership in Nonprofit Organizations: A Reference Book*, ed. Kathryn Agard (Thousand Oaks, CA: Sage Publications, 2011), 475–483; Yankey, John, and Carol Willen. "Collaboration and Strategic Alliances," in *The Jossey-Bass Handbook of Nonprofit Leadership and Management*, 3rd ed., ed. David O. Renz and R. D. Hermans (San Francisco, CA: Wiley and Sons, 2010), 375–400; Mendel, Stuart. "Response to Philanthropy: What Nonprofits Can Tell Grantmakers about Forming Meaningful Partnerships?" (unpublished colloquium presentation proceedings given at the 38th Annual Conference of the Association of Nonprofit and Voluntary Organizations Action, Cleveland, Ohio, 2009); Fairfield, Kent D., and Kennard T. Wing. "Collaboration in Foundation Grantor-Grantee Relationships." *Nonprofit Management and Leadership* 19, no. 1 (2008): 27–44, doi:10.1002/nml.203; Van Slyke, David M. "Agents or Stewards: Using Theory to Understand the Government-Nonprofit Social Service Contracting Relationship." *Journal of Public Administration Research and Theory* 17, no. 2 (2007): 157–187, doi:10.1093/jopart/mulo12; Austin, James E. "Strategic Collaboration between Nonprofits and Business." *Nonprofit and Voluntary Sector Quarterly* 29, no. suppl. 1 (2000): 69–97, doi:10.1177/089976400773746346; La Piana, David. *Real Collaboration: A Guide from Grantmakers* (New York: Ford Foundation, 2001); La Piana, David. *Beyond Collaboration: Strategic Restructuring of Nonprofit Organizations* (Washington, DC: National Center for Nonprofit Boards, 1998) <http://blueshieldcafoundation.org/sites/default/files/u11/Beyond_Collaboration .pdf>; Linder, Stephen H. "Coming to Terms with the Public-Private Partnership: A Grammar of Multiple Meanings." *American Behavioral Scientist* 43, no. 1 (1999): 35–51, doi:10.1177/00027649921955146; Andreasen, Alan R. "Profits for Nonprofits: Find a Corporate Partner." *Harvard Business Review* 74, no. 6 (1995): 47–50.

41. Gazley, Beth. "Why Not Partner with Local Government? Nonprofit Managerial Perceptions of Collaborative Disadvantage." *Nonprofit and Voluntary Sector Quarterly* 39, no. 1 (2010): 51–76, doi:10.1177/0899764008327196.

42. Bielefeld, Wolfgang. "Social Entrepreneurship and Business Development," in *Leadership in Nonprofit Organizations: A Reference Book*, ed. Kathryn Agard (Thousand Oaks, CA: Sage Publications, 2011), 475–483; Yankey, John, and Carol Willen. "Collaboration

and Strategic Alliances," in *The Jossey-Bass Handbook of Nonprofit Leadership and Management*, 3rd ed., ed. David O. Renz and R. D. Hermans (San Francisco, CA: Wiley and Sons, 2010), 375–400; Fairfield, Kent D., and Kennard T. Wing. "Collaboration in Foundation Grantor-Grantee Relationships." *Nonprofit Management and Leadership* 19, no. 1 (2008): 27–44, doi:10.1002/nml.203; Van Slyke, David M. "Agents or Stewards: Using Theory to Understand the Government-Nonprofit Social Service Contracting Relationship." *Journal of Public Administration Research and Theory* 17, no. 2 (2007): 157–187, doi:10.1093/jopart/mulo12; Austin, James E. "Strategic Collaboration between Nonprofits and Business." *Nonprofit and Voluntary Sector Quarterly* 29, no. suppl. 1 (2000): 69–97, doi:10.1177/089976400773746346.; Linder, Stephen H. "Coming to Terms with the Public-Private Partnership: A Grammar of Multiple Meanings." *American Behavioral Scientist* 43, no. 1 (1999): 35–51, doi:10.1177/00027649921955146

43. Bailey, Darlyne, and Kelly Koney. *Strategic Alliance among Health and Human Services Organizations: From Affiliations to Consolidations* (Thousand Oaks, CA: Sage Publications, 2000).

44. Hardy, Cynthia, Nelson Phillips, and Thomas B. Lawrence. "Resources, Knowledge and Influence: The Organizational Effects of Interorganizational Collaboration." *Journal of Management Studies* 40 (2003): 321–347, doi:10.1111/1467-6486.003.

45. Isett, Kimberley R., and Keith G. Provan. "The Evolution of Interorganizational Network Relationships over Time: Does Sector Matter?" *Journal of Public Administration Research and Theory* 15, no. 1 (2005): 149–165, doi:10.5465/APBPP.2002.7519436.

46. Selden, Sally Coleman, Jessica E. Sowa, and Jodi Sandfort. "The Impact of Nonprofit Collaboration in Early Child Care and Education on Management and Program Outcomes." *Public Administration Review* 66 (2006): 412–425, doi:10.1111/j.1540-6210.2006.00598.x.

47. Austin, James E. "Strategic Collaboration between Nonprofits and Business." *Nonprofit and Voluntary Sector Quarterly* 29, no. suppl. 1 (2000): 69–97, doi:10.1177/089976400773746346; Bartling, Charles E. *Strategic Alliances for Nonprofit Organizations* (Washington, DC: American Society of Association Executives, 1998); Osborn, Richard N., and John Hagedoorn. "The Institutionalization and Evolutionary Dynamics of Interorganizational Alliances and Networks." *Academy of Management Journal* 40 (1997): 261–278, doi:10.2307/256883; Gomes-Casseres, Benjamin. "Alliance Strategies of Small Firms." *Small Business Economics* 9, no. 1 (1997): 33–44; Kanter, Rosabeth Moss. "Collaborative Advantage." *Harvard Business Review* 72, no. 4 (1994): 96–108; Wasserman, Stanley, and Joseph Galaskiewicz. *Advances in Social Network Analysis: Research in the Social and Behavioral Sciences* (Thousand Oaks, CA: Sage Publications, 1994); Wood, Donna J., and Barbara Gray. "Toward a Comprehensive Theory of Collaboration." *Journal of Applied Behavioral Science* 27, no. 2 (1991): 139–162, doi:10.1177/0021886391272001.

48. Mendel, Stuart C., and Jeffrey L. Brudney. "Putting the NP in PPP: The Role of Nonprofit Organizations in Public-Private Partnerships." *Public Performance and Management Review* 35 (2012): 617–642, doi:10.2307/23484758; Seitanidi, Maria May. *The Politics of Partnerships: A Critical Examination of Nonprofit-Business Partnerships* (New York: Springer, 2010).

49. Ideas for the table taken from the following:

Alexander, Jennifer, and Renee Nank, "Public-Nonprofit Partnership: Realizing the New Public Service," *Administration and Society* 41 (2009): 364–386; Austin, James,

The Collaboration Challenge: How Nonprofits and Businesses Succeed through Strategic Alliances (Hoboken, NJ: John Wiley & Sons, 2010); Bailey, Darlyne, and Kelly Koney, *Strategic Alliance among Health and Human Services Organizations: From Affiliations to Consolidations* (Thousand Oaks, CA: Sage Publications, 2000); Brody, Ralph, *Effectively Managing Human Service Organizations* (Thousand Oaks, CA: Sage Publications, 2005); Gazley, Beth, and Jeffrey L. Brudney, "The Purpose (and Perils) of Government-Nonprofit Partnership," *Nonprofit and Voluntary Sector Quarterly* 36 (2007): 389–415; Guo, Chao, and Muhittin Acar, "Understanding Collaboration among Nonprofit Organizations: Combining Resource Dependency, Institutional, and Network Perspectives," *Nonprofit and Voluntary Sector Quarterly* 34 (2005): 340–361; Linder, Stephen H., "Coming to Terms with the Public-Private Partnership: A Grammar of Multiple Meanings," *American Behavioral Scientist* 43 (1999): 35–51; Mulroy, Elizabeth A., "Community as a Factor in Implementing Interorganizational Partnerships: Issues, Constraints, and Adaptations," *Nonprofit Management and Leadership* 14, no. 1 (2003): 47–66; Seitanidi, Maria May, *The Politics of Partnerships: A Critical Examination of Nonprofit-Business Partnerships* (New York: Springer, 2010); Selden, Sally Coleman, Jessica E. Sowa, and Jodi Sandfort, "The Impact of Nonprofit Collaboration in Early Child Care and Education on Management and Program Outcomes," *Public Administration Review* 66 (2006): 412–425; Yankey, John, and Carol Willen, "Collaboration and Strategic Alliances," in *The Jossey-Bass Handbook of Nonprofit Leadership and Management*, ed. David O. Renz and R. D. Hermans, 3rd ed. (San Francisco, CA: Jossey-Bass, 2010).

50. Forrer, John J., James Edwin Kee, and Eric Boyer. "'Dimensions of Cross-Sector Collaboration' and 'Cross-Sector Partnerships and Public-Private Partnerships,'" in *Governing Cross-Sector Collaboration* (New York: John Wiley, 2014); Bryson, John M., Barbara C. Crosby, and Melissa Middleton Stone. "The Design and Implementation of Cross-Sector Collaborations: Propositions from the Literature." *Public Administration Review* 66, no. suppl. 1 (2006): 44–55, doi:10.1111/j.1540-6210.2006.00665.x; Guo, Chao, and Muhittin Acar. "Understanding Collaboration among Nonprofit Organizations: Combining Resource Dependency, Institutional, and Network Perspectives." *Nonprofit and Voluntary Sector Quarterly* 34 (2005): 340–361, doi:10.1177/0899764005275411

51. Alter, Catherine Foster. "Building Community Partnerships and Networks," in *The Handbook of Human Services Management*, 2nd ed. (Thousand Oaks, CA: Sage Publications, 2009); Gazley, Beth. "Beyond the Contract: The Scope and Nature of Informal Government-Nonprofit Partnerships." *Public Administration Review* 68, no. 1 (2008): 141–154, doi:10.1111/j.1540-6210.2007.00844.x; Brinkerhoff, Jennifer M. "Government-Nonprofit Partnership: A Defining Framework." *Public Administration and Development* 22, no. 1 (2002): 19–30; Ahn, Roy. "Nonprofit/Nonprofit Collaboration in Boston." (2006) <www.barrfoundation.org>.

52. Krug, Kersti, and Charles B. Weinberg. "Mission, Money, and Merit: Strategic Decision Making by Nonprofit Managers." *Nonprofit Management and Leadership* 14 (2004): 325–342.

53. Austin, James E. "Strategic Collaboration between Nonprofits and Business." *Nonprofit and Voluntary Sector Quarterly* 29, no. suppl. 1 (2000): 69–97, doi:10.1177/089976400773746346; Hardy, Cynthia, Nelson Phillips, and Thomas B. Lawrence. "Resources, Knowledge and Influence: The Organizational Effects of Interorganizational Collaboration." *Journal of Management Studies* 40 (2003): 321–347, doi:10.1111/1467-6486.003; Guo, Chao, and Muhittin Acar. "Understanding Collaboration among Nonprofit

Organizations: Combining Resource Dependency, Institutional, and Network Perspectives." *Nonprofit and Voluntary Sector Quarterly* 34 (2005): 340–361, doi:10.1177/0899764005275411; Selden, Sally Coleman, Jessica E. Sowa, and Jodi Sandfort. "The Impact of Nonprofit Collaboration in Early Child Care and Education on Management and Program Outcomes." *Public Administration Review* 66 (2006): 412–425, doi:10.1111/j.1540-6210.2006.00598.x; Gazley, Beth, and Jeffrey L. Brudney. "The Purpose (and Perils) of Government-Nonprofit Partnership." *Nonprofit and Voluntary Sector Quarterly* 36, no. 3 (2007): 389–415, doi:10.1177/0899764006295997; Gazley, Beth. "Beyond the Contract: The Scope and Nature of Informal Government-Nonprofit Partnerships." *Public Administration Review* 68, no. 1 (2008): 141–154, doi:10.1111/j.1540-6210.2007.00844.x.

54. Mendel, Stuart. "Achieving Meaningful Partnerships with Nonprofit Organizations: A View from the Field." *Journal of Nonprofit Education and Leadership* 3, no. 2 (2013).

55. Wymer, Walter W., Jr., and Sridhar Samu. "Dimensions of Business and Nonprofit Collaborative Relationships." *Journal of Nonprofit and Public Sector Marketing* 11, no. 1 (2003): 3–22, doi:10.1300/J054v11n01_02; Andreasen, Alan R. "Profits for Nonprofits: Find a Corporate Partner." *Harvard Business Review* 74, no. 6 (1995): 47–50.

56. Ideas for the table taken from the following:

Carnwell, Ros, and Alex Carson, "Understanding Partnerships and Collaboration," in *Effective Practice in Health and Social Care: A Partnership Approach*, ed. Ros Carnwell and Julian Buchanan (London: McGraw Hill, 2005), 3–20; Granovetter, Mark, "The Strength of Weak Ties: A Network Theory Revisited," *Sociological Theory* (1983): 201–233; Knoke, David, and Song Yang, *Social Network Analysis*, 2nd ed. (Thousand Oaks, CA: Sage Publications, 2008); LeCompte, Margaret D., Jean J. Schensul, Merrill Singer, Robert T. Trotter, and Ellen K. Cromley, *Mapping Social Networks, Spatial Data, and Hidden Populations* (Lanham, MD: Rowman Altamira, 1999); Linder, Stephen H., "Coming to Terms with the Public-Private Partnership: A Grammar of Multiple Meanings," *American Behavioral Scientist* 43, no. 1 (1999): 35–51; Ralser, Tom, *ROI for Nonprofits: The New Key to Sustainability* (Hoboken, NJ: John Wiley, 2007); Takahashi, Lois M., and Gayla Smutny, "Collaborative Windows and Organizational Governance: Exploring the Formation and Demise of Social Service Partnerships," *Nonprofit and Voluntary Sector Quarterly* 31, no. 2 (2002): 165–185.

57. Carnwell, Ros, and Alex Carson. "Understanding Partnerships and Collaboration," in *Effective Practice in Health and Social Care: A Partnership Approach*, ed. Ros Carnwell and Julian Buchanan (London: McGraw Hill, 2005), 3–20.

58. Knoke, David, and Song Yang. *Social Network Analysis*, 2nd ed. (Thousand Oaks, CA: Sage Publications, 2008); Takahashi, Lois M., and Gayla Smutny. "Collaborative Windows and Organizational Governance: Exploring the Formation and Demise of Social Service Partnerships." *Nonprofit and Voluntary Sector Quarterly* 31, no. 2 (2002): 165–185, doi:10.1177/0899764002312001; LeCompte, Margaret D., Jean J. Schensul, Merrill Singer, Robert T. Trotter, and Ellen K. Cromley. *Mapping Social Networks, Spatial Data, and Hidden Populations* (Lanham, MD: Rowman Altamira, 1999); Granovetter, Mark. "The Strength of Weak Ties: A Network Theory Revisited." *Sociological Theory* 1, no. 1 (1983): 201–233, doi:10.2307/202051.

59. Ralser, Tom. *ROI for Nonprofits: The New Key to Sustainability* (Hoboken, NJ: John Wiley and Sons, 2008).

60. LeCompte, Margaret D., Jean J. Schensul, Merrill Singer, Robert T. Trotter, and Ellen K. Cromley. *Mapping Social Networks, Spatial Data, and Hidden Populations* (Lanham, MD: Rowman Altamira, 1999).

61. Linder, Stephen H. "Coming to Terms with the Public-Private Partnership: A Grammar of Multiple Meanings." *American Behavioral Scientist* 43, no. 1 (1999): 35–51, doi:10.1177/00027649921955146.

62. Frumkin, Peter. "Introduction," in *Strategic Giving: The Art and Science of Philanthropy* (Chicago: University of Chicago Press, 2006).

63. Bedsworth, William, Ann Goggins Gregory, and Don Howard. "Non-Profit Overhead Costs: Breaking the Vicious Cycle of Misleading Reporting, Unrealistic Expectations, and Pressure to Conform." Bridgespan Group (2008) <https://www.bridgespan.org/insights/library/pay-what-ittakes/nonprofit-overhead-costs-break-the-vicious-cycle>; Granovetter, Mark. "The Strength of Weak Ties: A Network Theory Revisited." *Sociological Theory* 1, no. 1 (1983): 201–233, doi:10.2307/202051.

64. Glasbergen, Pieter. "Setting the Scene: The Partnership Paradigm in the Making," in *Partnerships, Governance and Sustainable Development: Reflections on Theory and Practice*, ed. Pieter Glasbergen, Frank Biermann, and Arthur P. J. Mol (Cheltenham, UK: Edward Elgar, 2007), 1–25; Waddock, Sandra A. "Building Successful Social Partnerships." *MIT Sloan Management Review* 29, no. 4 (1988): 17–23.

2 Nonprofit Partnerships: The Gold Standard

Overview

Following the overview of nonprofit-first partnership in the introduction and chapter 1, this chapter begins to integrate our research data—the executive interviews—into the discussion in order to identify the benefits and challenges of partnership from a nonprofit-first perspective.

Introduction

As we discussed in the introduction and chapter 1, nonprofit-first partnerships describe partnership arrangements from the perspective of the nonprofit organization. Nonprofit-first is an essential element in establishing the most desirable partnership arrangements—the nonprofit partnership gold standard—because it prioritizes the perspective of nonprofit executives. The challenge in drawing on the wisdom of our nonprofit respondents is how to best aggregate and assess their interview data as a basis for our analysis of nonprofit-first partnerships. Our goal in this chapter is to identify the desired benefits of partnership from the nonprofit perspective.

According to our interviews, nonprofit leaders believe that they recognize a partnership opportunity when they see it. However, these same nonprofit leaders seldom, if ever, noted performance standards or partnership benchmarks as important tools of the trade. Instead, the partnership case narratives most often featured "soft" measures emphasizing what we have come to understand as the "emotional intelligence" of the organizational leaders or the participants' adaptability to the partnership organizational culture and behavior.[1]

This chapter presents our first extensive integration of the primary source material gathered through the interviews and survey with the fifty-two nonprofit executives. This examination will reveal the beneficial outcomes of partnership, as stated by those involved in these relationships, including aspects of their creation, performance, and impact on the participants.[2] We credit the nonprofit professionals who contributed important partnership cases with teaching us about the characteristics and the most rewarding outcomes of partnerships.

What Executives Think Partnership Is: Five Clusters of Partnership Categories

Several examples of the partnership case study data demonstrate the difficulty of defining partnership analytically. When prompted with this question, one nonprofit executive shared briefly and simply that a partnership "should advance both organizations." Another executive answered the same question by noting that partnership occurs when two entities work together intensely in some instances and less so in others. In a third example, an executive said that a partnership occurs when the parties work together to fulfill the goals of the project and the requirements of the grant that funded it. While other nonprofit executives offered more nuanced and lengthy answers, for the most part, their definitions lacked precision or concrete explication. Four examples offered by social services, philanthropic, economic development, and arts and culture nonprofit executives, respectively, illustrate the point:

> "The definition of a partnership is a collaboration that shares both risk and reward."
> "Partnership is a collaboration between organizations that includes sharing of resources toward common purposes."
> "A partnership is when both sides bring their expertise and competence, and the outcome and effort is enhanced by the collaboration. There are two types of partnerships. One is formal where something is agreed upon and put in writing. The other type is informal. Both types include an organization working together with another agency. A partnership requires the sharing of information, services, and resources."
> "A partnership is a collaborative effort among multiple agencies working toward the same goal, who have related missions."

As mentioned previously, all eighty-two partnership cases were contributed by the nonprofit executives who responded to our call for examples of partnership between their organization and another nonprofit, government, or business organization. Although we discuss the nomenclature of nonprofit subsectors in greater detail in chapter 5, for our purposes in this discussion, the fifty-two nonprofit executives interviewed represent organizations in six nonprofit subsector fields. The six subsector labels adhere to the classification system adopted by the US Internal Revenue Service (IRS) based on a nonprofit's primary mission. Nonprofit organizations in the United States are required to file Form 990, report annual financial activity, and so forth in order to qualify as tax-exempt organizations. The information provided in Form 990 is self-reported, while the exemptions status and subsector classification are then determined and assigned by the IRS.

Table 2.1 presents the subsector distribution of the fifty-two organizations that provided nonprofit-first partnership cases for this study.

Table 2.1. Nonprofit Organizations and Their Subsector Assignments.

Subsector Classification	Number of Organizations	Percentage of Sample
Arts, Culture, and Humanities	4	8
Education	5	9.5
Environment	3	6
Health	5	9.5
Human Services	16	31
Public, Social Benefit	19	36
Total	52	100

The fifty-two organizations in our sample constitute a highly diverse collection drawn from a pool of over 800 nonprofit organizations to whom we issued a call for voluntary participation in this study. These 800 organizations comprise the listing of nonprofit organizations that have worked with the Center for Nonprofit Policy & Practice at Cleveland State University over a ten-year period, from 2002 to 2012, and have consented to receive mailings (postal and email) from this institution. Across our data set of fifty-two organizations, no discernible pattern emerged with respect to the size of annual revenues, number of employees, population served, or organization age. The fifty-two nonprofits have a broad range of organizational characteristics, including dates of founding and continuous operations dating from 1903 to 2009; annual revenues ranging from a low of $18,600 to a high of $78,000,000; numbers of highly compensated senior staff as reported on Form 990 ranging from as few as a single individual to as many as eleven; missions, purposes, and subsectors that include the six subsector categories listed in table 2.1; and administrative capacities from grassroots organizations with volunteers providing essential services to large institutions with complex organizational structures, program divisions, and formalized bureaucracies. The fifty-two organizational participants also include a subgroup of nonprofits dedicated to philanthropic grant-making or federated giving organizations that we examine in detail in chapter 6.

The interview protocol began with a fundamental question: "Tell us what you think a partnership is." This question helped to establish a baseline of our participants' understandings of partnership. Based on the responses, we were able to categorize the elements of partnership that executives perceived as inherent to the concept. To standardize responses on the interview questions following, we explained that for the purposes of the interview, we considered a partnership to involve an exchange of some type between the partner organizations. Exchanges encompassed funding, personnel, facilities and equipment, expertise, information, knowledge, capacity, and access to other opportunities, or any combination of these resources.

We asked the nonprofit executives to tell us about their "important partnerships." We defined these partnerships as essential to the ability of the non-profit organization to meet its core mission. The purpose of delineating important partnerships was to make sure that the nonprofit executives framed and related their experiences in significant, rather than peripheral, partnerships. This definition also required the executives to think of both the processes and outcomes of their important partnerships. We then asked a series of open-ended questions regarding partnership to gain insight into partnership types. In these questions we asked about a variety of processes and results, including motives, roles, services delivered, financial and nonfinancial resources required or obtained, satisfaction with the partnership outcomes, perceived impact of the partnership, and lessons and advice to other nonprofit executives.

The professed motivations for partnership were grouped into five clusters of characteristics distinctive to important partnerships. We first grouped the definitions of partnership by the nonprofit executives along with their explanations of why they thought their partnership cases were important. We verified the clusters of motivations through identifying common themes among the responses to each interview prompt. The five clusters depict basic features that characterize the nonprofit-first approach to partnership.

Responses to our baseline questions concerning partnership varied from the terse staccato of a few short sentences to lengthy ruminations. In organizing the themes of such different answers, we focused on the most fully defined concept (typically the first mentioned) as the primary definition characteristic of the partnership. We also considered supplemental thoughts that may have been offered as qualifying, secondary characteristics, since these secondary concepts typically overlap in a manner that demonstrates partnerships form for a variety of reasons that are not mutually exclusive.

The results of our efforts to understand how our sample of fifty-two non-profit executives define, explain, and understand partnership are represented by the five clusters illustrated in figure 2.1 and explained in greater detail below. The five clusters identify:

1. partnership where mutual benefits enable each participant to achieve their respective goals and purposes, and are a main catalyst for the partnership;
2. partnerships in which the fulfillment of an organizational mission is the principal motivation for the endeavor;
3. partnership where participants share rather than exchange resources, and the shared resources motivate one or both participants to engage in the endeavor

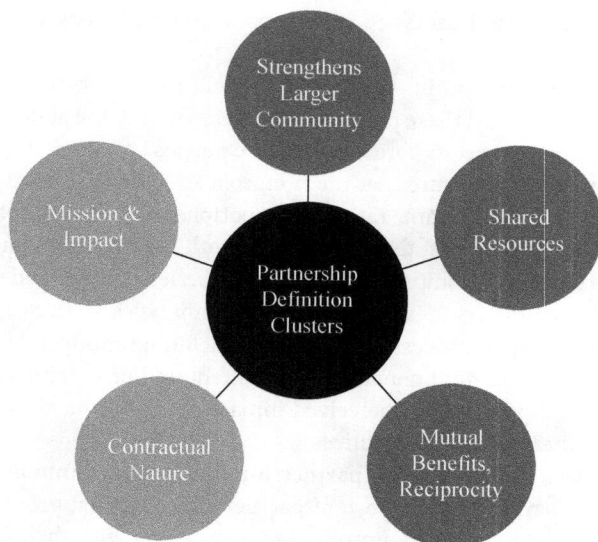

Fig. 2.1 Nonprofit-First Partnership Mission Drivers.

("sharing" includes the sharing of financial resources, practical knowledge of the endeavor, or relevant skills or information; aspects of organizational infrastructure, such as a human resources and personnel management capacity; and cultural values as expressed through the support of staff and utilization of volunteers);

4. partnership arrangements where the most central feature is a contractual agreement defining and governing the relationship; and

5. partnerships whose outcomes contribute to the greater good of the community, and to the creation of public value through mission fulfillment, policy and social change, and community problem-solving.[3]

The most numerous cluster of partnership cases among the categories illustrated in figure 2.1 were characterized not only by mutual benefit outcomes, but also by common acts of reciprocity and expressions of trust. Executives who mentioned reciprocity, fair play and trust as secondary themes looked to support their partners and the collaborative work of the endeavor, to build their institution and its capacity, and to create and connect with a larger network with which they might develop future projects. One example was offered by the executive director of a social services program dedicated to empowering disadvantaged youth by providing them with job-readiness and training skills. This respondent discussed the partnership of his agency with another social services organization dedicated to building similar job skills and placement programs for adults:

"The relationship scores 9 on a scale of 10 due to the good feelings and overall achievement of the goals of the partnership. While it would have been easier to work without a partner, going alone would not have been the best way, or even a successful way, given the requirements of the project.... Also, both organizations ... were willing to go beyond meeting the minimums of our memorandum of understanding ... so that both organizations took on a caretaker role regarding the health and well-being of the partnership."

The second-largest definition cluster involved partnership cases distinguished by mission fulfillment of the nonprofit-first participant. In this cluster, nonprofit actors sought partnership as a path toward innovation in their own organization. One example was provided by the chief executive of the local chapter affiliate of a national health education, research, and advocacy organization devoted to finding a cure for a genetic disease. The national organization was a private, not-for-profit research organization with an international network of scientists seeking to develop pharmaceuticals that slow the disease's progression. The local affiliate was described as a partner of the national office which was engaged in other partnerships to accomplish the mission of "curing the disease." This nonprofit executive stated,

> We do not separate out our partners in this work, but we must have them to perform our work. We consider them a network or chain of groups necessary to do the work/research called for in our mission. For example, we work with a partner to hold a fundraising event; donors make contributions that we then add to the big pot in the national office; we then work with a local hospital to apply those dollars to conduct research. Every link in this chain is needed to accomplish the work of our organization. We are a partner in partnerships.

The third cluster of partnership cases is distinguished by nonprofit organizations seeking to increase their impact by sharing resources gained through joint efforts. One example involves a partnership between a growing grassroots organization dedicated to advancing at-risk youth through performing and visual arts education and a large nonprofit health-care system. The larger organization sought out the grassroots partner as a way for health-care professionals to expose teenagers to careers in the medical field:

> The health-care system, which is one of the larger employers in our city, sought ways to engage low-income at-risk youth in an employee pipeline. Since their interests were with our target population, we cautiously entered into partnership. Our partner, the health-care institution, fulfilled its commitments to the kids by taking the lead on the topics discussed, and the kids benefited. They spent time with the children and allowed quality question and answer sessions. The services were fulfilling [and] provided enlightenment and value for our students, the target population. And the success was a pleasant surprise.

The fourth cluster of partnership cases was most readily defined as an arrangement codified by a formal contract. For example, the executive of a large, well-established social services agency providing services to children with developmental disabilities and their families related,

> The partnership described began as an informal, voluntary collaboration directly involving the County and indirectly involving public school districts for children requiring specialized education services and settings focused on autism. The partnership evolved, becoming more formal and defined by a formal contract for services delivery and funding. It is renewed each year through the budget development process of the County, which has continuously allocated funds to the partnership to serve youth requiring services in the public school system. In practice, we arrange and hold therapeutic classes for youth enrolled in our programs at several facilities around the county. The County also leases for $1 per year to us a building to hold the classes for youth and grants us the ability to provide professional development credits for public school instructors by facilitating collaboration with unionized public sector teachers employed by the school districts.

The nonprofit executive describing this partnership explained that though most of her partnerships with county government began as formal response to their requests for specific services for which a formal contact was typical, the manner in which the project evolved appeared to her to be one of mutual realization that an informal, ad hoc conversation could grow into a formal contract for services.

The fifth cluster suggests mission fulfillment centered on creating public value for the public good. The nonprofit executive of a large food bank explained her conception of partnership as follows:

> The Food Bank was founded on the principle of partnership [which] is critical to everything we undertake. Otherwise we would simply be a warehouse full of food. Our network of member agencies provides us a way to get food into the communities that otherwise would be difficult to both access food and distribute food to. Eighty percent of the food that comes through the Food Bank is distributed through/by our member agencies to those in need. We consider ourselves as a big sister in the partnership and are much like the agencies that we work with—working to feed hungry people.

What Executives Think Partnership Does

The examples of partnership motivations and assumptions within each cluster illustrate the diversity and complexity of the nonprofit executives' views on partnership. Nonetheless, three further examples demonstrate how the overlaps in partnership descriptions often made it difficult to assign clusters.

In the first example, the nonprofit executive described a partnership case that was established to meet the social services program goals of serving homebound elderly residents of three suburban communities. The partnership existed to improve the lives and independence of seniors in the area. Although the case exhibited partnership characteristics corresponding to four of the five clusters, the most distinctive characteristic described by the nonprofit executive was not fulfilling the mission of the nonprofit organization to serve the elderly residents, but rather that the assistance to the target population served the greater good of the community.

In a second example, the nonprofit executive expressed that an important outcome for her organization dedicated to eradicating a genetic disease was the publicity associated with working in collaboration with teaching and research hospitals. In her view, the publicity of the partnership outcomes validated advocacy, research, education, and service to the community, and the primary characteristic of the partnership was the credibility it gave her organization, which was then able to influence congressional funding priorities. This result helped to raise even more attention and funding for the cause. Although the primary cluster assigned to this case was mutual benefits for all the participants, we also recognize possible overlap into the mission and impact cluster.

In a third example illustrating the difficulty of assigning partnership clusters, a nonprofit coordinating agency whose members include large social services organizations formed a partnership to strengthen members' respective abilities to improve conditions for homeless individuals and families. The nonprofit executive stated that the partnership outcomes improved services to those facing homelessness through better funding and interaction with other organizations addressing the same issue. According to this respondent, the primary characteristic of the partnership was that the partnership's overarching purpose and defining characteristic was strengthening the community more generally, even though its intent was to alleviate a specific social pathology.

The complexity of assigning all eighty-two of the cases described by the nonprofit executives to partnership clusters called for a thorough reading and understanding of the underlying rationale the nonprofit executives offered for each partnership case. In figure 2.2 and in the next section of this chapter, we offer greater detail to trace the nuances of the cluster types and the cases which support them. In our view, the process of assigning the partnerships to clusters is instructive because the methods of matching the cases to a particular category inform our thoughts toward theory or theories for nonprofit partnerships based on the experience of those working in the field.

Cluster 1: Mutual Benefits

Figure 2.2 displays the percentage distribution of the five clusters. Percentages were calculated as a quotient of the simple fraction of partnership cases where

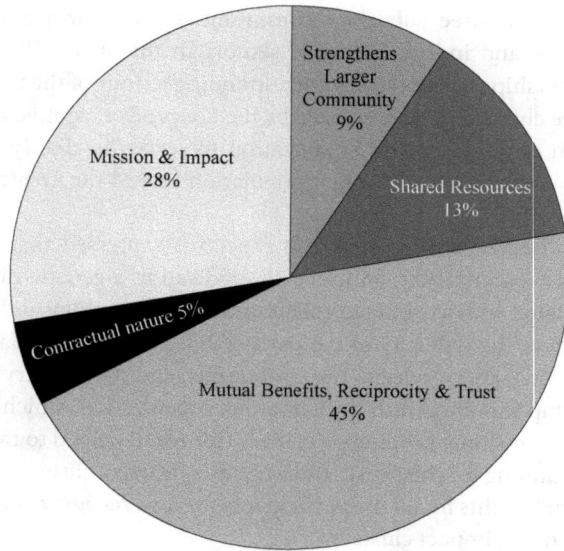

Fig. 2.2 Nonprofit-First Partnership Cluster Characteristics.

each of the categories was described as the first rationale of a partnership over the total number of partnership cases in our sample of cases.

The largest cluster by frequency comprises 45 percent of partnership cases and centers on mutual benefits of the outcomes achieved. In differentiating the definition clusters earlier in this chapter based on the motivations for partnership, nonprofit executives offered that mutuality also had strategic implications, which are derived through reciprocity of authority, dual ownership of the endeavor, perceived fairness, and funding equality of the partners. For example, a social services community-building and advocacy organization described partnership as a vehicle for organizations to help each other, with mutuality in power and authority within the relationship as the most distinguishing characteristic: "Partnerships exist because of a mutuality of agreement that there is a partnership, and it is the partners themselves who most consider the relationship as a partnership. Outsiders cannot attest to a partnership. Partnership members share equally the risks, the rewards, and the dynamic of the process, but have the flexibility to leave at any time."

Nonprofit executives noted the following organizational and leadership behaviors as evidence that a partnership is nurtured by mutual benefits: an intensity of effort by both partners on the work of the partnership endeavor; leadership fidelity to the partnership as a priority for the organization; and durability of the partnership as strategic, important and meaningful, and worthy of a longer-term commitment by both partners. In one case, a statewide organization focused on advocacy for best practices in public policy described partnership with its primary competitor organization in terms of political orientation as a reciprocal relationship between the two where each received technical assistance, publicity, and collaborative services as a benefit of the partnership. According to the nonprofit executive, the partner organizations set aside their political differences for the goal of producing a balanced conference. The ambition to create a neutral space recognized an equality of standing in the endeavor, a sharing of strengths, and compensation for their weaknesses for both. The executive observed that the value of the relationship arose from the leaders' commitment, as they made the endeavor a priority worthy of their time and attention.

> As a joint venture between organizations advocating public policy to very different and opposed political interests, the partnership ... allowed for a sharing of ideas across the broad political spectrum ... [and] provided access to populations and constituents typically isolated by politically ideological barriers. The promise for mutual benefits offered opportunity to stimulate trust-building and collegiality among public policy makers ... [and] improved the working relationships and discourse in the state ... around public policies important to each organization. Working toward the common goals of producing a policy paper and conference was a goal that the partners came to model for multipartisan partnership.... Our hope is that ... the partnership ... will transform the manner in which public policy makers and political leaders will interact with one another.

In an another partnership example involving a community development organization dedicated to urban development, redevelopment, and community investment, the nonprofit executive noted that operations and decision-making are equitable and replicable over time, originate at the highest level of leadership in both partner organizations, and feature full and honest disclosure: "We attribute our satisfaction with the partnership to the alignment that exists between all our partners on the strategies of the initiative to address vacant land reuse. The partnership isn't perfect, but the problems aren't anything that we feel is harmful to the initiative ... and sometimes things take longer than we would like ... but there is genuine trust and goodwill between the partners along with an equal commitment to the initiative.... Having a mutual respect and collegial relationship among the partners ... and having a little humor ... all contribute to the success."

A third partnership case described by the nonprofit executive of an interdenominational social justice organization promoting community dialogue to advocate for racial and cultural tolerance made the point that partnership occurs when each participant contributes and benefits equally. This executive attributed the process of creating partnership results to a trusting and respectful long-term commitment originating at the top levels of both organizations: "Mutual interests or a desire to have mutual return of benefits at the same time is important. For example, when the two participants are a nonprofit engaged with another nonprofit, an undercurrent of competition is present. An organization can be aware of this within five minutes of an exploratory meeting based on the tone set by the participants. You don't want to acquiesce to do things you might have not wanted ... so ... agreements in advance are really important ... including what each organization gains and needs from the partnership."

Cluster 2: Mission Fulfillment

The second cluster by frequency, comprising 28 percent of the total in figure 2.2, is best described as mission fulfillment and impact. The high proportion of cases comprising this cluster reveals an important pattern in the nonprofit executives' interview responses. Typically, nonprofit executives described two inseparable concepts to partnership: what a partnership is in terms of a process, and what a partnership does in terms of its purpose and outcomes. For example, the executive of a statewide policy and advocacy organization devoted to good government practice quoted previously defined partnership as "a reciprocal relationship between organizations where our organization receives technical assistance, publicity, ... collaborative services, and sponsorship of special events while our counterpart receives benefits it desires. Both organizations involved recognize an equality of standing, sharing of strengths, and supplement for weaknesses of both parties."

The executive director of an association of businesses and property owners in a central business district defined partnership as "two or more organizations or institutions with shared visions and goals work[ing] together in a way that is mutually beneficial."

The executive director of a social services organization devoted to providing training in job skills and preparedness as well as summer and full-time employment opportunities to at-risk youth defined partnership as "two different organizations, usually both nonprofit, [that] come together to do a project where money is shared, along with outcomes and accountability. It is important to have clear roles among partners. In a 'true partnership,' there is equal accountability and responsibilities. The secret of a good partnership is to be clear about what the tasks, accountability, and timelines will be."

The executive director of a short-term residential facility and program for recovering female substance abusers defined partnership as "an agreement between two parties who then work together for a specific goal."

The executive director of a community re-entry organization for formerly incarcerated individuals living in urban settings by providing life and employment skills and assistance defined partnership as follows: "A partnership relationship exists between two bodies in which there is mutually agreed-upon roles, benefits, and support of one another ... [toward] whatever ends [for which] the arrangement has been created."

When asked to define partnership, the executive director of a community performing arts organization whose target populations are at-risk youth and homeless adults, and whose mission was to use the healing power of the arts to increase quality of life in a designated urban neighborhood, stated, "A partnership must have a mutual benefit that will support or augment the mission of those engaged in the partnership. The mission of the partnership must also be crystal clear."

The executive director of a botanical garden in an urban neighborhood suggested, "A partnership is when one organization does something with another organization to get results they couldn't have gotten on their own."

In the vast majority of cases described by the nonprofit executives, the respondents emphasized the partnership outcomes or mission as the primary cause of realizing both the larger public good and the more specific mutual benefits to each organization. The dual nature of partnership outcomes—"transactional" in respect to an exchange (as opposed to "shared," which we discuss later) of resources or services between partners for a mutual benefit such as a return on investment, or "transformational" in terms of advances in organizational capacity, changes in public policy, or evidence of societal impact—are a significant aspect of partnership.[4] For example, the transactional and transformational nature of partnerships enable nonprofit executives to weigh whether the conditions of society can potentially be changed as a result of two organizations addressing a problem via their partnership. This standard of partnership offers nonprofit leaders with two means of measure for important partnerships. First, that mission fulfillment has transactional outcomes essential for both the participants and others related to the production of the partnership's work. Second, the action of partnership itself is transformative to the larger society, creating public value by creating systemic relationships where none existed and increasing the capacity of community leaders to solve problems.

The perspectives of transactional and transformational outcomes of partnership suggest that partnership is an essential means of nonprofit organization mission fulfillment: nonprofits interact with individuals, other nonprofits, public institutions, and businesses to fulfill their mission.[5] In the absence of partnership as a means to achieve their ends, nonprofits could not fulfill their missions. Consequently, partnership is a required outcome of nonprofit performance, rising beyond the level of a "best practice" and perhaps qualifying as a theory of nonprofit organizations.

Cluster 3: Sharing Resources

A third partnership cluster, comprising 13 percent of the total in figure 2.2, focuses on sharing resources and expertise as a way to amplify the efforts of both partner organizations toward the goals and purposes of the partnership. This cluster focuses on the synergistic aspects of partnership. Sharing was a way for each partner to both participate in innovative services or administration as its own return on investment and work at a scale of accomplishment that would not have been possible in the absence of the partnership. In these cases, nonprofit executives maintained that the manner in which partners supplemented each other's efforts was an important reason for engagement.

The notion of sharing as a desirable characteristic and outcome of partnership is multifaceted among our cases. Sharing between partner organizations can be a component of the delivery of a service or of the partnership endeavor itself. For example, one case described by the executive of a federated grant-making organization required that two competing social and human services organizations "share the work" to deliver services for the good of the community as a way to encourage them to form partnerships in the future. In this instance, sharing was a desired outcome to require the participants to change their behavior toward collaboration.

In another example, in a fundraising partnership among arts organizations in an urban revitalization zone of a city, the nonprofit executive credited the collaboration as enabling pooled salary, workload and supervision, funds for development prospect lists, resources for an experienced consultant, and a support staff infrastructure combining the operating budgets of the partners. The nonprofit executive stated that the partnership project changed as the partners shared greater resources, and the relationships matured to realize more benefits.

> Over time, the partnership has led to a migration of purpose to include a much larger set of goals to include the economic development of the community and five separate projects, the benefits of which we all share. We credit the expanded purpose to our increased trust in our partner executive directors, strong communication between the directors combined with frequent interactions, and the clarity offered to each partner by way of the five operating agreements created to share in the risks, costs, and benefits of the projects of the partnership. We value the partnership attributes: the knowledge and experience we have gained about real estate development, the increased profile and attention the organization has gained from the partnership, and the opportunity to raise major gifts from private and public sources.

A second case example involved two nonprofit business development organizations with different but complementary missions. The first focused on strengthening regional manufacturing industries through the innovative use of technology, and the second sought ways to incubate and nurture technology-centered start-up businesses focusing on alternative energy generation. Through the partnership, both organizations blended their program operations, leveraging staff expertise, market reach, and business venture opportunities while receiving in exchange major funding support for these activities from the US Department of Commerce. The revenue generated by the endeavor was shared equally by the partners. As the executive of one of the partner organizations claimed, "We attribute the common cultures, shared goals and mission, and similar backgrounds of both organizations as the major factors that contributed to the success of the partnership. Both parties bring private sector background to the table, and are able to understand both sides of private and nonprofit industries. This allows us to exchange information and teach each other, ultimately enhancing the partnership and making decisions that are truly collaborative."

A third example of sharing resources involves close working relationships between two social services organizations with similar-sized budgets and paid staff. The nonprofit executive described a deepening relationship between the partners that involved shared line personnel, pooled client referrals, complementary missions, and a continuum of service. The executive noted that the most distinctive characteristic of the partnership was sharing services, resources, and outcomes. The sharing became so strongly identified with and characteristic of the partnership that the collaborative endeavor eventually stimulated a merger between the two organizations.

Cluster 4: Greater Good, Public Good, and Public Value

Weaving throughout these cases is the conception of nonprofit-first partnership as a space where the greater good, public good, and public value are created. Briefly, these three ideas are established concepts in American civil society that result from altruism. In prior research, we have argued that public value is created by nonprofit organizations and philanthropic institutions fulfilling their missions in anticipated and unanticipated ways that extend beyond the transactional output of the partnership endeavor.[6] Greater good, public good, and public value outcomes occur from the formal and informal actions of individuals and public and private institutions that promote the common welfare or create benefits shared by everyone. The societal conditions that lead to beneficial results arise when individuals trust public policy makers and public institutions, have faith in the system of economy and justice, and enjoy (conceivably) a level playing field to achieve a measure of social, political, and economic security.[7]

As we have argued previously, public value can be observed in the desirable effects radiating out from a project beyond the immediate target group or clientele or area; that is, the positive externalities created. As reflected in the comments of nonprofit executives sharing their partnership cases, public value themes are byproducts of nonprofit-first partnerships. For example, nonprofit-first partnership arrangements are credited as stimulating public value and benefits through intangibles such as positive feelings of the partnership actors, improvements in the larger environment for collaboration, and redirected public dollars through advocacy.[8]

For example, in one case, the defining characteristic of the partnership was not cast as the target community receiving direct services offered by the partnership. Instead, the nonprofit executive relating the partnership case pointed to the impact of those services on the overall community in alleviating chronic pathologies, such as lack of attention to seniors, concerns for public health, youth poverty and homelessness, and unemployment. The executive justified this viewpoint by maintaining that the partners' developing bonds and fellowship and their growing network of social connections were benefits that helped drive the greater good as nonprofits perform their work and serve constituents, form and strengthen social networks, sustain social capital, build community, and nurture the bonds of trust that, together with the activities of government and business, comprise the fabric of civil society.

In another example of partnership characterized by the nonprofit executive as primarily contributing to the greater good, a nonprofit community development corporation sought to address large-scale community disinvestment in an urban neighborhood. Leveraging the community objective of accommodating artists seeking affordable, low-cost residence/work spaces in edgy urban settings, the organization formed a partnership with local government to form an arts district. This partnership had an impact not only on the target population, who were able to acquire idle buildings in a receptive community, but also on the community development corporation, which sought additional means of fulfilling its mission in the larger community. The greater good benefit to the residents was the lasting recognition that the partnership brought to the neighborhood as a safe, inviting space for the general public.

Yet a third partnership example involved a social service provider's influence on local government policy-making through drawing attention to the newest and best research on little-understood health conditions, such as autism, and the efficacy of group homes as an alternative to larger, more expensive public institutions. The executive director explained that the partnership with the county government raised the visibility of her organization as an expert provider of educational services to children diagnosed with autism to area families and school systems. Increased visibility led to more referrals to all agency programs, and to the creation of additional programs for autistic youth as well as youth with other needs. The executive also credited the partnership with contributing to the organization's core mission while improving service delivery competencies:

"We reached out to the superintendent to form a greater collaboration better aligned with the services of the County.... Our strategic plan directed us to form more partnerships as a way to have greater impact on the policies of the County regarding our target population.... The goal of this partnership was to provide quality services with the most effective use of resources that the County couldn't because it is a government agency."

Other examples of public value creation occur among the cases in which leaders sought ways to contribute new practices in the community emanating from the partnership's work products. One case example involved a partnership to promote and market the redevelopment of an older neighborhood through the creation and organization of a community festival. The partnership with local government attracted residents of all income levels to a celebration in a revitalized local park, raised regional awareness of neighborhood safety, educated participants on the local history of the city, and stimulated the education and involvement of children. The practical knowledge each partner gained was reported to public sector contracting agents and grant makers, who were then petitioned by the nonprofit-first partnership actors to change their policy and philanthropic initiatives for the neighborhood.

In another example, the head of a grassroots food pantry organization located in an inner-ring suburb in partnership with the mayor's office expressed satisfaction that the mayor personally took his telephone calls, which he considered an indicator that the partnership was a priority for the mayor. The nonprofit executive's perception of the importance of the partnership was further indicated by the mayor's help in solving problems in his organization so that the food pantry could better serve constituents in the city:

> There was a noticeable increase in public exposure and community awareness of our mission, programs, and ability to reach its target population.... The target population, who are homebound low-income elderly residents, are provided with better services and, because the food is donated to them, have less out-of-pocket expense for their monthly food costs. They also receive a monthly visit by our staff or volunteers, providing a human contact for individuals who may otherwise be isolated. The services provided were allocated to increased numbers of program participants in the city and also in surrounding cities due to improvements to our capacity to perform.

The nonprofit executive director of a local affiliate of a one-hundred-year-old social justice organization dedicated to the empowerment of minority populations told us that the partner organization brought intellectual and problem-solving resources to the endeavor, enabling both organizations to create valuable, impactful programs in minority business development that were replicated throughout their national headquarters organization. In the absence of the partnership, the social justice organizations would not have had the local political standing with funders to carry out the work in a field crowded with other business development service provider competitors:

> The partnership was originally set up to increase the number of minority-owned businesses in a geographical area and to create more jobs. It exists because there was a need to address high unemployment rates in the city and a need to stimulate business start-ups for minorities. We initiated the partnership because our partner's mission is based on public service to the community. We couldn't have done the work ourselves and needed the credibility of our partner. The partnership had an impact on our organization because it challenged us to alter our approach exclusively from social justice and social services to include economic development, primarily by bringing entrepreneurial language to our strategic thinking and program development for the central city population that wouldn't have otherwise considered it as a possibility.

Cluster 5: Contractual Nature

A fifth cluster, comprising 5 percent of the total in figure 2.2, concerns the contractual requirement, both verbal and written, as the most distinctive characteristic of the partnership. Although few nonprofit executives cast this characteristic of their partnerships as the most important and defining feature of their partnership cases, the value of a contract was mentioned as at least one important feature in well over half of the cases recounted. The executives whose cases were assigned to this cluster claimed repeatedly that their most important partnerships were characterized by a balance of concise, formal contracts with clear deliverables and performance parameters accompanied by informal understandings between the senior leadership of both partner organizations.

From this perspective, the contract served as a formal declaration with agreed-upon provisions. It presented the framework for governing the partnership relationship and holding each of the actors accountable for its share of the rights, burdens, and responsibilities. Unlike the other four clusters, which tend to emphasize aspirational outcomes and ambitions for the partnership, nonprofit executives who pointed to the presence of a contract as the most distinguishing feature of the partnership viewed the relationship through its operational necessities.

Describing a collaborative fundraising case involving arts and community development organizations, a nonprofit executive gave great credit to contracting as the reason that the partnership could take place:

> As two of the nonprofit organizations in the partnership consider the other a competitor, five elaborate operating partnership agreements were drafted to

protect the interests of each partner, while binding the partnership together through performance expectations of each.... The legal agreements enabled each partner to opt out at a penalty [and] provided the framework for problem-solving disputes that arose.... The operating agreements also set the conditions to require and orchestrate annual plans for achieving the partnership mission.... The nature of the agreements encouraged steady communication between the partner members as a way to avoid any break in the partnership until the goals of the partnership are met.

In another example, the nonprofit executive of a fast-growing social services agency, whose primary service population are developmentally disabled adults in group home settings moving into new communities with the purchase of single-family residences and multiunit apartment buildings, noted, "A true partnership comes together when two entities ... sign an agreement to work together toward a common goal.... A binding agreement in the form of a formal contract is indicative of a partnership, as opposed to a collaboration, which is a less formal, handshake understanding."

A second example related by a nonprofit-first executive of an agency devoted to strengthening men to be good fathers and role models to their sons, strongly asserted that a partnership is identified through either a contract or a memorandum of understanding between two or more organizations to perform a scope of services. In 2004, Cuyahoga County, Ohio, conducted a survey of its departments and programs intended to identify deficiencies in program delivery and provide access to services to support fathers. Based on the survey results, Cuyahoga County issued a request for proposals (RFP), to which this small faith-based grassroots organization responded and was awarded a contract for services based on its work with noncustodial fathers: "Cuyahoga County entered into a contractual arrangement for services because our mission is to work with the target population noted in the RFP. Both the population and services Cuyahoga County sought to provide closely matched to our purpose, which was 'to enrich the quality of life of families by focusing on prisoner re-entry, fatherhood involvement, job readiness, and closing the achievement gap for youth.'" Echoing the concept yet again, the leader of the local affiliate of a large global nonprofit organization offering housing and counseling services to the homeless described a nonprofit-first partnership as two or more organizations entering into a formal arrangement to work together: "The purpose of this relationship is to further our organization, but also to further their organization ... because ... it is possible for several organizations to accomplish more than can be done by one alone.... Though participation in the partnership ... is voluntary ... there is a formal contract with our partner that is reviewed and renewed annually."

"Important" Partnerships

In addition to asking nonprofit executives to define partnership, we sought their descriptions of partnerships they considered "important." Drawing on their collective responses, we concluded that nonprofit executives consider "important" partnerships as those that are essential to their organization's ability to meet its core mission. We also asked the nonprofit to describe partnership cases they considered important. In choosing cases to share, we asked the executives to provide an example of collaboration between their nonprofit organization and another nonprofit organization, a government actor, and a business. Using the same techniques described earlier in this chapter, we were able to cluster the eighty-two "important" cases into six categories based on the reasons executives believed the partnerships were important.

The nonprofit executives recognized that some partnerships are more important than others. Less important partnerships are those driven by motivations that executives consider contrived, superficial, or beyond their control. In those instances, external rules and procedures defined the relationship with the nonprofit organization in the role of simply meeting the requirements. Examples described by the executives referred to heavy-handed incentives that government officials and private philanthropic institutions sometimes offer through either public policy or collaboration requirements of RFPs. One executive, for instance, implied that his organization's participation was influenced by concerns that it would be excluded from future opportunities for funding or public discourse if it did not respond affirmatively to the partnership opportunity. Another executive acknowledged that the greatest risk to his organization is that the partner may not be able to live up to the partnership commitments or responsibilities, thus reflecting on the reputation of his organization as a partner for future opportunities. A third nonprofit executive shared that when government is a partner to a nonprofit, the relationship is usually more top-down and prescribed by public authority.

Table 2.2 presents six descriptive clusters of important partnerships. These clusters are comprised of thematic responses offered by the nonprofit executives describing why they felt the partnership was important. They include: strengthening each participant's ability to achieve its mission; engaging an issue critical to the community; increasing market share; building trust; attracting funding from third parties; and leading to program development and innovation. As in the earlier exercise involving the concept of partnership definition, the nonprofit executives often attributed more than one reason for claiming their partnership case rose to the level of "important." Table 2.2 presents all of the reasons that nonprofit executives gave as justification for each of the partnership cases cited as "important" (maximum three cases per respondent). We note from table 2.2 that eighty-two cases correlated to 279 explanations or justifications distributed across the six clusters.

Table 2.2. Descriptive Characteristics Clusters Arising from Important Partnerships by Sector.

#	Clusters of reasons executives gave for determining a partnership was "important"	Frequency aspects of this cluster were attributed	Nonprofit-Nonprofit	Nonprofit-Government	Nonprofit-Business
1	Strengthens each participant's ability to achieve its mission, allows participants to complement and supplement one another, and brings expertise and capacity to each member	120 43% of grand total	90 75% of total for this category	21 17.5% of total for this category	9 7.5 % of total for this category
2	Partnership engages a critical issue for the community, addresses a problem no entity can solve on its own, and creates a system for change or a system of program delivery where none existed before	54 19% of grand total	36 67% of total for this category	17 31% of total for this category	1 2% of total for this category
3	Partnership increases the market share, increases credibility, and brings diverse constituents together	39 14% of grand total	34 87% of total for this category	5 13% of total for this category	0 0% of total for this category
4	Partnership builds trust, raises awareness among service providers, and mitigates the risks of all parties	31 11% of grand total	24 77% of total for this category	6 19% of total for this category	1 3% of total for this category
5	Partnership constitutes program development or innovation for each participant	22 8% of grand total	14 64% of total for this category	7 32% of total for this category	1 4% of total for this category
6	Partnership attracts funding from third parties and creates revenue opportunity	13 5% of grand total	9 69% of total for this category	3 23% of total for this category	1 8% of total for this category
	Total	279	207	59	13

The process of assigning partnership cases to categories is illustrated in the following example. The nonprofit executive of a large organization serving autistic and developmentally disabled children and their families described an important partnership as essential to achieving the organization's mission while solving a problem for the community, performing advocacy with local public officials, and informing community civic stakeholders and grant makers. The partnership "is important because it deals with advocacy, community, and program problem-solving and decision-making about policy. Our chief executive officer regularly meets with the county executive counterpart on this partnership. The relationship has grown over time, and has survived the succession of a superintendent. The partnership has moved beyond simple contracts and grown into mutual respect between executives and have a sense of team efforts."

This case was coded in three of the important partnership categories listed in figure 2.2: engages with an important issue for the community; builds trust and raises awareness among service providers; and constitutes program development or innovation for its participating organizations.

Another example comes from an elite private school for girls that provides service-learning placements working in partnership with a nonprofit, faith-oriented, international community development organization. In the words of the nonprofit executive from the girls' school describing the case:

> While our partner is an organization that we work with on planning international immersion experiences for our students, we consider the partnership to be an important partnership because they have been able to go beyond just the service of the trip, and as such, the school and our partner benefit. Part of the process included persuading parents that our partner's program was not for religious trip/mission purposes which was their organizational mission and which was one of their goals for the collaboration. Some of the other outcomes included use of our students for a local speaker series and for fundraising by the students.

The partnership case enabled the school to arrange meaningful volunteer activities for youth and to raise its profile in community engagement while enabling the faith organization to strengthen its reputation among its peers and stakeholders and to increase grant dollars toward the fulfillment of its mission. From the perspective of the private girls' school, the partnership was important because it fulfilled the central tenets of each organization's mission, built trust in the community, raised money, and attracted positive attention to both institutions.

Cluster 1: Strengthen Each Participant's Ability to Achieve Its Mission

As figure 2.2 shows, more than 43 percent of the important partnerships cases featured arrangements that strengthened the nonprofit organization's capacity to achieve its mission. In their descriptions of organizations strengthened through important partnerships, executives observed that stronger arrangements arose when partnerships contributed innovations in service delivery, personnel management and fiscal administration, and fundraising or program impact that were not otherwise possible. For example, a community foundation established a pilot program focused on service delivery to youth in a public school district. Going beyond its traditional role as funder, the foundation convened, coordinated, and served as quality control for service providers to advance the program. The experience sensitized the foundation staff to the challenges the grantees face in service delivery, thus improving collegiality among the funder, grant recipient, and school district. The foundation pointed to this element of the partnership as an important, unanticipated innovation for the community philanthropic program: "As the mediating organization within the partnerships, this partnership was important because we learned the importance of strategy and thinking ahead of the partnership. As facilitator of the partnership and the smaller relationships within our program, we have learned to foresee change and adjust the strategy when necessary, and learned from change when it happens."

A second example involves a group home disabilities service provider to an adult population. The organization noted that the partnership with a peer service provider rose to the level of "important" because it extended the program's reach and allowed for new services, while at the same time building trust for future partnership endeavors. The nonprofit executive explained, "Both organizations foresee the need for new technology-enhanced services. We think that both our partner and ourselves can bring skills and expertise that neither could alone do, to ... expand the use of technology in services provided for people with developmental disabilities."

Yet another example involves a nonprofit organization serving youth in summer job programs that entered into a partnership with another nonprofit whose mission centers on employment training and job placement for adults. The partnership received public funding to provide continuous services that would not otherwise be offered, fulfilling an unmet need of the community. The nonprofit executive explained that the partnership was important because it allowed her organization to offer an innovative program, reaching new clients and fulfilling an unmet need in the community: "An organizational value is to actively seek collaboration and to engage in partnerships with other organizations. We consider collaboration and partnership as a part of our sustainability strategy toward achieving our mission, while protecting our core work focus and competencies from incrementally moving away from our mission. The project offered both organizations a way to obtain program funds, under our respective missions, to address training and employment needs of difficult-to-employ youth and adult populations, which are the respective service groups of both organizations."

Two other cases described as important nonprofit-government and nonprofit-business partnerships reflect the cluster 1 characteristics of strengthening the nonprofit's ability to achieve its mission, allowing the participants to complement and supplement each other, and bringing expertise and capacity to the nonprofit organization. In the nonprofit-government partnership example, a public sector contract to serve the homeless was consistent with the mission of the nonprofit partner as well as with the need of the county government to provide supplementary services. This same nonprofit organization also described the benefits of a partnership with a national retail chain business as boosting its credibility among peer service providers, while enabling the business to accept trained and externally supervised workers at reduced costs.

Cluster 2: Engage a Critical Issue for the Community

The second cluster includes 19 percent of the cases rising to the level of important partnership because they served to meet unaddressed community needs. Among the cases in this cluster, nonprofit executives noted that the unaddressed community needs had not been identified by public policy makers or grant makers but rather were innovative projects of the partnership. To several nonprofit executives, partnerships arranged to meet unmet community needs held greater importance precisely because the participants came together voluntarily without prompting from a third party.

One example involved the coordination of emergency response services in the form of communication equipment to the elderly. The partnership arose because the nonprofit organization mission was to serve a local community of independent-living senior citizens by matching their needs via 411-type phone services to appropriate service providers. When requests for information on home security and emergency response for an apartment complex known to house elderly residents became more frequent, the nonprofit initiated a partnership with a local business to create a product line for this market, paid for by public and private funding sources and coordinated by the nonprofit. In describing why this case was important, the nonprofit executive explained that the partnership mission was to install technology in people's homes that would enable them to summon help in an emergency: "The partnership was originally set up to install technology in people's homes that would enable them to summon help in an emergency. It exists because it provides a cost-effective method of providing people with services by monitoring in their homes so they can stay in their homes rather than be institutionalized. The partnership had an impact on the target population—ability to use nonintrusive technology to monitor people's well-being and keep them living independently at less cost than other options."

In this case, the nonprofit organization developed the relationship with the business because the nonprofit executive wanted to use a grant from the city to provide the services to low-income elderly people. The business entered into the partnership because it was a useful new service that could be provided for customers they had worked with previously, but in a different manner. The partnership resulted in a cost-effective method of keeping elderly people in their homes rather than in an institution, and it was facilitated by a public sector grant to the nonprofit organization.

Another example involved a nonprofit organization that provided food services to a growing population of homebound elderly not readily visible or represented by local advocates. Since the elderly were unable to receive food through the traditional food bank model, which requires recipients to travel to a central distribution site, a small community food bank formed to make deliveries to them on a monthly basis. Working in partnership with local government, the small nonprofit organization was able to use the official sanction of public sector leaders to serve this previously unserved population: "The factors that work toward meeting the goals of the partnership are that important, high-level members of city government, both in the Mayor's Office and City Council, are aware of the partnership and respond to us directly, as evident that they accept my telephone calls and call me back. These actions demonstrate acceptance of our mission by government as something worthy of their support and interest."

Cluster 3: Increase Market Share

The third cluster of important partnership cases listed in figure 2.2 reflects endeavors that increased the scope or scale of nonprofit program offerings. Executives described partnerships in this category as raising the nonprofit's program capacity and ability to provide services and/or reaching out to a greater number and diversity of people. In one partnership case, a nonprofit organization dedicated to urban land redevelopment worked with an extensive expanse of land that had sat empty for nearly fifty years following urban renewal demolition. Through the process of creating a community plan with local government, the nonprofit was able to envision and work toward the development of a new residential and commercial community. As resources became available for the new endeavor, the scope of the partnership grew beyond the original two members to include private housing developers and business enterprises. The nonprofit executive described the importance of the case as follows:

> The partnership was set up to work together to improve community development and to better the surrounding neighborhood. In addition, the partnership was committed to bringing businesses to the neighborhood institutions and

to figure out a way to unite the various organizations and entities, physically and economically. The effects of the partnership on our organization were in public exposure, community awareness of its mission, and establishment of creditability and viability. The target population was provided with a better neighborhood [in which] to live, increased the growth of the two universities, brought additional population into the neighborhood, and developed an artist community on Superior Avenue.

A second example involved a longtime social services settlement house seeking to draw positive attention to the community and attract middle-class residents and business activity in the neighborhood serviced. In partnership with local government, the nonprofit endeavor involved a summer festival program in a community park. As the nonprofit executive explained, "The purpose is to increase perception of the area as an arts venue and business opportunity, to increase opportunity for artists to exhibit their work, and to expose the children of the neighborhood to the arts and different populations of all incomes as a destination."

Cluster 4: Build Trust

Important partnership cases represented in the fourth cluster are those that were enriched by and evolved through the building of trust. Although it may seem surprising that trust was credited as a specific characteristic of "important" partnerships in only 11 percent of the cases, trust was often implicit in case examples. Many references to trust were indirect or reflected in different ways, such as expressions of confidence and expectations that the nonprofit executives had assumed reasonable risks in their partnerships and that commitments would be honored and reciprocated. Other indirect references attributed aspects of trust to communication and mutual respect between the participants.

Many more cases reflect implicit trust. For example, one executive shared that partnership offers opportunities to build understanding and collegiality among peer organizations. Another described expectations for mutual benefits and reciprocity between participants, durability of the relationship over time, and resiliency to withstand "hiccups" and overcome challenges. A third executive noted the success of the partnership endeavor as contingent on both organizations sharing the risks and rewards of the venture.

For our purposes, trust can be viewed through the framework presented by the Russell Sage Foundation.[9] In this series, trust is associated with decision makers obligated to choose a course of action whose potential costs depend on the actions of another person or organization. Trust involves accepting the risk that the other person will follow a more or less simple set of moral rules understood by both parties. In a partnership, trust enables each partner to predict the commitment, effort, and performance of his or her counterpart with a degree of confidence that binds the two together reflected by their sense of fairness and equity.

The cases in this cluster reflect two noteworthy observations about trust. First, building trust is an essential value and priority worthy of significant attention, time, and effort by the partner organizations. Second, a successful partnership can earn the trust of third parties, which may be able to bring additional funding or other sponsorship or support to the partnership endeavor. The trust of third parties grants legitimacy and adds value to a partnership in ways that strengthen it from the perspective of the larger society.

Although well-conceived and functioning partnerships are important because they drive the creation of public value, poorly performing partnerships can diminish public value, including the opportunity for third-party trust. As a result, partner organizations can be harmed through loss of funding, prestige and reputation, and opportunities. One nonprofit executive explained these perils:

> Our partnership was initiated by a community social service provider serving families and children based on friendly and ongoing conversations with us, another nonprofit, devoted to job training and employment skills. The family and children services partner told us their overarching reason to form the partnership was because it wanted to serve more people through existing programs, and we, the job training partner organization, had a strong capacity and expertise. Trust between we two was high at the beginning.... Soon, the endeavor began underperforming.... It lost money and the funders lost faith in the project.... The relationship deteriorated ... staff were laid off and the experience left hard feelings.

The executive recounted that his partnership was not well-conceived, performed poorly, and did not reach its goals. Although his organization gained capacity temporarily, it did not produce the results required in the contract underwriting the partnership. He noted that an unsuccessful partnership likely lowered his organization's chances of obtaining future awards through his community's RFP process because of the loss of trust.

Cluster 5: Organizational Innovation and Program Development

The fifth cluster of cases described as important partnerships in table 2.2 emanates from the ability to create new social innovations to address enduring challenges in the local community. The nonprofit executives noted that they were likely to enter into a partnership if they perceived a transformative and meaningful pay-off for the endeavor beyond the transactional work of the partnership. Transformative pay-offs hold two dimensions for the partner participants: those they may achieve within their organization, such as changed operating culture, procedures, and practices; and those that have observable impact outside the organization in the larger community.

Two cases illustrate the use of innovations as an outcome for partnership. The executive of a small philanthropic institution shared that both his organization and his more powerful philanthropic partner agreed on equal sharing of authority as an overarching value of the partnership. In his view, this simple but important element of the relationship–equity of partnership authority, which he considered an innovation and model in the field of grant-making—was the key feature enabling a successful services program provided to the target population of the partnership. His view was influenced by past experiences wherein nonprofit grant makers rarely, if ever, "shared authority." He claimed that this equity set the tone for collaboration and joint learning that facilitated problem-solving and a productive relationship.

A second example came from the nonprofit executive of an arts and culture organization focused on community planning and facilitating relationships in the community. The executive shared that his organization entered into the partnership because his board of directors believed that the nonfinancial resources and creative will for innovation within the local neighborhood community development corporation would create a model for urban redevelopment funded by others as the needs arose. The transformative community outcome aligned with aspects of the organization mission focused on changing public policy and other forms of advocacy. In his view, crafting a partnership between artists and economic development was an innovative way for both organizations to work together in a way that would not have otherwise occurred.

Cluster 6: Attract Funding From Third Parties

The availability of funding and/or the opportunity to obtain funding turned out to be a minor characteristic of an important partnership, as represented by the sixth cluster in table 2.2. The nonprofit executives explained that funding was important so long as it enabled the partnership to thrive, but it was less important as a sole motivator to enter into a partnership, as a reward for forming the partnership, or as a reason that a partnership rose to the level of being important. Overall, funding was seldom mentioned as a sole reason for partnership. For example, the executive of a grassroots social services agency, whose prepartnership operating budget was approximately $175,000, described the following: "We provided uncompensated 'in-kind' services such as use of our facility to deliver programs. The county contracting policy allowed only direct costs to be charged to the project. As a result, program coordination, management, and operating overhead were absorbed by us as the cost of doing business with the county. While the program revenue to us was essential to us for performing a work, we believe that the arrangement is reasonable, as the work of the project clearly falls within our organizational mission and priorities ... while our share of the responsibilities included our internal costs of operations."

Another example further illustrates the general complexity and subtlety of executives' perspectives regarding the role of funding in important partnerships. In this case, the nonprofit organization provided services for job readiness and employment placements for community re-entry of formerly incarcerated adult males. The partnership involved use of public sector funding to bring two nonprofit organizations together. The executive relating the case reported that his organization voluntarily entered into partnership with a larger social services agency, and together they responded to the county government's RFP. The motivation for the partnership was a mutual need to share and supplement service expertise between the two organizations. Because the public dollars available were insufficient to support the full operation of the partnership, the community re-entry partner provided a match of grant dollars using its own discretionary funds and facilities. In the end, the executive felt he had engaged in partnership for the right reasons, and had offered a positive model of voluntarily partnership formation to policy makers and grant makers seeking to spur partnerships. The nonprofit executive described the following rationale: "We provide discretionary dollars and facilities to the partnership while receiving computer equipment to administer the program.... Our nonfinancial contributions include skills and expertise with the target population, volunteer labor, [and] access to the target population; we receive connections to political decision makers, endorsements from important community stakeholders, and the ability to convene other organizations."

ONE PARTNER INFLUENCES CULTURAL CHANGE IN THE OTHER

Certain examples of the transformational power of partnership within an organization were also cast as important outcomes of collaboration. Some of the internal organization-transformation attributed to the partnership were fiscal controls or best practices adopted by the partners during the endeavor; increased ability to generate external communications such as public relations and marketing strategies; and enhanced procedures for holding employees to greater performance standards. Nonprofit executives also described subtler transformative changes in organizational culture, such as increased attention devoted to detail and record-keeping and the use of systematic data to assess organizational performance or improve planning. Several executives described that based on their exposure to partners, they were able to change organizational procedures in budgeting, accounting, program planning, and assessment. An executive of a small community food pantry noted that partnership provided him with advice and access to the partner organization's infrastructure for public advocacy and networking. This access dramatically changed the circumstances and overall sustainability of the nonprofit food pantry.

Two cases offered by the same nonprofit executive described transformation in his organization as necessary to adapt budgeting practices to bring the nonprofit into alignment with the government partner and desirable to advance human resources practices. The executive asserted that public sector contracting policy allows only direct costs to be charged to a project in cash accounting, while his agency utilized an accrual method of accounting. In the second case, the executive noted the moral values of his partner in employing the people the agency served: "The public sector funding for this project comes from three sources: a countywide property tax, and state and federal funds. Accountability is therefore an important characteristic of our partnership, and it was necessary for our organization to better align our budgeting and reporting to that of our public sector partner.... "Exposing our organization to the values of our partner influenced our operating values, specifically in our hiring practices to include our own residents who are partner-trained to work in our office."

Transformative community impact

With respect to the transformative effects realized externally on the community through the partnership, some of the important partnerships inaugurated innovative process improvements in service delivery. In several instances, the nonprofit executives pointed to innovation through new methods that improved the capacity of the partner organizations to perform their work and pursue their missions. One case example that illustrates this point involved combining the technology of two partners to form a common technology hub, remote monitoring, and a unified call center to better serve the target populations.

Innovation arose in a second case example when a more effective strategy was devised to achieve the desired outcome. The executive of a call-in community social services referral organization described a partnership with a large national commercial bank that helped bank customers remain in good standing with regard to holding clients' mortgages and loans:

> The partnership was set up to help customers of the Bank get linked to social services throughout America to assist them in addressing their debt issues. Since our organization is an information referral agency, it helped link the Bank customers to services such as debt management, foreclosure, debt consolidation, and credit consulting. The overall goal of the partnership was to link Bank customers to a service that will assist them with their financial issues; in

turn, this would help Bank customers keep their homes, and the Bank would not have to take a loss on the foreclosure of many of its home loans.

In another nonprofit-business case with a different nonprofit referral agency, the nonprofit executive devised a partnership whose purpose was to create safe living conditions for elderly inner-city residents. Using community stabilization grant funds made available by the city, the nonprofit approached a telecommunications business that installed technology in people's homes to enable them to summon help in an emergency: "We entered into the partnership because it was a great new service that could be provided for a population we worked with. The goal was to keep people independent in their own homes out of institutionalized care. The partnership had an impact on the target population by using nonintrusive technology to monitor their well-being and keep them living independently at less cost than other options. The project enhanced the credibility of both organizations and generated profits for each."

Transactional Outcomes, Transformational Outcomes, and Measurement of Impacts

The concept of innovation arising from transactional and transformational outcomes of partnership was a consistent theme throughout the case narratives. For example, returning to the nonprofit executive of the social services referral agency in partnership with a commercial bank, the executive explained,

> Our agency was looking for new sources of funding, and new ways to be engaged as an organization with businesses. The Bank received a good amount of public relations praise for their interest in helping their customers, and in theory for strengthening the ability of some customers to maintain their home loans. This partnership had many clear impacts on us organizationally. In order to meet the capacity of calls, our partner paid to improve our in-house technology, and helped us reorganize our staff to take more calls in the office. So far, the impact on the target population has been positive, and we have been able to provide customers with referrals that can help them.

Many nonprofit executives told us that they entered into partnership for the short-term purpose of building their organization's capacity to perform the transactional work of the partnership. Transactional work has been established in the scholarly literature as the sequential, incremental tasks and outcome requirements necessary to perform the endeavor and to achieve the goal of the partnership. Building the capacity of a nonprofit organization is also transactional, reflecting the enhancement of its program expertise, staffing, management, and/or leadership that may arise from its participation in the partnership.[10]

The nonprofit executives also related that their willingness to build organizational capacity by entering into partnership reflected the desire to strengthen their organization in both financial and nonfinancial ways. Financial support included in-kind contributions and commitment of resources such as equipment, discretionary funds, facilities, and salaried staff. Nonfinancial support included sharing or borrowing of skills and expertise, data and information, access to volunteers, market increase, influence on public sector decision makers, access to government agencies and other institutions, endorsements from third parties, the ability to convene wider groups of constituents, the ability to attract in-kind donated services, and the commitment of other organizations to a joint endeavor.

One example we mentioned earlier in this chapter was the case of a residential care facility in partnership with a job training and job services agency. The nonprofit executive maintained that exposing his organization to the partner's values influenced human resources administration, particularly hiring practices to include developmentally disabled residents trained by the partner organization.

Nonprofit executives also asserted that long-term strategies toward mission fulfillment involved transformational change. Some nonprofit leaders said that partnership activities that "moved the needle" or demonstrated impact offered the best opportunities to judge the efficacy of the partnership for both themselves and the larger community. Unfortunately, few examples demonstrated what those performance benchmarks might be, although one example suggested by the executive of a consortium of large, well-funded nonprofit education, health, and cultural institutions was typical of others who pointed to impact measures that they could use as signs of fulfillment of their mission: "The partnership had an impact on our organization as reflected by the partnership inducing us to form more partnerships, and the signal to people that we are successful. The partnership had an impact on the target population and on our member institutions, who tell us that the bottom line ROI for members provided cost savings, increased patronage [and] prestige, [provided] a positive place to work and live, and [provided] life enrichment for the community."

Several examples appear among the cases of impact measures leading to transformative changes in public policy. One case involved a consortium of three independent arts organizations coming together for a major fund development program and campaign that lasted for more than a decade. The partnership was aided by a community development corporation whose focus on partnership processes aligned with public policy priorities. The purpose of the partnership consortium also fit within the philanthropic community's desire to strengthen the arts subsector of the economy as a form of community economic development and neighborhood revitalization. The nonprofit organization claimed an impact in dollars raised, changes in community zoning, construction of new facilities and public streetscape infrastructure, increased property values, a rise in the number of commercial businesses in the neighborhood, increased parking fee revenue, and a decrease in the incidence of crime in the community.

In another example, nonprofit partners drove public policy by creating services for a senior population in need of food bank services that were not otherwise provided. Impact measures included a rise in the number of deliveries and a more frequent resupply of the food bank stocks. In a third example, a mutual benefit organization comprising an alliance of neighborhood community business-owners created a secure shopping environment for their customers to supplement the city's public safety services. Impact measures included a decline in the incidence of neighborhood pan-handling, trash accumulation, and litter; a rise in sales tax revenue to the city; and increases in philanthropic gifts and patronage in the downtown theatre district.

Conclusion

Nonprofit organizations enter into partnership arrangements for many of the reasons that we have investigated in this chapter. The more enduring and productive partnerships involve an exchange rising to the level of sharing between participants that may include knowledge and expertise, capacity to carry out work, enhanced credibility, and the imprimatur of each member for access to broader audiences, constituents, and potential funding.

In defining partnership and in ascertaining when or whether it achieves the status that it is "important," nonprofit executives told us that partnerships matter because they enable and empower the participants to create measureable change in a larger system of policy and practice. We suggest that nonprofit-first partnership impact arises as a result of efforts to create and achieve desirable outcomes that are attributable to the partnership. In addition, some change is likely to occur in the partner organizations, the recipients of services, and the stakeholders of the partnership, or among policy-makers, or in the larger policy environment. Our derivation of meaningful nonprofit partnership involves transactional as well as transformational outcomes that are impactful on the larger society, and fulfill the purpose of the partnership and the missions of the partner participants. We have also begun to identify "gold standard" criteria for forming important, meaningful nonprofit partnerships.

In this chapter, we explored the difficulty of defining partnership analytically. Nonprofit organizations enter partnership for different purposes. We proposed clusters of partnership based on the purpose of the partnership, whether the partnership arrangement was based on mutual benefits, an organizational mission, resource-sharing, a contractual agreement, or community betterment and public value.

After offering examples from each of these five clusters, we considered executives' designating certain partnerships as "important," and based on these responses proposed an additional means of grouping partnerships into additional clusters according to the perceived reasons for their importance. We elaborated these two different cluster systems in order to encourage more precise definitions, but also to begin identifying criteria for forming important nonprofit-first partnerships.

Notes

1. Boyatzis, Richard E., Daniel Goleman, and Kenneth Rhee. "Clustering Competence in Emotional Intelligence: Insights from the Emotional Competence Inventory (ECI)," in *The Handbook of Emotional Intelligence*, ed. Reuven Bar-On and James D. A. Parker (San Francisco, CA: Jossey-Bass, 2000), 343–362.

2. We will not cite specific primary sources because of our promise to the nonprofit executive participants that their participation would be held confidential and that they would not be identified in any way. Depictions of the organization types can be found in the data tables in chapters 4 and 5.

3. Mendel, Stuart C., and Jeffrey L. Brudney. "Doing Good, Public Good, and Public Value," *Nonprofit Management and Leadership* 25, no. 1 (2014): 23–40, doi:10.1002/nml.21109.

4. Mendel, Stuart. "Achieving Meaningful Partnerships with Nonprofit Organizations: A View from the Field." *Journal of Nonprofit Education and Leadership* 3, no. 2 (2013): 66.

5. Mendel, Stuart. "Roles of Government, Nonprofit Sector, Business and Family and Their Interaction in Democracy," in *Leadership in Nonprofit Organizations: A Reference Handbook*, ed. Kathryn Agard (Thousand Oaks, CA: Sage Publications, 2011), 38–45.

6. Mendel, Stuart C., and Jeffrey L. Brudney. "Cross-Sector Collaboration and Public-Private Partnerships: A Perspective on How Nonprofit Organizations Create Public Value in an Archetypical City in the United States," in *Creating Public Value in Practice: Advancing the Common Good in a Multi-Sector, Shared-Power, No-One-Wholly-in-Charge World*, ed. John M. Bryson, Barbara C. Crosby, and Laura Bloomberg (Boca Raton, FL: CRC Press, 2015), 225–244; Mendel, Stuart C., and Jeffrey L. Brudney. "Doing Good, Public Good, and Public Value." *Nonprofit Management and Leadership* 25, no. 1 (2014): 23–40, doi:10.1002 /nml.21109.

7. Ibid.

8. Ibid.

9. Cook, Karen S., Russell Hardin, and Margaret Levi. *Cooperation without Trust?* (New York: Russell Sage Foundation, 2005); Cook, Karen S., Margaret Levi, and Russell Hardin. *Whom Can We Trust?: How Groups, Networks, and Institutions Make Trust*

Possible (New York: Russell Sage Foundation, 2009); Ostrom, Elinor, and James Walker, eds. *Trust and Reciprocity: Interdisciplinary Lessons for Experimental Research* (New York: Russell Sage Foundation, 2003).

10. Selsky, John W., and Barbara Parker. "Cross-sector Partnerships to Address Social Issues: Challenges to Theory and Practice." *Journal of Management* 31, no. 6 (2005): 849–873, doi:10.1177/0149206305279601; Austin, James E. "Marketing's Role in Cross-sector Collaboration." *Journal of Nonprofit & Public Sector Marketing* 11, no. 1 (2003): 23–39, doi:10.1300/J054v11n01_0.

3 The Point of Partnering

Overview

This chapter is informed by understandings of nonprofit-first partnership that often dictate the success of such arrangements for their nonprofit actors. Building on the more general assessment of the introduction and chapter 2, we now pinpoint the implications of nonprofit partnership with other nonprofits, with government actors, and with business enterprises in order to determine how the involvement of these different actors changes the requirements and benefits that a nonprofit actor can expect.

Introduction

Three important insights from our discussion to this point offer a useful frame for understanding nonprofit-first partnership and are depicted in figure 3.1. The first insight is that partnership is recognized as a critical practice for nonprofit organizations. The second is that partnership engagement differs across different sectors, and that nonprofit executives have distinct expectations for achieving the benefits of partnership.[1] The third insight is that the nuances and subtle distinctions in the terminology of partnership are more than diplomacy or hairsplitting: instead, such language signifies important clarifications that have significant implications for the partner participants.[2]

In describing a partnership between a nonprofit organization dedicated to improving the conditions of a business district for its members, a nonprofit executive observed that business associations were obligated to "act as if they are businesses and speak the language of business. They must also be efficient and accountable to their donors and sponsors. In turn, businesses must use the nonprofit to perform advocacy work with government and to stimulate the conditions for economic development that support the conditions for business to thrive."

The comments of a pair of nonprofit executives encapsulate these insights. The first, the director of a social services agency devoted to job skills development and placements for youth residing in the city of Cleveland, noted, "This partnership is one of as many as 16 partnership arrangements with which we engage … all of which have different features and benefits.… An organizational value is to actively seek collaboration and to engage in partnerships with other organizations … while protecting our core work focus and competencies from incrementally moving

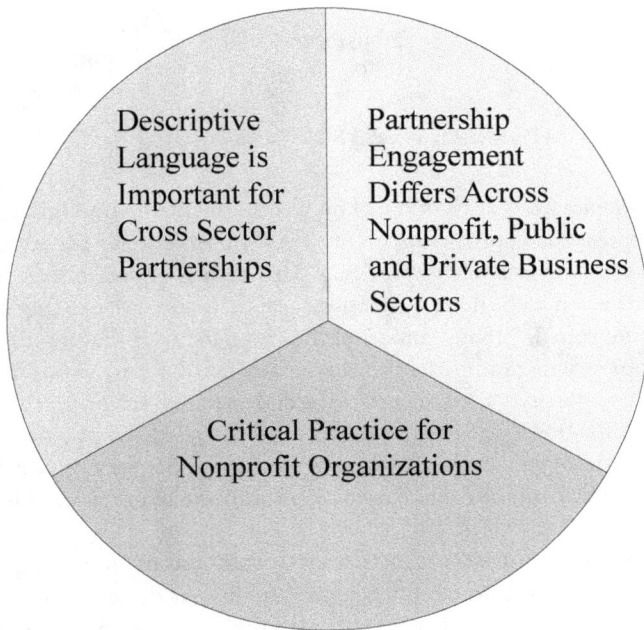

Fig. 3.1 Framing Insights into Nonprofit-First Partnerships.

away from our mission. We consider collaboration and partnership as a part of our overall sustainability strategy toward achieving our mission.... We are confident our partner would not describe ... collaboration the same way."

The second nonprofit executive, who leads a social justice organization that brings leaders of all faiths together to encourage understanding and community-building, stated,

> Yes, there is a difference between partnering with different industries.... Partnership between two nonprofits has undertones of competition. Many times, we did not want to acquiesce to do things to accommodate our partner ... and the agreements in advance were really important for the purpose of establishing limits for the partners.... There are other huge problems with nonprofit partners as well. Barriers to enduring relationships include ... [uncertainty] that both will take the same interest in the partner and their success.... When the relationship is between a nonprofit and a business or government, we did not sense competition as a factor whatsoever. In both types, we felt unrestricted in our efforts to seek end results without interference with the program delivery. Businesses and governments are easier because of the power struggle and the visibility.

$$\text{Transactional Outcomes} + \text{Transformational Outcomes} = \text{Benefits of Important Partnership}$$

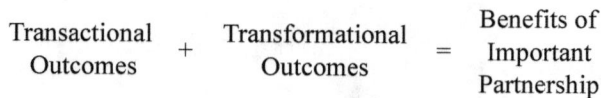

Fig. 3.2 Nonprofit-First Partnership Benefits Building Blocks.

Ample comments from our sample of nonprofit executives among the cases they supplied express viewpoints supporting these observations. The executive of a growing social services agency seeking partnership opportunities with other nonprofits as a way to build organizational capacity to serve existing clients and to reach more stated, "The intention of the partnership is that it will project an image of our organization as innovative, risk-taking, and entrepreneurial in our use of technology to enhance service delivery. The act of partnership with another organization also forces us to evolve by changing our practices and plans to account for joint endeavors. The changes in service delivery improve the quality of life for our clients and add employment training opportunities to our partner's clients and their families."

This chapter examines and illustrates the conditions under which partnership is more or less beneficial to nonprofit organizations. As depicted in figure 3.2, we show that partnership benefits accrue through the transactional actions of the two participating organizations as well as the creation of transformational outcomes to society at large. Our analysis of the cases provides examples of the ways in which the transactional and transformational benefits of partnership lead to the creation of public value and social value. We show differences across partnerships based on sector pairings: nonprofit-nonprofit, nonprofit-government, and nonprofit-business.

Validation Through Participation in Partnership

As illustrated in figure 3.3, many nonprofit executives look to partnership arrangements as a way to sustain their organizations financially, but the decision whether or not to enter into a partnership also includes nonfinancial considerations. Nonprofit executives expressed two important nonfinancial benefits.

The first is the potential that a nonprofit organization and its partner will be validated or granted a measure of recognition by third parties or the larger community as trusted institutional actors by virtue of participation in an important partnership. Such an imprimatur reinforces in turn the significance of the partnership endeavor. Several executives described the rewards for engaging in partnership as a return on their investment of time and effort through the endorsement of credible third parties. According to one nonprofit executive, endorsement implied that the partner organizations were trustworthy, capable, deserving of attention in the community, and worthy

Financial Non-Financial

Program Development

Build Revenue for Organizational Sustainability

Validation by Third Party Endorsement

Experiential Learning

Improve Personal Knowledge and Expertise

Continous Improvement of Programs Over Time

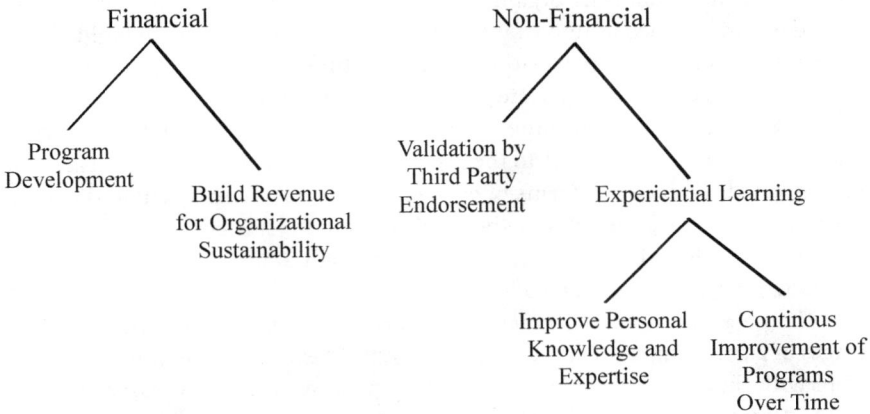

Fig. 3.3 Nonprofit-First Partnership Benefits Outcomes.

of policy makers' interest. For example, the executive of a statewide advocacy organization noted,

> We valued the partnership because it raised the stature of our organization, gave us confidence in the quality of our work, and lent credibility to our partner organizations, who are typically our political advocacy competitors. Effects on the target population are that the partnership was such an unusual union of political bedfellows that new audiences may feel compelled to listen to the joint and separate messages of all the partners. Plus, in working together, each organization may have a moderating effect on the views of the others politically and on their various constituents. This, we believe, is among the highest forms of advocacy in which it can engage.

In another example, the leader of a nonprofit research and community-coordinating institution promoting public sector support for the arts suggested that partnerships provided the opportunity to work with service providers in promoting the role and value of the arts in a thriving community. The partnership allowed his organization to tie the work of the arts community to more well-recognized economic development priorities. In this arrangement, the partnering organization served as an advocate and used its considerable strategic and operations expertise to improve business practices, conduct research, and collaborate on arts projects. This executive maintained that the partnership gave him new connections through which to advance his organization's credibility and influence among public policy makers.

The second nonfinancial benefit of partnership is a strong desire for continuous improvement in the delivery of partnership goals. When asked for their advice to other nonprofit organizations engaging in partnership, executives shared lessons learned as important to themselves personally and to building the capacity of their organization to succeed in future partnership endeavors. For example, the executive of a private grant-making institution entering into a partnership stated, "In the beginning, there were a lot of problems with our partner, and this required adjustments to the project.... We hung in, though, because we had invested too much in terms of opportunity costs to simply cut and run.... Despite many stops and starts, the work eventually started to move forward because of our learning curve ... and because of our adjustments ... overall this is a good program that will be offered again."

The ways in which such experiential learning eventually overcame the challenges of partnership indicates, first, that nonprofit executives enter into partnerships with the expectation that partnerships can evolve from the lessons learned by the actors. Second, it indicates that learning from the partnership experience is perceived as a benefit by the partners. Many nonprofit executives attested that the experiences of performing a partnership strengthened their organization and further justified their investment in the endeavor.

For example, the nonprofit executive of a growing grassroots after-school organization devoted to creating a safe space for adolescents observed about a partnership with the state Department of Education, "On a scale of 1 to 10, the partnership rated 7 because the partnership is going to end after a single year. It is an amazing partnership that would be even better in year two given our experience and our desire to make the project even better. Unfortunately, we can't use the lessons we've learned because the project will not continue."

The Most Common Nonfinancial Benefits of Partnership

The nonprofit executives rated their satisfaction with their partnerships on a 10-point scale where a score of 1 indicated a partnership that did not meet any of its goals and a score of 10 indicated a partnership that had met all of its goals. In 80 percent of the partnership cases, the nonprofit executives explained that at least one reason that their partnership failed to meet their performance expectations was because of vague, difficult-to-resolve challenges in the partnership design or arrangements. Process improvement and executives' own professional development are thus a desirable and overt benefit of partnership. In addition, in more than 87 percent of the cases, the nonprofit executives described learning from the partnership experience as a valuable benefit. Learning included a broad range of practices and skills. At one extreme, simple exchanges of information contributed to better ways of understanding the nature of the work to be performed, and at the other, learning influenced the perspective, and in some cases the actions and performance, of the partner. As a nonprofit executive director of a grant-making institution noted, "One of the factors for why the partnership was able to meet its goals is that our partner had a building rehabilitation operation already in place, and they also had the ability to conduct sales of homes that were rehabbed. They taught us how to price complex projects. Our experience and abilities were in putting financing packages together needed to secure the funding for rehabbing of the homes for this project.... They also used our model on other project work they performed outside the partnership."

In the most successful instances of experiential learning emanating from partnership, one or both partners gain a better grasp of collaboration itself. The executive director mentioned above offered an apt example. In reflecting on her organization's requirement that grant recipients enter into partnership arrangements, she indicated that her foundation had little experience in partnership engagement itself. Forming its own partnership thus became a critical learning experience for her organization, as leadership came to better understand the work required of a joint endeavor and the obligations that each partner must meet in order to make that endeavor succeed. Based on her newly gained experience as a partner in a relationship with a peer institution, the executive modified the grant-making program expectations of her own foundation to adjust for increased costs grantees might incur from the required partner arrangements.

In some cases, nonprofit executives described another type of beneficial experience often gained through partnerships. In one instance, executives' time investments were repaid by improved partnership program operations and outcomes. The executive rated as 7.5 on a 10-point scale a partnership of more than five years of community organizations dedicated to mutual fundraising because both participants needed to improve their understanding of the programs' effects on other stakeholder groups. A second nonprofit executive rated his partnership as 7 because it met a high number of its goals, but the organizers did not pay sufficient attention to project outcomes that should have signaled to them the need to make mid-course corrections. As a result, a primary goal that this partnership failed to meet was to continue the program.

Challenges to Partnerships

Despite the many nonfinancial benefits of partnership, executives also named significant challenges, as illustrated in figure 3.4. One of the most daunting included a broad range of new burdens specific to the ongoing act of partnership, such as the challenges of hiring, training, and supervising new staff dedicated to the partnership endeavor; aligning two fiscal operating systems to comply with the accounting standards of a third-party funding source; and establishing clear lines of communication and responsibility across two organizational cultures, integrating a new program into an existing culture of work.

In most partnership cases described by the nonprofit executives, the effort put into overcoming the burdens of partnership also became a means of

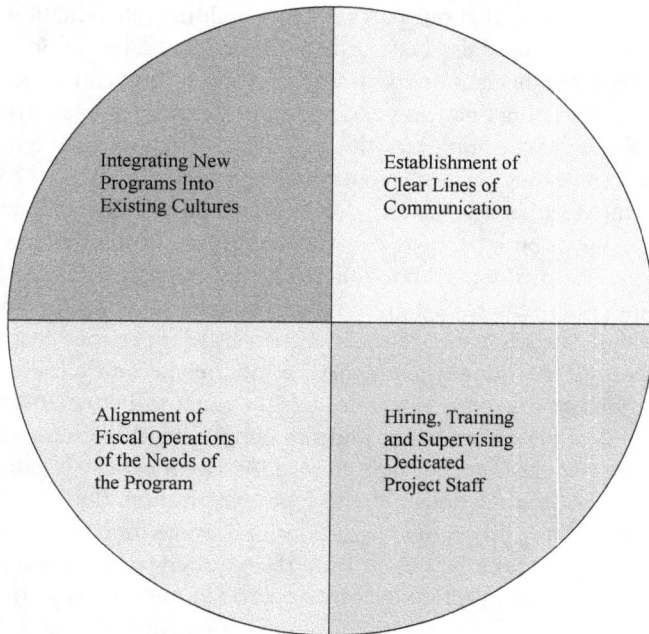

Fig. 3.4 Challenges to Nonprofit-First Partnerships.

strengthening the nonprofit partner's capacity to set and reach goals. In some instances, the challenges were quite modest. The executive of a large social services organization in partnership with another sizeable organization devoted to complementary purposes noted, "Some of the burdens were as simple as finding time to communicate with our partners." More complex issues, though, involved responsibilities for measuring the performance and the impact of the partnership.

Other challenges dealt with basic understanding of the partner's limitations. One executive, for instance, shared that an important takeaway of his experience was to understand the partner organization's strengths and limits, and to take them into account in future partnerships. He further explained that some government agencies engaged in partnerships may change the agenda and commitment to an endeavor depending on the outcome of an election. He also gave the example of a partnership that began with one set of senior staff that was abruptly replaced by another without the benefit of a transition plan. As a consequence of this change, his organization was left responsible for ensuring that the partnership continued to function. The burden of having to assume the full stewardship of the partnership, which began as a public sector initiative, compelled the nonprofit partner to create an exit strategy and eventually to leave the partnership.

Table 3.1. Reasons for Cross-Sector Partnerships.

Nonprofit-Nonprofit (56%)	Nonprofit-Government (34%)	Nonprofit-Business (10%)
1. Mission Purpose	1. Leveraging Tax Dollars	1. Business Development
2. Simpatico Mission	2. Principal Agent Theory	2. Market Share
3. Shared Information	3. Greater Good and Public Value	

In a second example of the benefits of learning from experience, one executive shared that the primary factor working against meeting his partnership's goals was the nature of government funding. For example, the project work of the partnership required task completion and verification, submitting of detailed invoices, and then a thirty-day payment turnaround for all approved invoices. Typically, this process did not occur as a seamless set of transactions. The executive reported that the primary lesson that informed his learning was that public sector funds were released only after the completion of government procurement and contracting processes. In the meantime, the nonprofit partner organization had loaned its own discretionary dollars to the endeavor due to its government partner's lengthy reimbursement timelines.

Nonprofit-Nonprofit Sector Partnership Benefits

Among the eighty-two examples of important partnership cases collected in our research, 56 percent occur between two nonprofit participants; nearly one-third, or approximately 34 percent, occur between a nonprofit and government actor; and the approximately 10 percent remaining occur between a nonprofit and a business. Table 3.1 documents these proportions and the affiliated reasons for cross-sector partnerships nonprofit executives gave and that we describe in the following paragraphs as distinctive of their partnership pairings.

Respondents presented three primary reasons for the nonprofit-nonprofit partnership pairings. First, executives shared that nonprofit organizations with similar or complementary missions are usually aware of one another, see each other as both peers and competitors, and can frame the benefits of partnership as a rationale to achieve their respective organizational missions. Despite the pressure of competing for limited funding opportunities, organizations with mutual missions and interests already have this common baseline understanding and drive to form partnership arrangements with each other. One executive director noted that in her case partnership began when she contacted an arts education organization because its musicians frequently performed at art gallery openings held by her nonprofit organization. The musical performances created a positive ambiance for visual arts patrons and guests while providing the music students with additional opportunities to perform. In addition to merging the artistic products, the partnership also achieved the benefit of bringing two arts constituencies together.

A second reason nonprofit organizations often form partnerships is as a strategy toward fulfilling their own missions. In seeking a nonprofit peer, two nonprofit executives are more likely to coordinate by merit of familiar concepts, sources of income, ability to attract philanthropic giving, and technical language. For example, the same nonprofit executive noted above stated that the partnership with the arts education organization was gratifying for the staff because it was easy to launch, and the new shared program broadened the scope of an existing initiative. The executive appreciated the good working relationship and personal rapport between the two nonprofit partners, and noted that mutual understandings helped keep the costs for the arrangement very low.

A third reason nonprofits benefit from partnerships with one another is that these arrangements have a better chance of success than partnerships proposed or prompted by a third party outside the partnership. According to nonprofit executives, the process of mutual partnership formation typically takes place between complementary organizations that come together through some combination of similar resource needs, aligned mission or vision, or shared perspectives on public problems needing attention. "We felt... the partnership itself as being important, and our major funder for the partnership (the State of Ohio) really liked the partnership and the partnership's ability to leverage their funding into other/new dollars."

Two examples illustrate these points about mutual interests as a catalyst to the formation of nonprofit-nonprofit partnerships that would not have occurred with public or business partners.

First, the executive of a statewide political advocacy organization noted earlier in this chapter prompted a partnership with advocates of the opposing political affiliation because the participants shared mutual interests related to the declining civility in public discourse as well as among public policy makers and political parties. Because each partner identified with a different part of the political spectrum, and those differences typically inhibited their collaboration, the partnership was conceived to utilize their combined staff and convening power to draw attention to policy issues and processes that they hope will contribute to the public good. The nonprofit executive stated,

> As a joint venture between organizations advocating public policy to very different and opposed political interests, the partnership allows for a sharing of ideas across the broad political spectrum represented by the partners, their constituents, and other interested parties. It also provides access to populations and constituents typically isolated by political ideological barriers; offers opportunity to stimulate trust-building and collegiality among public policy makers; and improves the working relationships and discourse in the state of Ohio around public policies that are important to each

organization. Modeling a multi-partisan partnership involving a common goal of producing a policy paper and conference has the potential to transform the manner in which public policy makers and political leaders will interact with one another.

A second partnership was initiated by an interfaith social justice organization in the aftermath of the September 2001 terrorist attacks. According to the nonprofit executive, the partnership gave a voice to faith communities that previously had few institutional voices or advocates to raise awareness and understanding.

> The partnership was originally set up to create an educational forum to improve understanding of beliefs that were not one's own. The partnership exists because our organization had existing relationships with the Sikh, Hindu, Muslim, Jewish, and Christian communities, who were each members of the partnership. This initiative brought everyone together to create a single event which we considered an important partnership. Our desire is that the event will stimulate dialog and pathways for future dialogue between the communities [and] better understanding and opportunities for advocacy by the groups with one another and with other players beyond our community.

Another frequently mentioned benefit realized by two nonprofit actors in a partnership was that both organizations shared their exclusive data and the expertise of program staff in ways that were more reciprocal than competitive. According to one nonprofit executive, providing access to propriety information was no small matter, but doing so as a practice of sharing helped meet the partners' highest aspirations: using their organizational data enabled the partnership to create a more efficient and well-targeted program. Upon completion of the project, the partners agreed that the most important innovations of their endeavor were not lower costs, but the principle and practice of adaptation and a higher public profile for the target population than would have been possible otherwise.

Nonprofit-Government Sector Partnership Benefits

Scholars of public administration and management credit the nonprofit sector with mission fulfillment as supportive of the general good and also as a supplement and complement of government.[3] The nonprofit executives in our sample, however, related that public sector mission fulfillment differs in important ways from nonprofit sector mission fulfillment.[4] According to scholars, public sector organizations seek engagements that offer efficient use of tax dollars to produce value beyond a dollar of investment for a dollar of service. Nonprofit missions as defined by scholars of nonprofit management theory, by contrast, are realized through engagements where a societal condition requires institutional action by intermediary actors to fulfill a need or induce remedy or change.[5]

As a result, the challenge in tracing partnership benefits between the two sectors is that public sector actors consider contract-for-hire relationships with nonprofits "partnerships."[6] Although the nonprofit executives in this study maintain that a partner-as-funder can rise to the level of partnership when a steady dialogue and interchange occur between the participants regarding the outcomes and processes of the endeavor, they also note that very few of their contracted government relationships exhibit either the characteristics or the benefits of partnership in the sense that nonprofits intend or as they understand them. Instead, the nonprofit executives maintained that government drove arrangements whose primary features were contracted performances that prized accountability, compliance, and transaction outcomes.

Although these types of arrangements between public and private actors are frequently cast by government as a partnership, nonprofits asserted that partnership with the public sector was achieved through other means. They did offer some examples of collaboration with government that rose to the level of partnership. For example, one executive of a nonprofit social and human services agency explained that his view of nonprofit-government partnership required starting with the understanding that public agencies have different constituencies than nonprofits. Because they ultimately have to be responsible to the public, they are frequently limited in their ability to respond to their nonprofit partners. Still, in his experience, variations exist across government agencies: some exhibit flexibility and are designed to be responsive and adaptive to their nongovernmental partners; others are part of a larger public agency bureaucracy and are slower to meet obligations to their partners. Like many of our nonprofit respondents, his overall conceptualization of nonprofit-government partnership was that the relationship is top-down and prescribed by government. In the nonprofit view, these arrangements are not partnerships because government rules and procedures control the relationship, subordinating the nonprofit to simply meeting the public sector requirements.

The interviewees also suggested that the goals of public sector actors for partnership often differ from those of nonprofit actors. Public sector funding is typically a mechanism of nonprofit-government partnership that reflects the power, credibility, and authority of government leaders' mission to achieve a greater purpose and good.[7] For example, one nonprofit executive described a partnership with government that funded community-wide arts and cultural organizations. Prior to the partnership, his organization had no access to public funds; with the partnership, a new revenue stream was created through an approved "sin tax" on cigarettes and alcohol consumption in the county. The nonprofit executive explained that maintaining the custodial or stewardship role of the partnership endeavor, which he asserted meant that internal performance deadlines were kept and meetings to communicate and overcome problems were held, rested with his organization. This role also meant, as he explained below, that his organization accepted the responsibility for the partnership to communicate to the public the value of tax dollars committed to supporting arts and cultural institutions in the city.

> There are two primary partners: our nonprofit organization and a special division of government funded by a tax levy in tobacco and alcohol sales. The partnership is voluntary and has a formal contract. It is cast as a partnership because the relationship speaks to both missions of our organization and our public sector partner. The partnership is ongoing and began in 2005 due to legislation in the Ohio Revised Code, section 2281. The partnership is renewed annually, but the latest contract commitment to us is for two years. We know the partnership is important because it allows arts and cultural organizations an opportunity to work with us to influence public policy, research, and capacity-building for the subsector of arts community organizations. Because of its importance and our role as the private actor in the partnership, we take the responsibility to ensure that the case for continuing the tax is made to the community and the voters.

Nonprofit-Business Sector Partnership Benefits

Even though the number of cases of nonprofit-business partnerships in our sample is small ($n = 8$ cases), the benefits and outcomes identified seem to differ from those of nonprofit-nonprofit and nonprofit-government partnership cases.[8] Engagement and community service are elements of these partnerships; however, the nonprofit executives described their nonprofit-business partnerships as based primarily on market share and business development. Typically, the partnership outcomes were facilitations of transactions such as providing basic business services. In one example, a nonprofit executive for a social services organization dedicated to client referrals for all kinds of social, legal, and economic support explained that his organization referred callers regularly to the regional office of a large global banking institution. The bank would connect the referred clients to financial services such as debt management, foreclosure assistance, debt consolidation, and credit counseling. The linkage was the partnership mechanism between the nonprofit organization and the business, both of which received positive attention for helping the hotline referrals. The benefits to each partner arose from simply performing the functions they would ordinarily carry out to the benefit of the nonprofit, the clients, and the bank such as branding in the larger community by demonstrating that people in need were able to increase their own capacity to pay their home mortgages and other obligations.

Desirable Conditions Leading to Partnership Benefits by Sector Pairings

Based on the nonprofit executives' case narratives demonstrating important and desirable conditions that support the creation of benefits for partnership, we

Table 3.2. Benefit Causes Underlying the Three Dyadic Sector Partnership Pairs.

Nonprofit-Nonprofit	Nonprofit-Government	Nonprofit-Business
1. Active Involvement of Executive Director, Demonstrating Priority of Partnership	1. Shared Staff and Data	1. Funding Scholarships
2. Leverage Knowledge and Expertise	2. Increase in Awareness of Target Population	2. Alliance with Business Community Sponsorships
3. Strengthen Shared Values	3. Active Involvement of Government and Nonprofit Leaders	
	4. Mutual Engagement of Partners	
	5. Opportunities for Mutual Advocates	
	6. Convenes Constituents	

identify and depict in table 3.2 the causes underlying nonprofit-first partnerships that are specific to the different partnership dyads

Nonprofit-Nonprofit

The first major benefits cluster of answers provided by nonprofit executive respondents reflects benefits that are derived from the direct involvement of the nonprofit leader in the partnership. Each nonprofit executive sharing this insight asserted that the involvement of organizational leadership signaled to the partners and other stakeholders involved that the partnership constituted an organizational priority. The result of the partnership was active involvement of the senior leadership of the participating organizations in the rapid problem-solving and the addition of resources through an expedited path that cut through the bureaucracy of the partnering organizations.

The nonprofit interviewees also explained that the opportunity cost of the involvement of the executive, whose time and resources are the most limited in the organization, is a "wager" or risk undertaken by the organization that the partnership will produce a return on investment that justifies it as an organizational priority (and the use of the executive's scarce time). One executive noted that the return on investment for his organization due to the partnership was that it raised the stature of the organization among third parties, instilled confidence among the staff in the quality of their work, and lent credibility to their partner organizations. He maintained that his commitment to the partnership could be seen as the time he dedicated to its shared mission and to communicating with the partner organization. The executive further explained the value of reciprocity: "Factors that worked towards meeting goals were ... openness, honesty, trust, tolerance, flexibility, and humor between the leaders of both organizations.... We made a commitment ... to deliver on our promises as a value, because to not do so would have been to deliver upon our partner, harm."

A second major benefits cluster that nonprofit organization partners accrue in partnership with other nonprofits is new or leveraged knowledge and expertise gained when program staff are shared. This sharing between the two organizations allows the partners to influence each other. Although sharing information, program methodology, and responsibility between the partners was unexpected at the outset, the nonprofit executives viewed sharing as added value. "The partnership exists because by working together the program funding is doubled, along with two different perspectives on the opportunity to provide services and to share staff expertise. The strength of the partnership was our differences: we were able to act as an intermediary for a large grant-making institution and provide them with cover from controversy. The partnership worked out great in practice. The roles were very clear and the two partners have [each] established the other as a priority."

In a third major benefits cluster, partnering nonprofits can often strengthen both shared and individual values and practices. For example, one nonprofit executive explained that his large social services agency maintained a partnership with a smaller peer organization. The executive observed that cross-training and career development practices in the smaller social services agency were effective in keeping staff motivated and working with greater intensity, while also creating avenues for staff succession and continuity in program delivery. The nonprofit executive maintained that these concepts and practices became a shared value influencing hiring practices in both organizations, which in turn strengthened the bond of partnership between organizations. "Exposing our organization to the values of our partner influenced our operating values, specifically in our hiring practices to include our own residents who are partner-trained to work in our office."

The three preceding clusters of partnership benefits described by the nonprofit executives engaged in nonprofit-nonprofit partnership were complemented by several categories of benefits that were mentioned less frequently. These minor clusters of benefits include: nonfinancial contributions of facilities, equipment, and office supplies; access to legislators, public officials, civic leaders, funders and sponsors, board members, and other third-party constituents; and access to volunteers, which also occurred rarely in the minor cluster of nonprofit-nonprofit partnership benefits.

Nonprofit-Government

The major benefits clusters in these partnership dyadic pairs reflect benefits derived from the nonprofits' partnerships with government. The nonprofit executives elaborated that nonprofit-government partnerships were most effectual when the arrangement involved the leadership of the nonprofit organization and senior leadership from the public sector, which might include the legislative, executive, or administrative offices of government.

An important and distinctive benefit occasionally described by the nonprofit executives was the opportunity for advocacy by the nonprofit partner with elected legislators and other policy makers. The following three case examples illustrate this point.

First, a small community social services organization looked to the separate offices of the mayor and the city council in order to receive funding and access to city departments for the coordination of service delivery to local residents, community education, and in-kind services such as additional space, dissemination of information, and opportunities for fundraising. The factors that led to meeting the goals of this partnership were that important, high-level members of city government both in the mayor's office and the city council became aware of the partnership and responded to the nonprofit directly. As the executive told us, "There is a demonstrated acceptance of our mission by government as something worthy of their support and interest.... We have expertise and capacity that the City lacks to fulfill its commitment to the residents ... and are a knowledge resource for the city."

In a second case example, a social services agency focused on youth and teen fathers partnered with the county Department of Human Services to drive referrals and the entrance of new clients into public sector human services counseling. The nonprofit executive explained that from his point of view, the partnership with the county educational services center was mutually beneficial; he identified repeated project renewals by the County as one measure of government commitment. Both partners demonstrated willingness to compromise in solving problems and overcoming barriers. He also observed that both organizations had strong individuals driving the endeavor, solid second-tier program leadership, and sufficient support staff committed to the program. As he related, "The relationship is 9 on a scale of 10 ... due to ... the intent of the County to address the needs of the target population. ... I consider the County a true partner ... and the positive relationship with the County is because ... of a regular evaluation that is neither punitive nor inhibited and helped by open and easy communication with County administrators ... The multi-year nature of the contract awarded through an RFP tell us that they appreciate us."

A third example involved a social justice workforce development organization focused on community re-entry of formerly incarcerated city residents trained to provide social services to the elderly. The partnership project broke new ground in the respect that it wove together three separate public policy agendas: it facilitated services to seniors living in public housing; it addressed the need to employ formerly incarcerated individuals, who are frequently shut out of employment markets; and it improved public safety for city residents. "The factors that contributed to these goals are that our public partners ... recognized the partnership as a low-cost way to provide services to elderly residents while aiding in the re-entry of a difficult-to-serve population of working-age city residents. Simultaneously, the success of the project reduced the apprehension that many employers and people in the larger community hold regarding the presence [of] and willingness to employ formerly incarcerated individuals. As a nonprofit devoted to the re-entry population, we believe that we are serving the role of value guardian for the partnership."

Other highly rated benefits of nonprofit-government partnership mentioned by over 70 percent of the fifty-two nonprofit executives included: perceived endorsement of one partner for the partner agency as a result of the partnership project; sharing staff across the partnership project who contributed labor and proprietary data (but not necessarily expertise); increase in the public consciousness of the target population by virtue of their receiving the services provided by the partnership endeavor; and the ability to convene public and private constituents. Mentioned less frequently were partnership benefits of in-kind resources; such as equipment and office space; funding contributed by the nonprofit from its discretionary funds; volunteer involvement; and increased target market share.

Nonprofit-Business

The major cluster of benefits in this dyadic pairing group reflects advantages and benefits realized from partnerships formed between nonprofit and for-profit organizations. Nonprofit executives recounted a total of eight partnership cases between their organization and private businesses.

Within this major benefit cluster lie four categories, each defined by a distinctive perspective on the underlying motivations for nonprofit-business partnerships. The first sub-cluster includes nonprofits seeking sponsorship dollars from businesses. The second sub-cluster comprises nonprofits seeking to benefit from businesses that fulfill community service, public-values generation, or corporate social responsibility. The third sub-cluster involves the nonprofits lending their credibility to businesses for program expertise or to boost operational profitability and efficiency. The fourth sub-cluster consists of nonprofits lending their credibility to businesses that are trying to enhance market share: in this model, the clients or patrons of the nonprofit begin to associate the business with the "doing good" glow of the nonprofit.

NONPROFITS SEEKING SPONSORSHIP DOLLARS FROM BUSINESSES

One nonprofit executive shared a partnership case in which his organization, a statewide affiliate of a national health organization performing research and education to eradicate a particular disease, worked with the regional manager of a global corporation. The health organization was able to demonstrate its appeal as a partner to local and regional corporate sponsors, and the partnership was formed to raise money to support the research and operations of the national office of the nonprofit organization. Businesses were offered membership in the "team," which signaled to the local community that the business was a responsible corporate citizen, thus raising public perceptions of its corporate image. As the nonprofit executive noted, "The partnership was important because it was beneficial to both sides. The perception by the general public that their customers and corporate values appealed only to motorcyclists in leather and steel helmets was harmful to their business growth trajectory. The partnership served our partner's interest in softening and broadening their image, while we needed to raise money."

NONPROFITS SEEKING TO BENEFIT FROM BUSINESS CORPORATIONS
FULFILLING COMMUNITY SERVICE, PUBLIC-VALUES GENERATION,
OR CORPORATE SOCIAL RESPONSIBILITY

Another nonprofit executive described the origin of a nonprofit-business partnership as initiated by the business to make the community more inviting to commercial enterprise and residential neighborhood stability. The partnership began as a funding relationship between his nonprofit and a community bank that had its headquarters in an urban neighborhood and eventually grew into an important partnership centered on services to youth. Although his nonprofit organization entered into the partnership seeking unrestricted operating support for its work in the community, the nonprofit understood the bank's motivation to find ways to help stabilize the neighborhood as a desirable place for the business to maintain its headquarters. The nonprofit executive also noted that the bank was a business anchor and gathering place for the local community, which lacked such amenities. In pursuit of these mutual benefits, the two organizations created a project to address the educational future of the neighborhood's youth and their families.

A second case example of this type comes from the executive of a social justice organization that brings leaders of all faiths together to encourage understanding and community-building:

> The partnership was originally set up to create an event (conference) that presented the issues of racial disparity in health care.... The partnership exists because it amplified our organizational credibility to a national audience on the topic ... while ... making use of the existing credibility of both partners to attract high visibility and national stature speakers and draw local health-care

experts.... The goal of the partnership was to create awareness of the issue of inclusion and race health disparity and motivate people to move the health-care plan industry and their corporate clients in a more inclusive direction. The factors that worked toward meeting the goals of the partnership were that neither partner overshadowed the other; we had the ability to be creative with the program; mutual and timely support and advice between partners; neither intruded upon the turf of the other; the partners were non-competitive.

NONPROFITS LENDING CREDIBILITY TO
BUSINESSES FOR PROGRAM EXPERTISE

A third example consists of a partnership whose output includes arranging business placements for clients to whom the nonprofit organization provides training, social services, and hopefully relief from some social pathologies. Two cases in this cluster involve nonprofit social services agencies that partner with businesses to employ youth trained in entry-level jobs as well as adults re-entering the community. One nonprofit executive explained that she valued the partner-ship with the business because a successful partnership of this type engenders respect among her peers.

> The partnership with a business is an ongoing relationship that began in 2008 because we find and train youth in low-income communities in Cleveland and East Cleveland, from which our partner, a national chain of retailer outlets selling clothes, housewares, and accessories at a discount, draws upon for qualified applicants for employment in its stores.... We entered into this part-nership with [the] business by making the case to the business as relating to their profit goals and not based on philanthropy and donations.... The success of the relationship is a point of pride and accomplishment for our organization and positions us as an expert among our peers.

The partnership assists the nonprofit by providing jobs to at-risk youth, and the business receives employees. The business also offered feedback to the nonprofit partner on the quality of its youth participants as workers.

NONPROFITS LENDING CREDIBILITY TO BUSINESSES
DESIRING ENHANCED MARKET SHARE

Nonprofit organizations can also lend their credibility to a business seeking to enhance its market share, as illustrated in the following case example:

> The partnership was originally set up to expand the capacity of the microenterprise lending in Northeast Ohio. This was to help small businesses who would not be credit-worthy otherwise. The partnership was initiated by the regional district office of a large commercial bank after the demise of a small nonprofit intermediary organization that served as a microlender to small businesses. The nonprofit partner was a small community foundation

dedicated to strengthening entrepreneurial business start-ups. The goals of the partnership were to leverage more access to capital for aspiring entrepreneurs, but also to affiliate the bank as a friendly face to small business enterprise. The partnership had an impact on the target population, which was an increase in access to technical assistance and capital in the form of banking products.

Partnership Benefits and Public Value

We have described the benefits of partnership drawn from the viewpoint of nonprofit executives engaged in these endeavors. The benefits we ascertain from the executives are linked to the beliefs that their organizations would receive a reasonable return on investment to the relationship, and that the partnership endeavor rose to the level of "important." One executive shared that his partnership had an impact on his organization through an increased operational budget, a larger staff, and an increase in clients served. He also pointed to stronger client retention.

Beyond the immediate and tangible transactional benefits of partnership for the partners, the nonprofit executives point to benefits that they believe contribute to a greater societal good. In many of the case narratives, the executives stated that the processes and activities of the partnership realize benefits for both partner participants as well as the greater society. Executives named forming and strengthening social networks, sustaining social capital, building community, and nurturing the bonds of trust that comprise civil society as transformational outcomes arising from partnership processes. The outcomes of such transformations can potentially resonate well beyond the work of the partnership and extend into benefits for the larger community, examples of which were suggested by nonprofit executives contributing cases as reduction in overall rates of crime rate, poverty, and illiteracy. In other cases, the benefits of partnership were credited as enhancing the standing of a partner as a community institution.

Transformational benefits are reflected in outcomes such as positive participant impressions, improvements in the conditions of society, and public dollars redirected through advocacy. The executive of the social services organization mentioned above explained that transformational benefits arising from his partnership were less directly observable or measurable. For example, he claimed that the benefits rose to the level of community impact because the increased number of clients served translated into a reduction of "distress" in the larger community.

Other examples of transformational benefits arising from partnerships are outcomes that strengthen the network of service providers, promote social change, improve public policy, or create public value. The nonprofit executive of an organization devoted to strengthening arts organizations receiving tax dollars explained that transformational impacts worked in two directions. From one perspective, the arts and cultural sector gained access to public sector funds that did not exist before the partnership. The creation of a public sector contribution to the arts enabled a new source of sustainability for private organizations that had not been available previously. From another perspective, arts and cultural organizations receiving public sector funding had greater responsibility to communicate the value of the arts to the public and to cast the dollars as an investment by the public, who could then contemplate the arts community as drivers of economic development and improved social and educational services to the region.

A third nonprofit executive stated that the partnership was established in order to build a community improvement district. The institutions that formed the partnership sought urban revitalization through property and institutional development, and the nonprofit members wanted to create plans for the strategic growth of all member institutions. The partnership provided transactional benefits to its members, who gained from collaboration and shared resources, and to the larger community, which then created the conditions for positive change in an urban neighborhood threatened by economic disinvestment and decline.

Conclusion

A central element in our inquiry into nonprofit-first partnerships has been the lens of sector pairings that form these arrangements. We show that nonprofit-nonprofit, nonprofit-government, and nonprofit-business partnerships produce differences in expectations, approaches, and methods, as well as outcomes meriting our attention. Among nonprofit-nonprofit partnerships, we note eight distinct and frequently mentioned outcomes listed in table 3.3 and described on next page.

First is an emphasis that both partners share the benefits and outcomes of the partnership while still pursuing their own missions. Second is a demonstrable commitment reflected by the hands-on involvement of the leaders in both organizations to the partnership and its outcomes. Third is mutuality in authority and responsibility between the partners. Fourth is that the risks and rewards are shared between participants. Fifth is a perceived reciprocity of financial and nonfinancial contributions by both partners toward carrying out the work of the partnership. Sixth is the willingness and interest of the parties to continue or renew the relationship beyond the partnership. Seventh is the perception that the process of partnership is itself a valued outcome of the endeavor. Eighth is the idea that the partnership contributes to the greater good and the creation of public value.

In nonprofit-government partnerships, by contrast, we note three main clusters of benefits. These outcomes are related to, but different than, the benefits noted for nonprofit-nonprofit partnerships. First is an emphasis on clarity in the roles and expectations of each member. Second is the requirement for a formalized agreement on the partnership, usually in the form of a contract for services between the two partners. Third is the understanding that relationships are

Table 3.3. Distinct and Frequently Mentioned Nonprofit-First Outcomes Associated with Cross-Sector Types.

#	Nonprofit-Nonprofit	Nonprofit-Government	Nonprofit-Business
1	Both partners share benefits and outcomes while pursuing their own missions	A priority is the emphasis on the roles and expectations of both partners	Desire to improve market share, reduce costs of doing business, and create profits
2	Both partners demonstrate commitment reflected by hands-on involvement of the organizations' leaders	The presence of a formal written agreement or contract between actors	Expectation by both partners that they will be flexible and adaptable to achieve their mission
3	Both partners perceive a mutuality of authority and responsibility	Agreement by both partners that the work of the partnership is focused on transactional outcomes and performance accountability	Businesses may support the nonprofit in its mission fulfillment, but that is secondary to profit achievement goals
4	Both partners share risks and rewards		Nonprofits may support business profitability goals if the business aids them in reaching their goals
5	Both partners perceive reciprocity of financial and nonfinancial contributions		
6	Both partners perceive the willingness to continue the partnership beyond its expiration		
7	Perception that the partnership itself is a worthy outcome beyond the work of the partnership		
8	Perception that the partnership contributes to the greater good of society		

focused on transactional work products and accountability for performance as specified in the contract agreement.

Although the nonprofit-business partnership dyads were the fewest in number as related by our nonprofit respondents, four benefits distinguish these ventures from the other two types of sector pairings. First is the for-profit businesses' concern with market share, reduced costs, and profit creation as motivations to engage with nonprofit organizations. Second is the understanding that many of the nonprofit partners enter into partnerships with business with the aspiration that the business will be flexible and adaptive to the circumstances of the partnership. Third is the realization that businesses enter into partnerships with nonprofits for motivations other than the desire to engage in social enterprise or social innovation. Fourth is the insight that nonprofit partners were motivated to form partnerships with businesses based on the part the business would play in program completion, resources development, and a perceived legitimacy arising from the association.

The three insights that framed our growing understanding of nonprofit-first partnerships in this chapter have led us to identify both transactional and transformational benefits for the nonprofit participants. Nonprofits are validated by partnership and may gain both financial and nonfinancial benefits; the specifics of such gains, however, differ by nonprofit-nonprofit, nonprofit-government, and nonprofit-business pairings. In this chapter, we developed clusters of benefits based on these three major pairings in order to better understand the benefits and values that each type can offer the nonprofit actor and the larger community thus served.

Notes

1. Forrer, John, James Jed Kee, and Eric Boyer. *Governing Cross-Sector Collaboration* (Hoboken, NJ: John Wiley & Sons, 2014); Bryson, John M., Barbara C. Crosby, and Melissa Middleton Stone. "The Design and Implementation of Cross-Sector Collaborations: Propositions from the Literature." *Public Administration Review* 66, no. s1 (2006): 44–55, doi:10.1111/j.1540 -6210.2006.00665.x; Austin, James E. *The Collaboration Challenge: How Nonprofits and Businesses Succeed Through Strategic Alliances* (Hoboken, NJ: John Wiley & Sons, 2010), 109.

2. Teisman, Geert R., and Erik Hans Klijn. "Partnership Arrangements: Governmental Rhetoric or Governance Scheme?" *Public Administration Review* 62, no. 2 (2002): 197–205, doi:10.1111/0033-3352.00170; Linder, Stephen H. "Coming to Terms with the Public-Private Partnership: A Grammar of Multiple Meanings." *American Behavioral Scientist* 43, no. 1 (1999): 35–51, doi:10.1177/00027649921955146.

3. Powell, W. W., and Steinberg, R. *The Nonprofit Sector: A Research Handbook* (New Haven: Yale University Press, 2006); Bryson, John M., Barbara C. Crosby, and Melissa Middleton Stone. "The Design and Implementation of Cross-Sector Collaborations: Propositions from the Literature." *Public Administration Review* 66 no. s1 (2006): 44–55, doi:10.1111/j.1540-6210.2006.00665.x.

4. Benington, J. and Getters, M. "10 Partnerships as Networked Governance?," in *Local Partnership and Social Exclusion in the European Union: New Forms of Local Social Governance?* (Abingdon, UK: Routledge, 2013), 198; Young, Dennis R. "Complementary, Supplementary, or Adversarial? Nonprofit-Government Relations," edited by Elizabeth Boris and C. Eugene Steuerle entitled *Nonprofits & Government: Collaboration & Conflict. Urban Institute Press* (2006): 37–80, doi:10.1515/npf-2015-0040.

5. Young, D. R. "Alternative Models of Government-Nonprofit Sector Relations: Theoretical and International Perspectives." *Nonprofit and Voluntary Sector Quarterly* 29, no. 1 (2000): 149–172; McDonald, Mary B. "Understanding Social Capital, Civic Engagement, and Community Building," in *Leadership in Nonprofit Organizations: A Reference Book*, ed. Kathryn Agard (Thousand Oaks, CA: Sage Publications, 2011), 46–55.

6. Gazley, Beth, and Jeffrey L. Brudney. "The Purpose (and Perils) of Government-Nonprofit Partnership." *Nonprofit and Voluntary Sector Quarterly* 36, no. 3 (2007): 389–415, doi:10.1177/0899764006295997; Young, Dennis R. "Alternative Models of Government-Nonprofit Sector Relations: Theoretical and International Perspectives." *Nonprofit and Voluntary Sector Quarterly* 29, no. 1 (2000): 149–172, doi:10.1177/0899764000291009; Salamon, Lester M. "The Nonprofit Sector and Government: The American Experience in Theory and Practice," in *The Third Sector: Comparative Studies of Nonprofit Organization* (Berlin and New York: Walter de Gruyter, 1990), 210–240, doi:10.1515/9783110868401.219.

7. Rainey, Hal G., and Barry Bozeman. "Comparing Public and Private Organizations: Empirical Research and the Power of the *A Priori*." *Journal of Public Administration Research and Theory* 10, no. 2 (2000): 447–470, <http://jpart.oxfordjournals.org/content/10/2/447. abstract>; Moore, Mark H. *Creating Public Value: Strategic Management in Government* (Cambridge, MA: Harvard University Press, 1995); Oliver, Christine. "Determinants of Interorganizational Relationships: Integration and Future Directions." *Academy of Management Review* 15, no. 2 (1990): 241–265, doi:10.5465/AMR.1990.4308156.

8. Eikenberry, Angela M., and Jodie Drapal Kluver. "The Marketization of the Nonprofit Sector: Civil Society at Risk?" *Public Administration Review* 64, no. 2 (2004): 132–140, doi:10.1111/j.1540-6210.2004.00355.x; Sagawa, Shirley, and Eli Segal. *Common Interest, Common Good: Creating Value through Business and Social Sector Partnerships* (Cambridge, MA: Harvard Business Press, 1999).

4 Good to Great: Recognizing the Signs of High-Quality Partnerships

Overview

In this chapter, we consider partnerships as evolving, and examine how importance, meaning, and satisfaction all play into this ongoing relationship. Following up on earlier insights in chapter 3 regarding the ways that different sector partnerships affect the nonprofit organization, we examine the nonprofit executives' interviews to compile performance standards that nonprofit leaders can use to monitor and predict the progress of their partnerships.

Introduction

In this chapter, we mine the case study data on partnership satisfaction, factors of partnership that worked for and against achieving the stated goals, and advice that the nonprofit executives offered to their peers contemplating engaging in partnerships. We also consider how nonprofit-first executives see partnership processes as evolving and their assessments that partnerships need not be perfect to be important or meaningful or worth the risk. This chapter also presents partnership performance indicators, which can serve as practical signposts for whether partnership arrangements are positive and on track to meet their stated goals.

Partnership Anecdotes

As mentioned previously in the introduction of this book, a pillar of the research methods for our study involved the presentation to the nonprofit executive respondents of a rating system and the request that they apply it to their important partnership cases. We used a simple scoring system of 1 to 10, where a score of 1 indicated that a partnership had met none of its goals, and a score of 10 indicated that the partnership had met all of its goals. In seventeen of the eighty-two partnership cases—about 21 percent or slightly more than one in five of all partnerships comprising our case study data-set—the nonprofit executives rated the partnership as having a perfect score of 10. In their comments regarding these cases, the nonprofit executives praised the commitment of their partners and the alignment of interests between the two organizations as major reasons for the superior performance. Other reasons cited included: trust between the participants, parity with respect to organizational resources and capacity, preparation and advance planning, willingness to share resources and information, and good communication between the partnering organizations. The nonprofit executives also maintained that partnerships were validated when both the partnership mission and the two participating actors' respective missions were fulfilled. In the best of these cases, the partnerships were validated as well by the partners' desire and intention for future collaboration.

In contrast to the positive characteristics contributing to the partnership success of these seventeen cases with perfect scores, other executives mentioned contrary conditions that led to difficulties in their respective partnerships. These "nonpositive" factors were present in some measure among all eighty-two cases—including the seventeen scoring a perfect 10—and were related in the interviews to us as we sought insights on the factors that posed barriers to success, increased risks of failure, or led to negative partnership outcomes. The challenges, obstacles, and pitfalls of partnership shared by the executives extend over a broad range of issues, including disparity in authority between participants; absence of relationship reciprocity, mutuality, and respect; and misaligned organizational capacity and culture. Some of these challenges were situational complications or temporary conditions with single or limited occurrences, while others were systemic, resulting from a design flaw of the partnership and appearing to be deeply woven into the fabric of the particular partnership. In some instances, the executives said that although they expected partnerships to have challenges, the obstacles could be very difficult to resolve. Figure 4.1 summarizes the concepts for nonprofit-first partnership success and nonsuccess.

In one example, a nonprofit executive engaged with the county pointed to unequal power in the dyadic relationship as a significant barrier to partnership performance. She traced the power dynamic to the fact that some partner organizations have greater funds and authority and therefore more clout, autonomy, and ability to make demands of the others.

> The project also fatigues our staff and leadership, and adds administrative costs and overhead which is not recognized or compensated by the County as part of the contract arrangement. The unfortunate aside is that we tend to subsidize the work with volunteer hours beyond the scope of the contract to meet the obligations of the contract, and it is frequently these "value added" features that enable the project work to succeed. For example, making our staff work long, late hours to register low-income youth [and] providing food and complimentary parking and copy services to facilitate enrollment and engagement of recipients, which are not billable to the County on public funds as part of the compliance.

Overall, we note three characteristics in the nonprofit executives' reported experiences in high-quality partnerships. First is an appreciation for the

Frequent Attributions for Partnership Success

Commitment of Partners

1. Trust Between Participants

2. Parity in Organizational Resources and Capacity

3. Preparation and Advanced Planning

4. Willingness to Share

Alignment of Interests
Between Partners

5. Good Communication Between Partners

Frequent Attributions for Partnership Failure

Situation

1. Disparity in Authority in the Partnership

2. No Sense of Partnership Reciprocity and Nuetrality

3. Misaligned Organizational Capacity and Culture

Design Problems

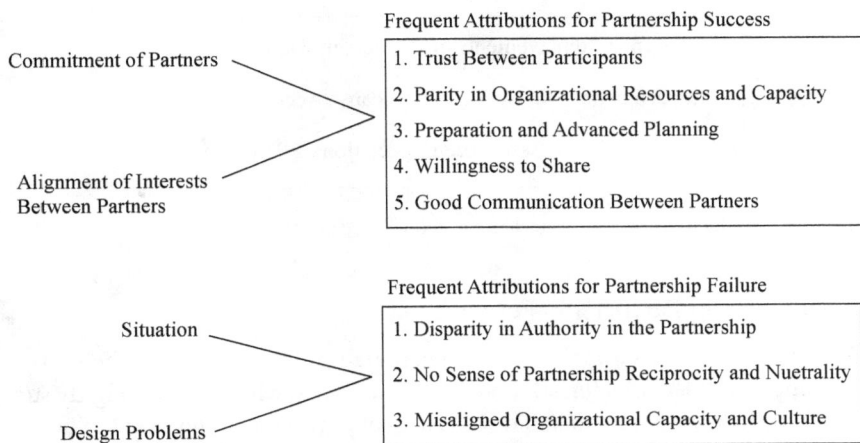

Fig. 4.1 Nonprofit-First Partnership Characteristics (Positive and Nonpositive).

partnership's accomplishments attained through attention to the partnership itself. For example, an executive of a philanthropic institution explained that his very successful partnership required daily attention despite its achievements. He attributed its successful outcomes to active participation, care-taking, and overall "paying attention" by both partners.

A second characteristic was that most nonprofit executives anticipated that their partnership could accomplish its goals despite being imperfect. They also expressed faith that as their partnership matured, and as the respective actors became more experienced in partnership, that the partnership would yield even better outcomes. One executive, who was engaged in a complex partnership and subsequent merger of health-care and advocacy organizations, maintained that the partnership required a steady commitment to dialogue and adjustment. She asserted that the partnership outcomes resulted from continuous improvements in the relationships and performance of the participants throughout the endeavor.

The third characteristic involved expectations of reciprocity, which was seen as an underlying value of partnership.[1] Across the cases, the nonprofit executives stated that their initial conception was of a contractual exchange of goods and services with another organization. For some of the partnership cases, reciprocity was institutionalized in a contract that defined the roles and responsibilities of each partner while also placing limits on them. Reciprocity also included elements that were less tangible, such as soft-skill interactions promoting friendship, collegiality, and shared outcomes among the partners. Figure 4.2 lists the three concepts.

1. Recognize Achievements of Partnership Daily

2. Imperfect but Still Successful Because Accomplish Goals

3. Reciprocity is a Base/Core Expectation of Participants

Fig. 4.2 Three Outstanding Characteristics of Experience on Partnerships.

Benchmarks of Partnership Performance

To understand the factors that inhibit partnerships from achieving their goals, we compared the characteristics noted by executives who reported highly successful partnership with the characteristics of partnerships reported to be less successful. In most instances, these characteristics confirmed one another. For example, one organization pointed to leadership as a reason for the partnership's success, while another named the lack of the participants' commitment as a key cause of disappointing partnership performance. For example, as one nonprofit executive reported "While the partnership was successful and met its goals, there were certainly challenges.... Sometimes there was a lack of transparency among the partners, as one organization leader was unable to attend to the partnership consistently. Also, individual staff were impediments to the partnership and ultimately contributed to there being less than 100% trust among the partners." Another nonprofit executive stated, "The partnership was able to overcome issues raised by a stream of steady and quality communication, sensitivity to others' points of view, honoring deadlines and responsibilities, providing feedback, shar[ing] goals, developing trust, and continuing to earn that trust from the dedicated interest of the leaders of both participants."

From the cases, we were able to identify two themes consistently characterizing top-performing partnerships (those scored as 10 on the scale). The first was that top-performing partnerships arose from relationships that were consciously nurtured and developed by both organizations. This kind of relationship created deep interorganizational bonds as participants gained experience with each other over time. For example, many nonprofit executives alluded to increased appreciation for their partners as their partnerships overcame challenges in achieving their shared mission. Some executives also related that as they accrued more experience in participating as a partner, their expectations and abilities in partnership activities increased.

A second theme of the highly successful partnerships encompassed fluidity and adaptability. Executives stated that they often learned from multiple partnership experiences, because each partnership had its own dynamic. Some respondents opined that even the best partnership arrangements had room for improvement in design, operations, and outcomes, even if all goals were met, making the case that partnerships evolve and must have an ability to adjust to changed circumstances. For example, one nonprofit executive stated,

> Our view of partnership with government has evolved incrementally over time and experience in successive projects. Each project with government causes our leaders and staff to learn more and be better. For example, we now know that government can't both lead and manage because of the different parts of government. There is a gap between the people in government making the policy and those implementing policy in terms of their experience and confidence, who don't have [the] ability the take risks and be accountable.... We've learned that our role is to be flexible when working with government because they can't be.

The nonprofit executives also related that they entered into partnerships cautiously and looked for signs or indications that the partnership would succeed and merit their investment of time and effort. In many instances, the executives referred to a desire for formal performance indicators that would indicate whether or not their partnership was on a positive trajectory. As one executive further explained, "An organizational value is to actively seek collaboration and to engage in partnerships with other organizations. We consider collaboration and partnership as a part of our sustainability strategy toward achieving our mission, while protecting our core work focus and competencies from incrementally moving away from our mission.... We are both experienced and cautious in seeking partners and forming partnerships ... and we consider how well our partners have worked in the past with others and their reputation in the community."

As an initial check, respondents told us they considered whether the partnering organizations had previous experience with partnerships and whether they would exchange financial and nonfinancial resources. Previous experience with partnership meant better training and expectations among involved personnel and an overall better understanding of the work that a partnership would entail. The exchange of resources demonstrated a willingness to commit and collaborate, as evidenced by sharing funding, personnel, facilities and equipment, expertise, information, knowledge, capacity, or access to other opportunities. Some executives with prior experience in partnerships suggested less precise and more intuitive indicators of future success, such as the partner's performance in past partnership engagements, a trusted third party's validation of the partner, rapport between the organizations' leaders, mutual respect, and ease of communication and willingness to solve problems among organization staff. One nonprofit executive offered the following advice to others about partnership based on her experience merging five sister organizations:

- Make sure the focus is the mission for the partnership
- Make people feel safe and important
- Keep focus on the visionary transformational goals of the partnership
- Pay attention to each other
- Be careful about making promises you cannot keep or deliver on

Table 4.1 elaborates on the seventeen partnership cases that the respondents rated as having met all their goals. The seventeen cases are comprised of eight partnership cases between a nonprofit and government, seven between a nonprofit and another nonprofit, and two between a nonprofit and a business. The table column headers organize the partnership characteristic data. The first column refers to the code we assigned to each nonprofit organization contributing cases and therefore is an identifier. The second column lists the sector pairing partnership and the subsector type (discussed more fully in chapter 5 but described here as the type of nonprofit services defined by the mission of the organization; for example, social services, health and welfare, education, arts and culture, and community and economic development), followed by the rationale for rating the partnership a score of 10 along with clarifying comments in the next column. The last column of the table includes advice from the nonprofit executives for other nonprofit leaders for building high-performing partnerships. Together, the last two columns provide rationales drawn from the case study narratives in which the executives explained the factors that worked for and against achieving the partnership's goals.

Important and Imperfect

Table 4.1 demonstrates two useful findings to advance our understanding of the internal workings of highly successful nonprofit-first partnerships.

First, even when nonprofit executives credited their partnership as having met all its goals, the search for "continuous improvement" or the premise that the partnership could "always be better," was expressed many times. For example, three of the eight nonprofit-government cases included circumstances where the participating organizations overcame their own negative reputations with the partnership target population over time as a result of the partnership. In two of the seven nonprofit-nonprofit cases credited with meeting all partnership goals, the nonprofit executives described an emerging equality between the participants as an important element to partnership success. In both of the nonprofit-business

Table 4.1. Cases Rated as having met all their Goals with a Score of 10.

Org ID Code	Sector Pairing	Subsector	Reasons for a Partnership Satisfaction Score of 10	Suggest Best Practices Partnership Behavior Drawn from Respondent "Advice to Others"
3	Nonprofit / Business	Social Service	Steady stream of communication to over-come misunderstandings.	Maintain sensitivity to the partner viewpoint and understand their expectations of you.
6	Nonprofit / Government	Social Service	Overcame negative **stereotypes of target population** in community.	Be sure the purpose of the partnership conforms to mission of organizations.
8	Nonprofit / Government	Culture, Social Services	Overcame **negative attitudes toward of** target population in community.	Don't over-think the collaboration but agree on the depth of collaboration.
9	Nonprofit / Government	Social Services and Education	Mutual goals, similar missions, and excellent communication overcame legacies of negative feelings **between partners.**	Respect among organizations CEOs and leadership staff led the way for strong advocacy for one another and willingness to invest time and effort in the relationship.
9	Nonprofit / Government	Social Service	Transition in leadership forced the focus of new director on the partnership endeavor.	The partnership can achieve all its goals if it is a priority for both partners.
13	Nonprofit / Government	Econ Dev, Education, Advocacy	Collaborative vision to achieve outcomes led to an expansion of the partnership to other participants.	Must have a shared vested interest to overcome external politics that would have otherwise inhibited the partnership.
17	Nonprofit / Nonprofit	Social Services	Merger between two organizations arose from strong desire on the part of both agencies to create something new and meaningful for the community.	Since both agencies really 'wanted it' and initiated it, their funder provided them with a pilot process and structure to work through problems and difficulties.
21	Nonprofit / Nonprofit	Advocacy, Health, Social Services	It met all of its goals gradually, over time.	Follow the exact intentions of the partners and the most difficult part will work effortlessly. Little ambiguity, so little need to negotiate once the partnership began.
23	Nonprofit / Nonprofit	Education, Culture	The partnership exceeded all of the expectations and met all of its goals.	No organization should feel as if they were subordinate in the partnership. Because the development of the program was democratic and each organizations'

(Continued)

Table 4.1. (*Continued*)

Org ID Code	Sector Pairing	Subsector	Reasons for a Partnership Satisfaction Score of 10	Suggest Best Practices Partnership Behavior Drawn from Respondent "Advice to Others"
				goals did not become subservient to others, making compromise at the end of the day not feel like compromise.
27	Nonprofit / Nonprofit	Philanthropy, Econ Dev	In a short period of time the program had a successful launch and a second project in the subsequent year.	Equality in partnerships is very important, so that neither organization achieves the mission without the other.
29	Nonprofit / Nonprofit	Education, Culture	Partnership completely met all the goals and the partner committed additional, unanticipated resources to the cause.	Commitment by partner led to an ease in obtaining funding.
32	Nonprofit / Government	Environment, Advocacy, Education	Healthy collaboration that appears as if the two organizations are seamless in their work.	Both sides demonstrated a high level of commitment due to accountability built into the partnership and the sense of a 'meshed' endeavor.
34	Nonprofit / Government	Economic & Community Development	Expected this just to be a funding relationship, but the partner continued to engage and advocate for the plan beyond the partnership.	As a small organization, we had to leverage relationships to accomplish our goals.
35	Nonprofit / Nonprofit	Culture, Education	Every part of it works. Audiences love it, people look forward to it, and it's relatively easy to maintain.	Partner with organizations similar in size, outlook and philosophy.
35	Nonprofit / Nonprofit	Culture, Advocacy	All expectations were met and exceeded. The grant maker validated the partnership and views the effort as a "poster child" for collaboration.	Thoughtful and specific time commitment by both made it possible.
48	Nonprofit / Business	Health, Education	Met all of its goals attributable to two leaders on the same page setting the stage for the whole culture of the relationship.	Partnership elevated the profile of both and raised more resources to engage in research, services delivered and participation throughout the state.
48	Nonprofit / Government	Health, Advocacy	Goals were met.	The person leading the relationships is the difference maker.

cases, the importance of "improved communication" was credited as essential to the success of the partnership.

A second common assessment among the partnerships that scored 10 was that the processes of partnership allowed for a sense of forward motion. The partnership was seen as a relationship that evolved among participants, one which had to be reviewed and adjusted over time to reach its goals.

Partnerships scored as 10 typically alluded to mutuality and a sense of teamwork. Nonprofit executives sought partnership as a method of mission fulfillment because partnership with another nonprofit or a government agency or private business can leverage or extend their mission impact beyond the limits of the nonprofit's fiscal and human capital. Without mission fulfillment as the normative purpose for a nonprofit organization's partnership undertakings, a nonprofit leader would have difficulty defending the decision to commit resources to the endeavor. To form successful partnerships, executives must believe that such arrangements can satisfy their own organization's mission at least to some extent, and that the mission of the partnership itself aligns with their own organization's interests.

In the scholarly literature and described in various levels of detail in our partnership cases, for example, in the best of circumstances, partnerships can form from the independent and voluntary enterprise of the participants who come together to solve a problem or issue in which both have an interest but that neither can accomplish alone.[2] Drawing on the full body of data collected in the eighty-two cases, the shape and design of important and successful partnership formation appear to follow a consistent design. Initially, the transactional steps of forming a partnership in our partnership cases are described by nonprofit executives as following a nonsequential pattern which may constitute a "scorecard."

The scorecard illustrated in figure 4.3 reflects the elements of partnership formation that nonprofit executives might consider a checklist of process outcomes they might formally or informally look to identify in the partnership. These include whether or not mission fulfillment for each partner is evident; whether both partner missions align with that of the partnership endeavor; whether the intended benefits to the organization and the larger community are evident; whether or not early-stage trust-building occurs from actions that indicate the partnership is an organizational priority, such as the direct involvement and commitment of senior leaders; evidence the partners share resources and risks; evidence of reciprocity in terms of workload and institutional authority; whether the partners have a track record of prior success in partnership endeavors; and the likelihood of anticipated and unanticipated return on investment for each party, such as enhanced organization reputation.

	Is mission fulfilled for each partnership?
	Are missions aligned with partnership endeavor?
	Are there designed benefits from partnership?
	Is there early stage trust building?
	Is there involvement of senior leaders?
	Is there evidence of shared resources and risk?
	Is there reciprocity of work load and authority?
	Is there a track record of partnership success?
	Is there a potential for reputational return on investment?

Fig. 4.3 Scorecard of Early-Stage Transactional Steps for Important Partnerships.

Establishing That Mutuality of Interest Requires Work

The pattern of mutual interests underpinning partnership is well established in the scholarly and popular literature.[3] Participants in the best-performing partnerships in this study identify a mutuality of interests through which joint problem-solving and overcoming challenges worked to create bonds between participants that extended beyond the partnership to the greater community; such bonds help to form the basis of civil society in the United States.[4] The discovery and fulfillment of mutual interests typically occurred when partners identified a community need independently and voluntarily engaged in collaboration to address it.

At the same time, recognizing mutual interests and accepting the burden of work required to realize them frequently became steps necessary to surmount obstacles across the partnership cases. For example, in the case of a partnership between two organizations with complementary missions, both organizations utilized different job-readiness and skills training models to address the special needs of two different difficult-to-employ populations. The initial discussions involved ways that the partners might overcome the differences in program approach and what the implications of change might mean for each partner. A central facet of the partnership was to use the mission of the partnership endeavor to create a new service program using the staff expertise and resources of both organizations. "Since our missions were complementary and the partnership involved bringing two existing skill sets together in a manner that helped perform the work of the grant, staffing of the partnership did not include new hires initially, but reassignment of existing staff.... Neither of us wanted to increase costs but to find ways to make better use of our program staff.... This allowed for a fast track to plan and merge programs, we thought, temporarily."

In a second example, a nonprofit executive noted that his partnership was formed by the organizations to carry out the program services outlined in a proposal to state government. The arrangement was codified after a lengthy effort to agree on performance responsibilities, scope of work, reporting to the state government, and many other details in a memorandum of understanding drafted between the two organizations. "This agreement was between equals outlining roles and responsibilities of each of the partners ... and took a long time to complete because we felt that we did not want to delegate authority of oversight to our partner."

Partnership Willingness and Readiness

Underlying the partnership case descriptions is the awareness that partners may or may not be similarly ready and willing to enter a partnership. Ideally, readiness to enter a partnership is demonstrated by willingness and commitment to engage in joint problem-solving. One partnership case offers the illustration of commitment to resolving problems as an indicator of the willingness and readiness of organizational leaders to engage in partnership and to take actions necessary to achieving success. The nonprofit executive of an organization devoted to residential group homes described a case between his organization and a social services partner organization in which a period of difficulty escalated to the point where executives could not overcome the challenges of the endeavor. Two board members took it upon themselves to broker a meeting between the two organizations to consider ways in which the organizations might better cooperate. The board members, committed to the success of the partnership, were able to draw on their own resources and professional connections to employ computer-aided technology for program purposes to fulfill the mission of the partnership to improve the lives of people with developmental disabilities. Reflecting back on the incident, the executive noted that the outcome of the board member involvement was an indication of their readiness and willingness to ensure the partnership's success.

Partnership willingness has two facets. The first refers to the organization leaders' desire, openness, and intention to seek partners and partnership opportunities. The second refers to organization leaders' active and assertive commitment to achieving successful outcomes. Across our sample, partnerships achieved greater goal satisfaction when partners adjusted to one another and were able to make accommodations for future obstacles both anticipated and unanticipated. For example, one nonprofit executive attributed her partnership success to the organizations' desire to make it work and to go beyond meeting the minimum aspects of their written partnership agreement as needed. As a result, both organizations took an ownership role in regard to the health and well-being of the partnership. In another example, the executive stated that the partnership relationship was very difficult because it took a long time for the partners to respect each other, overcome the egos involved on both sides, and develop the fortitude to manage the involvement of local government actors who she perceived as being motivated by "political theatre" and not the long-term societal impact of the partnership endeavor. The executive attributed her reticence to engage in partnership to her organization's prior experiences of costly, unsuccessful partnerships. She confided that these prior negative experiences had given her a reluctance and a "better safe than sorry" takeaway for any further partnership endeavor with other organizations. Once she overcame her mindset by thinking through her organization's readiness for partnership, she was once again ready to enter into partnership.

The second facet of partnership willingness arises from external circumstances that may drive an organization toward partnership by necessity. Examples include changes in the politics of the local community or the policy environment of the state, or in the imposition of partnership by a third party. In a case involving the merger of five regional affiliate chapters of a national organization focused on women's health, reproductive health, and health advocacy, the executive shared that the partner organizations knew changes in state governor's administration and in members' party affiliation of the state legislature meant that the individual chapters could not survive alone because of their own inability to raise funds to sustain their individual identities. The executive explained, "Interest and willingness to come together changed quickly with the new political realities in state government ... and in the ability of our stakeholders to influence policy.... This was essentially a strategic decision that ... required greater coordination ... to continue the work of our mission and missions.... The time it took to position all five organizations so that everyone was ready for a merger was lengthy ... and was complicated but worth the hard work."

Partnership readiness is a category related to but distinct from partnership willingness. Readiness refers to an organization's capacity to engage in partnership endeavors. For example, one case involved a partnership between two nonprofit economic development organizations centered on different types of businesses when they responded jointly to a US Department of Commerce request for proposals. The nonprofit executive relating this case noted that both organizations were experienced at working with third parties to create businesses and shared a readiness to enter into the partnership, as reflected by the ease with which they came together to respond to the RFP and attracted third-party support. Partnership readiness became an issue due to external marketplace conditions, such as finding companies the partnership was intended to serve, as few

Indicators of Partnership Readiness	YES	NO
Discretionary Funding		
Viable Market Opportunity		
Available Personnel		
Facilities and Equipment		
Expertise		
Information		
Knowledge		
Capacity		
Access to Other Opportunities to Leverage and Impact		

Fig. 4.4 Scorecard Assessment of Partnership Readiness.

viable business development candidates existed. Thus, although the partners and funding streams were ready, the marketplace timing of the partnership was not at the right stage to engender successful partnerships.

Assessment of partnership readiness lends itself to a scorecard checklist of indicators whose presence can define an organization's capacity to engage in partnership. Potential indicators of partnership readiness include: a roster of financial and nonfinancial resources, such as availability of discretionary funding in the existing budgets of each partner; evidence of and viability for market opportunity for the partnership endeavor; available personnel in one or both partners; availability of facilities and equipment; organizational capacity in terms of staff expertise, information, and knowledge; and access to other opportunities to advance or growth of the partnership for purposes of leverage and impact. Figure 4.4 illustrates these criteria.

An element of partnership readiness that respondents thought contributed to poor partnership performance was the timing of the partnership. Timing was reflected by three dimensions consistently described in the partnership cases. First, the nonprofit executives questioned whether both organizations had been able to commit the necessary resources and attention to the arrangement and perform the work required to deliver on its purpose at the time of the partnership. Second, the executives noted that the partners might have been in different stages of organizational development and lifecycle, and although perhaps willing to enter into partnership, might not have been ready to realize or effectuate a successful collaborative endeavor. For example, one nonprofit executive shared that during the early stages of his partnership, the partner organization did not have trained or dedicated staffing for the initiative. Over time, the partner organization assembled a staff of ten to run the program and eventually assumed operation of the program, thus removing his organization. The executive attributed the challenge to the timing of the endeavor as his organization was growing from a grassroots to a more professionally administered organization at the time, and the partner organization was not ready to wait. While the partnership mission was fulfilled in the short term, the longer-term result was an abrupt end to the partnership.

The third element of partnership readiness refers to the amount of time used to plan and prepare the partnership arrangement. This step included sorting out roles through early-stage discussions and preparation, the desire for formal memorandums of understanding or contract documents to govern the partnership relationship, and the participants' overall sense of their state of preparation to work together. Many examples occur across the cases. For instance, the executive of a small social services agency working with community youth shared that while he believed the partnership with a competing organization also serving youth would be ongoing, it was also limited in its ability to meet primary goals. The partnership came together hurriedly to meet the requirements of a grant proposal, since the funder had a policy not to fund similar organizations separately, and this requirement was reflected in the need for transitions in leadership and program staff and the balancing of different priorities between the partners. Consequently, the partnership was a relationship of convenience, with little involvement between the two organizations beyond each providing its share of services.

Operational Barriers

Nonprofit executives described three types of barriers to achieving partnership outcomes: barriers that arose through the operations of the partnership; barriers that resulted from poorly conceived, designed, led, or managed partnership arrangements; and barriers that originated with larger forces beyond the control of the partnering organizations. Some nonprofit executives pointed to differences in the organizational cultures of the participants, which might involve ethical issues such as accounting practices or interpretation of performance reporting. Yet other differences noted by the nonprofit executives involved matters of fiscal compliance to third parties, boards of directors, and constituents or human resource policies and procedures. Barriers to partnerships meeting their goals were often attributed to such matters as difficulty in meeting deadlines, sharing resources, or having to wait for partners while bearing the strain of helping them. The most significant challenges, however, arose from differences in operating and regulatory cultures between the partners and the third-party funders or partnership stakeholders. For example, two nonprofit executives explained,

> Our partnership scored 4 out of 10.... Partly this was due to the difficulties we had in staffing as we relied on volunteers to perform much of the work, while our partner had paid staff and much more experience working with the funder.
>
> ... Performance could not have been better because we did not possess the sophisticated financial back office ... to maintain records in the manner demanded by our partner and the county. While this was an issue we had expressed at the beginning ... we were disappointed that our partner did not help us ... align our systems.

Attending to Partnership Leadership and Management

Forming and performing a partnership has many parts necessary to synchronize the operations, program development and delivery, fiscal controls and accounting, and assessment. The partnership process and work typically advance to greater sophistication over time at certain benchmark points, such as the crystallization of the collaboration project, the decision to enter into the partnership, the departure point of joint work efforts, etc. Over time and with the progression of tasks toward mission fulfillment, the partnership must evolve and deepen as the participants gain a better understanding of the work and their partners. The nonprofit executive of a small teen fatherhood initiative expressed his belief that partners "are well served when both express a desire for learning to make it a better project next time."

In the best-performing partnership cases nonprofit executives expressed that the skills of the partnership leaders evolve and grow to reflect their on-the-job learning experiences and demands of the partnership. In one example, the executive stated that the presence of committed executive directors in both nonprofit organizations, dedicated high-level staff and organizational program staff, and a general will to cooperate between the organizations contributed to meeting the goals of the partnership. One much-repeated warning by the nonprofit executives was not to delegate authority or leadership too far down the organizational hierarchy for managing or operating the partnership. Rather, for a successful partnership, the leaders of the organizations must be attentive and involved to solve problems, inspire staff, drive the partnership, and demonstrate to external stakeholders that the partnership is a priority for the partners.

Conversely, other cases demonstrate that when leadership from the partnering organization failed to allocate strong or engaged personnel to the partnership, the effort slowed or faltered. Problems often stemmed from the lack of staff capability, commitment, and person-power in the endeavor. The nonprofit executives also attributed problems to misaligned skill sets among the staff assigned to the partnership across organizations, sudden or unanticipated staff reassignments, and unexpected duties such as staff engaged in service provision also assuming interorganization liaison functions of the partnership. In one case involving a large social services organization and a much smaller grassroots organization, the problems in performing the work of the partnership were exacerbated by the reliance on part-time volunteer workers in the smaller organization as a counterpart to the full-time, paid professional staff in the larger organization.

Attending to Partnership Design

Another partnership challenge concerns faulty design in the partnership program. In at least one instance, poor program design arose from the flawed assumption that volunteers could readily perform ongoing professional functions. One of the factors that worked against the partnership meeting its goals was that some functions were performed by volunteers who, although caring and committed, were frequently absent or quit on some occasions because of the rising time demands and increasing complexity of the work, thus taking valuable institutional knowledge with them and leaving behind unstable program capacity. In another case, the contingency planning for the uncooperative, elusive, or unpredictable behavior of homeless drug recovery clients receiving services was insufficient, with the result that the partner organizations expended more time and resources than planned yet still produced poor outcomes.

Forces Beyond the Control of the Partnering Organizations

Yet other barriers to partnership identified by the nonprofit executives included larger environmental factors such as the state of the regional or local economy, regional or local politics, and priorities of third-party funders. One case narrative involving home ownership and rehabilitation attributed the low partnership performance to the mortgage lending crisis and housing market crash of 2008, which ended public sector support of the partnership endeavor. Another partnership involving a community organization seeking to coordinate services to low-income individuals noted that the target population was too big, and public policy insufficient, to address the magnitude of the problem. Other cases involving funding from the federal government administered through local authorities attributed the less-than-ideal partnership performance to federal regulations, complex bureaucracy, and lengthy decision processes that worked against the partnership. Two nonprofit executives shared similar perspectives on their partnerships:

> Our partner was a bank that was very slow to make adjustments to their attitudes toward the primarily low-income clients we referred to them, who

sought to keep their homes ... in their defense, they were looking to the federal government for answers to the crisis....

Although we maintained cordial communications ... local and state government seemed stuck with the current practices and could not ... give us answers.... This places considerable strain on our resources as ... we began receiving more requests for help than we could accommodate. We had to cease the program until the environment improved and the city could come up with more money to prevent the huge rise in foreclosure actions.

Importance of Reciprocity in Partnership

A somewhat unremarkable and overlooked but all-important concept that emerged from the partnership cases was the perception by nonprofit executives of a lag in transaction reciprocity between partners. Unlike expectations of mutual benefits governing some partnerships, partnerships grounded in reciprocal exchanges were less about outcomes. Instead, such exchanges were more about the generation of trust among participants and the desire for longevity of the partnership. Delays in anticipated actions had a corrosive effect on the partnership as described by nonprofit executives. Several cases illustrated the idea that time spent in the service of the partnership was an important indicator of reciprocity. By way of illustration, one executive of a social services agency with many partnerships across all three sectors lauded the notion of reciprocity as a key concept that the partners themselves determine, as he said outsiders were not in a position to attest to a partnership. He also contended that meaningful partnerships occur between peers who share risks and a common purpose. According to him, organizations entering into partnership should expect the partnership to take time to incubate and mature, and success cannot be measured in weeks or months, but perhaps years.

In a second case—which we described earlier in this chapter—that might be considered as an example of "counter-reciprocity," the executive of a small faith-based, grassroots organization devoted to teaching fatherhood skills expressed disappointment as early reciprocal behaviors of the partners did not seem to progress or grow beyond contractual performance. Despite the initial enthusiasm, the partnership ended because the larger organization became the sole service provider for the county, effectively pushing out the smaller organization. The executive reflected that the early limited reciprocity was a sign of the longer-term intentions of the partner organization.

Advice to Other Nonprofit Leaders

We can understand the obstacles to partnership as variable predictive indicators of problems that will likely interfere with meeting partnership goals. We might also piece together from these cases a listing or scorecard of partnership progress benchmarks portending whether a partnership is on a path to meet its goals. For example, challenges to partnership among the cases were frequently overcome by a stream of steady and quality communication, sensitivity to others' points of view, honoring deadlines and responsibilities, providing feedback, sharing goals, developing trust, and continuing to earn that trust. Collectively, we glean from the nonprofit executives that a meaningful and important partnership requires that participants share risks and rewards; include a process to consider carefully the mutuality of purpose of a partnership; and come to terms with the pace at which benefits accrue and in what ways rewards are distributed equitably.

Some of the advice offered by the nonprofit executives speaks directly to tangible actions that a nonprofit leader can consider as achievement benchmarks for partnerships (see table 4.2). The data entries for the two columns under Partnership Behavior correspond to the reasons nonprofit executives offered in the seventeen cases for their important partnerships meeting all their goals and achieving a perfect score of 10. The Partnership Behavior category is subdivided to explain the actions of the participants and the intent of their actions based on the explanations executives gave as "advice to others." The next two columns of table 4.2 are drawn from the partnership behaviors that suggest progress toward goals and outcomes. The first column entries assess whether or not a behavior has occurred and allow for comparison; the information in the second column suggests an accomplishment measure of that behavior offered by the nonprofit executives.

The information presented in table 4.2 can help nonprofit participants gain a sense of whether their partnerships will achieve outcomes beyond the simple accomplishment of the partnership work, and to judge the relative worth or efficacy of these endeavors. The use of a standard for comparison offers the possibility of identifying or perhaps predicting poorly performing partnerships and organizing a range of performance characteristics by which a collaborative endeavor rises or will rise to the level of successful partnership. Such a template for assessing partnership efficacy can offer a tool to recognize, or even modify, poorly performing partnerships.

Good to Great: Recognizing the Signs of High-Quality Partnerships

Based on the interviews with nonprofit executives in this chapter, we have assembled practical standards for successful partnerships. Focusing on partnership cases from the respondents, we used the executives' reasons for those ratings to determine various characteristics of partnership success as well as measurable benchmarks, including development, adaptability, and previous experience in partnership. These findings emphasize that importance and imperfection are not mutually exclusive in partnership, and that mutuality and reciprocity are

Table 4.2. Partnership Performance Indicators and Benchmarks.

Partnership Behavior		Partnership Performance Process Indicator	Performance Benchmark
Action	Purpose of Action		
Steady stream of communication to overcome misunderstanding	Maintain sensitivity to the partner viewpoint and understand their expectations of you	Is there a mechanism for ready and easy communication?	Scored measure on a scale of 1-10 of communication where 1 = none; 10 = perfect
The partnership mission in sync with missions of organizations	Working toward the same goal outcomes for the same reasons	What is the frequency of workflow bottlenecks and the ease or lack thereof in resolution?	Agreement (formal or informal contract) for a process for adapting to changed circumstances
Create trusting relationship	Forming new relationships or repairing old relationships	Do the participants advocate for the partnership and their partner?	Partnership as documented mutual priority for each participant; voluntary commitment of supplemental resources; perceived reciprocity using a scored measure on a scale of 1-10 where 1 = none; 10 = perfect
Impactful performance of the partnership	Creating a new way to resolve longstanding, chronic community problems	Do the partners agree the partnership endeavor has impact, and is that validated by an independent party?	Subsequent projects or desire to engage in subsequent projects
Fulfillment of the partner's and other stakeholders' goals and expectations	Accounting for the circumstances under which the goals were met	Did the partnership meet all of its goals and why? Is there a willingness to re-partner?	Scored measure on a scale of 1-10 where 1 = partnership that met none of its goals, while a score of 10 = the partnership met all of its goals
Partners solve problems of the partnership	Creating the conditions for durability and resiliency in the relationship	Do both partners serve to steward reciprocity in the partnership?	Scored measure on a scale of 1-10 of satisfaction where 1 = partnership that did not achieve reciprocity for both members, while a score of 10 = partnership that was perceived to be equal and fair in terms of reciprocity

important factors in these endeavors, yet they may require time and effort to develop. We also learned that partnership willingness and partnership readiness are separate elements, and that the first does not determine the second. Although partnership readiness is more measureable, it can be hindered by various operational barriers, creating obstacles that may prevent successful partnership. Nonprofit leaders can use this information to bolster their own partnership endeavors.

Notes

1. Ostrom, Elinor, and James Walker, eds. *Trust and Reciprocity: Interdisciplinary Lessons for Experimental Research* (New York: Russell Sage Foundation, 2003).

2. Yankey, John, and Carol Willen. "Collaboration and Strategic Alliances," in *The Jossey-Bass Handbook of Nonprofit Leadership and Management*, 3rd ed., ed. David O. Renz and R. D. Hermans (San Francisco, CA: Wiley and Sons, 2010), 375–400.

3. Austin, James E. *The Collaboration Challenge: How Nonprofits and Businesses Succeed Through Strategic Alliances* (Hoboken, NJ: John Wiley and Sons, 2010), 109; Brinkerhoff, Jennifer M. "Government-Nonprofit Partnership: A Defining Framework." *Public Administration and Development* 22, no. 1 (2002): 19–30, doi:10.1002/pad.203; Benington, John. "10 Partnerships as Networked Governance?," in *Local Partnership and Social Exclusion in the European Union: New Forms of Local Social Governance?*, ed. Mike Geddes and John Bennington (London and New York: Routledge, 2013), 198–219; Calabrese, Raymond L. "Building Social Capital Through the Use of an Appreciative Inquiry Theoretical Perspective in a School and University Partnership." *International Journal of Educational Management* 20, no. 3 (2006): 173–182, doi:10.1108/09513540610654146.

4. Van Til, Jon. *Growing Civil Society: From Nonprofit Sector to Third Space* (Bloomington: Indiana University Press, 2000); Putnam, Robert D. "Bowling Alone: America's Declining Social Capital." *Journal of Democracy* 6, no. 1 (1995): 65–78; Brinkerhoff, Jennifer M. "Government-Nonprofit Partnership: A Defining Framework." *Public Administration and Development* 22, no. 1 (2002): 19–30, doi:10.1002/pad.203; Brinkerhoff, Jennifer M. "Assessing and Improving Partnership Relationships and Outcomes: A Proposed Framework." *Evaluation and Program Planning* 25, no. 3 (2002): 215–231, doi:10.1016/S0149-7189(02)00017-4.

5 Nonprofit Partnerships by Subsector

Overview

In this chapter, we separate the partnership cases into subsectors. Two underlying considerations drive our interest in subsectors. First, subsector operations are the primary affinity peer organization groups in which nonprofit executives operate in the larger societal systems of institutional actors. Second, the agency of subsectors shifts the gaze of our inquiry into nonprofit-first partnership discovery to the partnership mission, rather than the partners' own missions and sector origins. Figure 5.1 illustrates these affinity relationships wherein nonprofit actors form alliances and carry out the work of partnership for outcomes and benefits to the community via, for example, social services, arts and culture, education, and health and wellness.

In order to prioritize the partnership mission over individual actors' missions, we make use of three pre-existing nonprofit classification systems that place individual organizations into subsector categories, and we reference the helpful aspects of each to group and examine partnerships by subsector. Use of a three-pronged classification system is necessary for several reasons: the difference in theoretical basis for each system (one as mission-based outcomes, another as goods and services outputs and outcomes, and a third allowing for philanthropic outcomes), variations in the nomenclature of each system, and the necessity of accounting for the three-mission fulfillment principle that we discuss later in this chapter. The combined classification schema allows us an analytic tool to examine and mesh nonprofit institutions engaged in partnership for distinct nonprofit-first partnership purpose.[1] In our view, understanding subsector partnerships will help nonprofit actors achieve partnership outcomes more successfully by prioritizing commonalities among partners of different service orientations and missions.

Introduction

In this chapter, we examine characteristics attributable to partnership arrangements in certain nonprofit subsectors. One noteworthy finding of our focus on partnerships by nonprofit subsectors is that actors with different missions and mission outcomes are frequently brought together by the innovation required to create a partnership mission and by various third parties offering incentives to generate such novel partnerships. In many of the cases, cross-sector partnerships contributed to partnership purposes that differed from the

**Hierarcy of
Nonprofit-First
Operations Affinities**

**Mission-Based Institutional
Partnership Affinity by Sector**
• Nonprofit
• Public (Government)
• Private (Business)

**Institutional Affinity Partnership
Peer Groups by Sub-Sector**
• Social Services
• Education
• Arts & Culture
• Healthcare

**Mission Fulfillment
Constituency Receiving
Benefits and Services**

*In partnership case
narratives, nonprofit
executives describe their
partnership operations in
terms of peerage subsector
represented here rather
than the "sectors" depicted
as the larger sphere.*

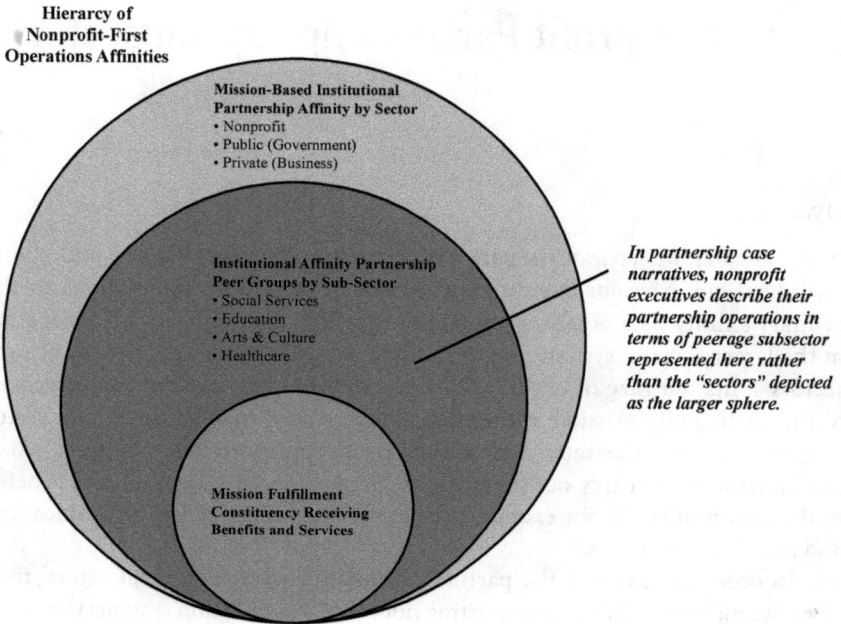

Fig. 5.1 Hierarchy of Nonprofit-First Operations Affinities.

subsector classifications of the partners. This realization required that we divide and analyze partnerships by subsector according to the mission specialties. Since "philanthropy" was not part of either of the two dominant nomenclature systems for subsectors but considered by us to be similar in nature to a subsector, it is discussed partially here and more thoroughly in the next chapter.

We hope to accomplish four things with this inquiry into partnership subsectors. First, we look to identify aspects of specific subsector partnerships that might otherwise have been overlooked by our earlier focus on the macro-sector pairings (i.e. nonprofit-nonprofit, nonprofit-government, and nonprofit-business). Second, we intend to identify and parse any nuances attributable to the subsectors that might help partnership participants increase the likelihood of successful, meaningful, and important partnerships. Third, we intend to sharpen our conception of partnership indicators so that policy makers, grant makers, and others desiring to stimulate partnerships in specific subsector service fields may recognize and nurture effective partnership. Fourth, we hope to develop more sophisticated expectations regarding the processes and results of nonprofit-first partnerships.

The purpose of the partnership fulfills a third mission separate and distinct from the missions of the two partnering organizations. In our partnership cases, the partnership missions depicted active bridging or serving as institutional intermediary functions to create change in society or in the conditions of society contributing to problems. Assigning the partnership to a specific subsector category required us to blend three commonly accepted systems from nonprofit and civil society scholarship to account for partnership purpose, rather than individual organizational purposes, across our cases. As we explain below, the three classification methods differ according to mission area versus type of economic activity.

Interrelating the three classification systems allowed us to assign partnerships to a subsector, even though the partnering organizations may operate in substantively different mission field areas such as human and social services, arts and culture, education, health care, community and economic development, and environmental or societal mutual benefits. To illustrate the point, consider that a community development organization devoted to neighborhood revitalization might form a partnership with an arts organization to raise funds for a new building and community arts programming for the overarching purpose of creating higher property valuations in a targeted neighborhood.

Based on the nonprofit executives' rich practical experience, we identified specific characteristics for partnership outcomes and purposes that were relatable to the subsector pairings. We then applied qualitative research methodology to mine these characteristics.[2] Although this methodology has been validated repeatedly as a means of surveying primary source materials, we encountered limitations. One limitation involved the number of cases per subsector. Because the subsectors containing smaller numbers of partnership cases necessarily lack the same opportunity for empirical verification as the full sample of cases, our analysis of partnership subsectors must remain more tentative, but is worthwhile nonetheless. Another limitation were the limits in data collection that did not account for a self-reported subsector assignment by the partner of the nonprofit organization contributing the partnership case study.

The Subsectors Through the Lens of Three Classification Systems

The three classification systems are similar, with overlapping but distinct category differences. Because some nonprofit organizations in our sample follow multifaceted missions that cross the boundaries of classification into more than one system, applying the accepted classification nomenclature to group them and their partnership proved challenging. Examples include health-related organizations that blend the use of dance and music arts for physical therapy and health awareness and nutrition; community development corporations engaged in urban planning, housing redevelopment, and business start-ups; and mental health and social services organizations involved in job readiness, educational achievement, and after-school programming.

Table 5.1. National Taxonomy of Exempt Entities (NTEE) Designations.

NTEE Code	Number of Organizations	Percentage of Sample
Arts, Culture, and Humanities	4	8
Education	5	9.5
Environment	3	6
Health	5	9.5
Human Services	16	31
Public and Social Benefit	19	36
Total	52	100

To address these challenges, we utilized elements of three existing subsector classification systems recognized in the scholarly literature of nonprofit studies. We also compared the classifications in separate data tables above to illustrate how the same fifty-two organizations might be legitimately classified into differing subsector categories. We then created a third table using the classifications on two axes of a matrix to assign the partnerships to a subsector based on the partnership mission and outcome purposes.

The National Taxonomy of Exempt Entities system

The first and most prominent classification system is the US Internal Revenue Service (IRS) National Taxonomy of Exempt Entities (NTEE) system. The NTEE designations are based on organizational mission and statement of purpose, type and sources of income, and use of that income.[3] We emphasize that the organizations' assignment to the subsector categories listed in Table 5.1 is based not on their partnership mission, but instead on the mission of the nonprofit organization.

The IRS uses the information filed in IRS Form 990, which is the annual tax filing for exempt organizations in the United States, for classification purposes. The organization's self-reported information is used to assign the nonprofit to a specific subsector designation within a tiered system of twenty-six topical codes of tax-exempt categories. The designations are codified by federal legislation that constitutes the list of sanctioned tax-exempt functions.[4] The NTEE system is accepted in the United States as the standard for subsector classification and is also used by the Foundation Center, a private organization which is the leading source of information about philanthropy worldwide,[5] to catalog both grants and grant recipients. Table 5.1 lists the NTEE and Foundation Center subsector categories of the fifty-two nonprofit organizations contributing nonprofit partnership cases to this study. The subsector categories include arts, culture, and humanities; education; environment; health; human services; and public and social benefit.

Table 5.2. ICNPO+ Designations.

ICNPO+ Code	Number of Organizations	Percentage of Sample
Culture	4	8
Education	5	10
Health	5	10
Social Services	17	32
Environment	1	2
Development	9	17
Advocacy	2	4
Philanthropy	9	17
Total	52	100%

The International Classification of Nonprofit Organizations System

The second nonprofit subsector classification system was devised by Lester Salamon and Helmut Anheier to account for cross-national differences in the non-profit sector around the world and is a system recommended in the United Nations "Handbook on Non-profit Institutions in the System of National Accounts."[6] The Salamon and Anheier classification system, which has been revised over time, referred to here as the International Classification of Nonprofit Organizations (ICNPO), has been in use since the late 1990s and is widely accepted among countries outside the United States, including Canada, the United Kingdom, Poland, and Israel. The basis for classification is not by organizational mission, but by major economic activity, usually measured by the types of goods and services produced by the organization.[7] Although our partnership cases are all in the United States, we believe the application of this nomenclature can also reinforce our subsector assignments by virtue of the attention given to economic and community development and other categories that are not granted the same status as subsectors in the NTEE system.

In table 5.2, the ICPNO classification system is used to assign subsector categories to the fifty-two nonprofit organizations in our sample as a comparison to the NTEE assignments listed in table 5.1. In addition to variations in nomenclature between the two subsector classification methods, the categories in table 5.2 are based not on the partnership mission, but on services on which the organizations expend their revenues to fulfill the mission of the nonprofit organization contributing the partnership case to the study. The subsector categories include culture; education; health; social services; environment; development; advocacy; and philanthropy. As we explain in greater detail below, an important caveat to the ICPNO nomenclature is our addition of the category of "philanthropy" as a subsector, drawing on the scholarship of Michael O'Neil rather than the category included in the ICPNO system. We took this extraordinary step to account for a distinct set of nonprofit partnership cases in our data, which is solely drawn from the contextual constraints of philanthropy in the United States rather than on the theory that might possibly have been conceived to address the exigencies of global philanthropy.

Philanthropy as a Subsector

We have tapped a third subsector classification system to account for a subsector category we've labeled "philanthropy." Michael O'Neil's perspective on philanthropy is not accounted for explicitly in the NTEE subsector categories, but does include overlap with the ICPNO. We rely upon the O'Neil classifications to accommodate our cases for a distinct category of funders and grant makers operating in the United States.[8] O'Neil's classification system is based on donors and funders seeking to do good in society by focused philanthropic investment and their influence on society through the institutions of business, government, and civil society.

Although not a subsector *per se*, philanthropy, in our perspective, identifies a subset of our nonprofit-first partnership cases that involve private philanthropic grant-making foundations, federated fundraising and grant-making institutions, and other nonprofit organizations that serve as intermediaries for funders to distribute dollars to nonprofit organizations providing direct services to the community. Although the ICPNO classification does account for "philanthropy and intermediary" organizations, we believe it necessary to restrict the classification of partnerships to the US context to avoid unnecessary association with global grant-making behaviors and purposes that might tend to distract from our research partnership cases. We also found attention to grant-making and philanthropy equally important, and thus we use the terms interchangeably in the discussion of their involvement in nonprofit partnership. Although we devote chapter 6 to an examination of the nine grant-making institutions that contributed partnerships to our study (thirteen cases), we also distinguish it as a subsector in this chapter using the ICPNO + philanthropy (O'Neil) classification system.[9]

In table 5.3, we have plotted all eighty-two partnership cases based on the three classification systems on an *x-y* axis. This method accommodates for differences in nomenclature across the three systems of subsector classification. The assignments of partnerships are based on the subsector origin of the partners from the perspective of the nonprofit executive contributing the case and applied to the two categories of nomenclature. The subsector designation for each partnership was determined by the pairing of the two partner organization missions and verified by a careful assessment of the partnership mission. The subsector partnership mission case designations, depicting the combining of three missions, are listed in table 5.3.

The Subsectors

Table 5.3 draws our attention to the subsector categories and concentration of partnerships across our sample of cases. Assignments of partnership cases to a

Table 5.3. Combined NTEE/ICNPO+ Categories of the Nonprofit Partnership Cases.

NTEE ⇨ ICNPO + ⇩	Arts	Education	Environment	Health	Human Services	Public Benefit	Unlabeled	Total	%
Culture	4		1					5	6%
Education		4	1	2		2		9	11%
Health				2	1			3	4%
Social Services	1	1		1	15	4		22	27%
Environment			1			1		2	2%
Development					4	9	1	14	17%
Advocacy		1		2	5	6		14	17%
Philanthropy	1		1	1	1	7	2	13	16%
Total	6	6	4	8	26	29	3	82	100%
	7%	7%	5%	10%	32%	35%	4%		100%

particular cell of the table were made by matching the partnership mission to the categories crossing the axis of the matrix. The partnership cases that fall into the NTEE column header categories labeled public benefit and human services are the largest groupings of partnership cases, with the social services category comprising the largest concentration of ICNPO+ row headers.

Other combinations of subsector partnership categories of significance include those devoted to economic and community development and advocacy. According to Lester Salamon, advocacy is representing alternative perspectives and pressing them on public and private decision makers.[10] Philanthropy also constitutes a significant cluster of nonprofit organizations and partnership cases, which we exclude here because a full chapter is dedicated to a discussion of the treatment of philanthropy as a subsector cluster of partnerships in chapter 6. The next-largest clusters of cases include advocacy, health, arts, and education.

Based on the largest concentrations of partnership cases, we examine five distinct major subsectors of paired categories from the NTEE and ICNPO+ classifications encompassed by the partnerships. Because of the low number of cases in the remaining categories (environment and unlabeled), we do not include their typology, as we consider them minor categories of partnership types for this study. Five classification systems emerged on the matrix: human and social services; public benefits arising from economic and community development, and with attention also for public benefits arising from advocacy; health; arts and culture; and education. Table 5.4 summarizes the key distinctive subsector characteristics identified in the five subsector categories (excluding philanthropy).

Human and Social Services Partnerships

Four important characteristics are evident from the partnership cases distinctive of the human and social services subsector. First is the size of this cluster of cases relative to the other subsectors listed in table 5.3. Forty-eight of the eighty-two partnership cases comprising our interview data involve some combination of assignment to this partnership subsector. The NTEE human services subsector category comprised the second-largest concentration of partnerships, with twenty-six cases assigned. Twenty-two social services partnership cases among the ICPNO+ philanthropy subsector categories rank it as the most numerous category across the eighty-two partnership cases. One reason for the large concentration of partnership cases in this subsector is that many of those listed in this category receive public funding. The 2009 US Congress assessment of government-supported employment states that organizations devoted to human and social services purposes and outcomes are second only to health care with respect to receipt of public dollars in the nonprofit sector.[11]

A second important characteristic of human and social services subsector partnerships is complexity. Nonprofit executives who contributed the cases assigned to the human and social services subsector partnerships agreed that competitive grant and contract processes from the public sector often drove the partnership actors to craft innovative partnerships. These public sector–stimulated endeavors require considerable sophistication on the part of the nonprofit actor. For example, in several cases, these partnerships are not technically dyads but more complicated arrangements that go beyond the one-to-one sector partnership framework we have discussed. Nevertheless, nonprofit executives perceive their human and social services subsector partnerships as dyads when they have a formal performance contract with a funder—usually a government agency, but sometimes a nonprofit intermediary organization—to coordinate functions, allocate funding, and hold partnership participants accountable for partnership mission fulfillment on behalf of a third-party policy or grant maker. In our partnership cases in this subsector, nonprofit executives point to mutual benefits, an expanded client base, and increased mission fulfillment as underlying reasons to collaborate with government and service-provider networks. They also note that the outcomes of service to their constituents are amplified through the intentional leveraging of public funds.

In one case, the nonprofit executive a described a continuing policy of the US Department of Housing and Urban Development (HUD) that evolved over the 1980s of issuing annual, competitive grant notices for funding homeless programs. In recounting the context for her case involving a social services agency working to place low-income citizens in affordable housing, the executive explained that to stimulate collaboration and encourage services innovation, grants for homeless assistance under the 1987 HUD McKinney-Vento Act were consolidated to a Notice of Fund Availability or Super NOFA in 1995. This nonprofit executive maintained that the annual Super NOFA process is complicated and highly technical; in addition, over the past twenty years or so, policy has imposed higher thresholds for community involvement and agency accountability. Communities that did not form partnerships to produce a consolidated application did not receive federal aid. As a result, local municipalities are highly motivated to collaborate with nonprofit organizations, since these organizations can be cast as the partnerships required for HUD funding.

In this situation, Cuyahoga County (Ohio) had been awarded a multiple-year contract with annual funding ranging between $13 million and $20 million. This complex partnership involved certain core principles regarding acceptable performance outcomes. Homelessness had to be addressed through comprehensive approaches, and participating service providers had to collaborate to form a network for the endeavor.

The third important characteristic of the human and social services subsector partnerships is related to the second and frequently occurs in tandem: the intent of leveraging resources as a tactic of public managers, grant makers, and others seeking to produce public value benefits. Many examples of leveraging occur across our sample of partnerships. One example of leveraged funding drawn from the human and social services subsector cases involved a partnership between a social services organization and a school of medicine using funding provided by the public sector. The partnership was established to provide rehabilitation therapy, occupational training, and case management services to people dealing with hearing loss or communication deficits. The partnership outcomes also included career skills preparation for speech pathologists and enabled research in areas of common interest to the two institutions. The use of public funds required that both organizations contribute discretionary dollars from their own operations as a one-to-one match of federal support. Nonfinancial in-kind support was also required as a match to share the costs of the endeavor. These two sources of direct and indirect support to the project demonstrated to all parties that each dollar of public funding was producing two or more private dollars of resources to support the partnership outcomes. As the nonprofit executive stated, "The greatest impact on the organization has been the institutional credibility that we receive as a result of this long-standing partnership. It has aided them in our ability to raise money for the organization and to illustrate to our constituents in the legislature that a dollar invested in us produces many dollars of value."

The fourth important characteristic of the human and social services subsector partnerships is positive outcomes derived from unanticipated benefits. Unanticipated benefits often occur across subsector partnerships (see earlier chapters). Among our cluster of twenty-two social services partnership cases, fifteen occurred between two human and social services partners, while the remaining seven took place across subsector pairs that included combinations of social services with arts and culture, development, education, health, and public advocacy and policy. In all seven instances, nonprofit executives considered the success and importance of subsector partnership combinations differently from their home subsectors as both unexpected and "value-added."

One example of unanticipated and value-added benefits is illustrated by the partnership between a speech pathology services agency providing community diagnostic and health services and a professional school in a research university:

> The partnership is important because it has been sustained for such a long time, involves multiple levels with our University partner, and is the only one of its kind in the country.... We feel that we meet the needs of the University and they provide us with institutional credibility because the relationship with [them] means something to people we need to impress.... It has aided in our ability to raise money.... Additional benefits are that it is like having a big brother—and it's good to have a big brother ... for example when we go to the state capital to advocate for our organizations and services, we can bring the Dean of the College with us, who also serves on our board.... The Dean is pretty powerful advocate and we get more attention when we bring him than when we don't.

In the partnership case described above, the partnership was originally established to stimulate quality field placements and job skills training for graduate students. One designed benefit was the service of the dean on the nonprofit's board of directors. Unanticipated and value-added benefits accrued, as the nonprofit executive noted, when the executive traveled to the state capital to advocate for speech pathology services accompanied by a dean of the university. The dean became a powerful advocate for the services of the speech pathology organization, and consequently the executive perceived more attention and credibility from legislators than he alone would have received.

Unanticipated benefits were also a strong outcome characteristic in our earlier Super NOFA case. In that example, the social service provider was required to join a statewide network of similar providers, since the network received and allocated all federal funding to the individual nonprofit services agencies that performed the work of their specialty programs. While the primary goal of the partnership was to help people with disabilities secure and retain employment, a secondary, unexpected benefit described by the nonprofit executive was the ability of the network strengthened by the public sector project work to convey its deaf clients' abilities to potential employers, businesses, and the broader community.

Public and Societal Benefit Partnerships

As we mentioned earlier, the human and social services subsector partnerships are typically perceived as dyads, even when a third-party funding source is an active participant in a partnership. Another facet of this category in the partnership cases in our sample is that the work outputs are limited to services provided to local neighborhood communities and specific target populations. By contrast, the public and societal benefit partnership cases are multilayered, with many players embedded within larger networks to affect the broader community. Nearly all of the partnership cases in this subsector involved a nonprofit intermediary organization responsible acting as grant maker coordinating funds or services as the principal participant to its partners. For example, one partnership was established to address the rapidly growing problem of foreclosure in Cleveland and the county. The partnership developed into a large-scale community partnership, where many organizations worked with the County and one another, both within and beyond contractual agreements, to arrest foreclosure. Several partnership participants credited the program with saving homes and stabilizing neighborhoods across Cleveland and the county.

Like the human and social services subsector partnerships, the partnerships in the public and societal benefit area are complex but more systemic in nature. Their participants share the belief that these partnerships are formed and designed to benefit and develop a larger community, such as a city, county, or region. The twenty-nine partnerships comprise the largest concentration of cases assigned to a NTEE subsector category. Among the ICNPO+ philanthropy subsector classification, this cluster is not as common.

Two important characteristics are distinctive of the public and societal benefit partnership subsector. First, most of these partnerships have broad service constituencies and partnership mission fulfillment goals that articulate social change and speak to public policy. As one nonprofit executive advised, this facet of the subsector enabled his organization devoted to human welfare and social policy to amplify its reach beyond the organization's traditional client base and constituencies and utilize partnership to leverage dollars and relationships for the greater good. Second, many of the public and societal benefit subsector cases involve intermediary organizations whose *modus operandi* was to use existing networks of organizations or stimulate new ones.[12] In these instances, the working goals of the partnerships had transactional outcomes as well as strategic outcomes ultimately designed to strengthen the network through further partnerships.

Several cases demonstrated examples of intermediaries—a nonprofit organization that coordinates functions, allocates funding, and holds partnership participants accountable for partnership mission fulfillment on behalf of a third-party policy or grant maker—driving the development of a partnership network. One such example involved a multiorganization capital fundraising program in a designated neighborhood. The initiative brought together three independent arts organizations that were continuously coordinated by a community development corporation over a ten-year period. The partnership involved separate but linked fundraising programs that occurred in successive phases, involving all three organizations. Each phase became a more effectively run endeavor due to the increasing working familiarity between the partners, the consistency in planning and institutional knowledge drawn from the experience gained on each project, and the succession of mission fulfillment achievements.

In a second example, an intermediary organization served its dues-paying members (mostly large health, education, and cultural institutions) by driving an urban and city-planning agenda for an urban neighborhood. In our interview, the executive explained that the goals of the partnership were to advocate on behalf of neighborhood institutions; provide collective neighborhood services such as public safety, parking, and planning; stimulate community and economic development; generate economies of scale through shared services; and create a welcoming environment in which employment at member institutions would flourish. In his opinion, the partnership had an impact on member provision of dues, cost savings, and community life enrichment over the long term. "The partnership was set up for the purpose of community revitalization through development, to serve and advocate for the local community. Member organizations pay a fee to belong and serve on our board. This establishes self-interest and self-serving partnerships.... The partnership is a multilayered partnership that forms working relationships that will help the individual members serve to themselves but to the benefit of City of Cleveland.... One way is because individual member institutions create community plans for strategic growth of member institutions that provide services to a district of the city."

A third example of public and societal benefit partnership involved an association of business merchants in a downtown commercial district. The partnership was established to promote community reinvestment through interactions with the public and private sectors. For example, the partnership worked with local government for local business district assessments in lieu of property tax payments to pay for dedicated safety ambassadors to remove trash and provide a presence on public sidewalks to serve as the eyes and ears of the police downtown. The nonprofit executive contributing the case described several public value and greater good outcomes emanating from the partnership:

> The partnership was set up to assess property owners to employ safety ambassadors to help and keep a look-out downtown. They also act as the eyes and ears of the Cleveland Police downtown. Trained unarmed police officers have radio connectivity to off-duty policy offers, who communicate with on-duty offers to respond to situations. The off-duty officers help get a quicker police response and connect with on-duty police. This increases safety downtown. In exchange, the police department instituted [a] downtown services unit to increase downtown officers for the district. It is to create more city involvement and is a win-win situation.

The public benefit NTEE subsector has a second major cluster of partnership cases in addition to economic and community development centered on advocacy. In our partnership case data group listed in table 5.3, the six cases assigned to the advocacy subsector are characterized by service to the community through partnerships, providing an institutional voice for an issue or particular population. Among these cases are examples of cross-subsector partnerships that amplify impact.

To illustrate these points, we turn to the example of a community foundation dedicated to promoting healthy communities that entered into a partnership because health disparities across minority populations were consistent with fulfillment of its mission. According to the nonprofit executive describing the partnership, no other local actors addressed this issue. The goal of the partnership was to create awareness and influence health-care plan providers to be more inclusive in their coverage. The partnership led to national interest and had a much larger impact on the issue and policy discussion than had been anticipated by the participants. "The partnership was originally set up to reduce [the] amount and impact of child lead poisoning in [the] area and coordinate efforts among partners to solve the problem.... The partnership purpose required coordinated efforts around child lead poisoning prevention and ... a strategy to inform public policy. The partnership had an impact on the organization—because lead poisoning had been cut in half, and the partnership outcomes can prove a direct impact of its program.... This will inform our advocacy with legislators and local government ... and foundations."

A second example involved a partnership that facilitated arts and cultural organizations' ability to influence public policy, research, and organizational development and capacity-building. The partnership involved the annual allocation of tax dollars levied on users of alcohol and tobacco products. The art community's desire to maintain this level of public support required a steady dialogue between the recipient organizations and the nonprofit intermediary whose responsibility it was to convey the impact to taxpayers and to articulate the needs of the arts community that merited this public support. "Arts organizations have greater opportunity to prove to the public their value, because they must report back to the community the exchange that takes place by using tax dollars to support art. The partnership ... created new programs ... and free programs that make the community a better, more vibrant place.... An important part of our mission is to communicate to the public the ROI."

Health Subsector Partnerships

The eight nonprofit partnerships devoted to the NTEE health subsector listed in table 5.3 span a broad range of ICNPO+ philanthropy categories that include education and research; social services; law, advocacy, and politics; philanthropy; and youth. The partnership cases also share mission outcome purposes, including educational outreach for public awareness, funding for development for research, and advocacy around specific public health priorities.

Nonprofit executives sharing their cases emphasized that the partnership mission for this subsector is subordinate to that of their own organization. For these cases, the partnership was a device for their own mission fulfillment rather than an endeavor requiring their commitment beyond the transaction work of performing the partnership work. Partnership mission fulfillment required each participant to merely complete their assignment. As a result, benefits arising from the partnership beyond the stated purpose of the partnership were welcome but not a factor in their decision to enter into a partnership or to judge its importance. For example, one executive noted that her organization works with a partner to hold a fund-raising event to which donors make contributions that are allocated to a hospital for research purposes. She explained,

> We try to get pharmaceutical firms interested in looking into new drugs for the disease to support our organization with funding.... Their desire is for us to help them find hospitals to conduct the research.... We work in a collaborative way with our partners to hold joint conferences and conduct joint research programs for the disease.... We could not have done any of our work

without the funds our partner provides or helps us obtain, but they really have no involvement in our work beyond the dollars ... and the most important factor for any success we've had is money—which is why the donor partners are so important to this partnership narrative.

In contrast to the social services partnership category, where the partnership relationship between actors is organic, integrated, and involves improvement in program delivery and operations as desired outcomes, the health subsector partnerships were characterized as formal, limited, and administratively mature. Several examples illustrate these points. In the case quoted above, the executive shared that her partnership was originally established to raise money to support research and operations, while also impacting the organization's image and raising its profile. In her opinion, partnership is a "tool of the trade" and a key to future success.

In a second case contributed by the same executive, the partnership outcome was to provide locally raised funds to its national headquarters chapter, which had assigned it an annual fund development goal.

Several reasons can explain the perception that health subsector partnerships tend to be more formal, limited, and administratively mature. First, the respondents typically described these partnerships as contractually limited pathways to fulfilling the partners' own organizational missions. The nonprofit executives who offered these cases suggested that any innovations derived from the partnerships were intended, at least initially, to strengthen their capacity to perform their organizations' work and nothing more.[13] The executive of a healthcare organizations noted, "the partnership was originally set up for two reasons: to raise money to support our research and operations goals, and to impact our partner's image with the intent that they expand the customer base for their products. We both wanted to use this partnership as a mechanism to achieve our own purposes rather than ... for ... vaguely ... defined greater good ... to the community."

A second reason involves the notion that partnerships stuck to a single, familiar model of transactional relationships, designed to be repeated annually for the purposes of fund development or issues awareness to the community. For example, as one nonprofit executive noted, "The partnership was originally set up to annually solicit local philanthropy and to provide awareness for infant mortality issues by educating the public through special events in accordance with the national office of our organization."

Allegiance to a single model promoted by a national home office organization meant for these nonprofit executives that a successful partnership engagement could, but might not, lessen risk-aversion for greater, more complex engagements. In most of the eight cases, improvements in the partnership were based upon the experience gained from repetition of designed partnerships, and eventually contributed to the participants' decision to continue or renew their partnership. "The agency sought a sponsor for major fundraising events ... but we really expected to stick to our national funding model.... The national office tends to limit our creativity and to stick to their formula for fundraising.... We sought a relationship because of overlapping client bases and saw this as a way to be innovative within the restrictions with which we operate with little risk."

A third reason was attributable to the governance by home offices that local affiliates of national organizations are obligated to observe. Across our partnership case examples, the health subsector organizations are independent affiliates of national organizations with a local governing board. Although this structure allows for a measure of local governance autonomy, the local organization usually acts as a geographic site for an umbrella organization whose policy-setting board of directors places limits on deepening local partnerships.[14]

Arts and Culture Subsector Partnerships

Four of the six nonprofit partnerships devoted to the NTEE arts, culture, and humanities subsector listed in table 5.3 are concentrated in ICNPO+ philanthropy culture and recreation categories. The other two engaged in partnerships whose missions placed them within the social services and philanthropy subsector areas.

Two common themes appear among the six arts and culture subsector partnership cases. First, the partnerships were characterized by an interest in increasing audience, member, or other market share development. In one example involving a youth arts organization and a local orchestra, the goal of the partnership was to work with children to create a string orchestra of thirty participants in the first year, sixty in the second, and ninety in the third. Because string instruments are among the least accessible musical instruments in the inner city, the program creates awareness and knowledge among youth while preparing them to appreciate and participate in the musical arts as adults. "The partnership worked well.... The exhibition and music programming were great and well-received.... We could not have offered the outreach to the schools and community alone. The number of attendees to our performances went up, as did the number of African American attendees."

The second theme evident in the arts and culture subsector cases is an emphasis on the partnerships' informal origins and the role played by individual relationships between the leaders of the partner organizations. For example, two executives described their important nonprofit partnerships as based on their personal networks of peers, but also as envisioned and created through unplanned interactions at fundraising events or other gatherings. In fact, one of these executives opined that nonprofit partnerships are less formal, take more of the leader's time and effort, and are harder to terminate than partnerships that are convened by third parties because they exist on the level of personal interaction. "The partnership began when we two key leaders began an informal conversation on ways both organizations might work together after meeting by happenstance at [a] fundraising function for another organization.... We wanted to expand the audience of people willing to come to the performances by children and to get a greater diversity in our program participants."

Education Subsector Partnerships

The nine nonprofit partnerships in the education subsector listed in table 5.3 are spread across four NTEE categories and three ICNPO+ philanthropy subsector categories. The nonprofit organizations involved in the education subsector include a broad array of participants, such as stand-alone nonprofits with independent boards of directors, a local independent high school, a university, and local affiliates of national organizations.

The partnerships in the education subsector cluster are similar to those in other subsectors with one important caveat: the nonprofit executives consistently described the partnership purpose or program as evolving over the life of the joint endeavor. One executive attributed the improvements in program design and partnership operations to the annual cycle of the academic year and to the need for new programs to become institutionalized after an initial period of development and working through the problems. In the culture of educational institutions, annual cycles involve renewing a partnership each year, which typically includes annual performance assessment and recommendations for improvement.

In one case, the partnership started as a way for students from a private high school to support a local nonprofit organization in the community through an annual fundraiser. Following the event, which brought the students in direct contact with less-privileged students, the partnership eventually evolved into the promotion of literacy through a service-learning program. This program reflected joint mission fulfillment on the part of both organizations through its pairing of existing complementary programs, one devoted to local community service learning for high school students and another youth program seeking peer mentors and coaches, with a desire to provide better experiences for students at both institutions. The nonprofit executive who contributed that case explained, "The partnership grew out of our existing fundraising partnership event we hold on behalf of a nearby nonprofit devoted to youth in the city ... and works smoothly and generally 'like clockwork.' The partnership addresses what our needs [are] to get our students to work with an organization to fulfill our community service-learning activities.... We also believe that the partnership addresses the some of the needs of our partner to have volunteers available for their youth program participants."

A second case involved international travel for high school students as part of their civic education experience. The partnership was intended to provide students with international experiences by having one participating organization recruit the students, while the other organized and sponsored the trips abroad.

In a third case, the partnership was initiated to gain the partners more exposure by increasing foot traffic for their educational exhibits. The nonprofit executive shared that the partnership was initiated by the funders' expectation that they support established partnerships. The partnership was also described as allowing both organizations to share in mutually beneficial risks, rewards, and pooled marketing dollars for purchasing and advertising. The partnership is renewed annually and receives third-party grant-funding.

In a fourth case, the partnership was set up to address the a shortage of nursing and radiology technicians. The two partners—one a technical community college and the other a major nonprofit hospital system—realized they had a mutual problem and needed to work together to address it. The partnership was designed to take advantage of public job growth and skills development programs to fill the needs of service industries, particularly in health care and health administration. The partnership is designed to be a long-term endeavor reviewed annually and follows a continuous improvement scheme as a formal contract specified in the partnership agreement. As the executive described,

> A partnership is something that changes depending on who you are partnering with and what [the] circumstances of the collaboration are.... In this case, we agreed to participate in a grant for three years, and had to undergo some program changes to meet the goals of the partnership. We designed a new curriculum for people in this program and moved the program to night and weekend courses to allow the students to continue working their positions with their employer, our partner.... The pilot grant period was extended for one year, and after the grant we continued to work on this project together outside of the original contract. Since there is no longer funding, the specific program cycle does not exist ... but the night and weekend classes still do exist ... and we tweak our program offerings so that the pipeline of employees still have the opportunity to go to school while working in this program.

Conclusion

In previous chapters, we learned that the language applied to partnership purposes and outcomes across nonprofit, government, and business sectors differed in important ways. We believe that by understanding behaviors and characteristics by partnership sector and subsector, nonprofit actors can gain important information to promote successful partnership outcomes.

In this chapter, we have examined differences among partnership subsector categories. The salient subsector partnership characteristics are drawn from our data of eighty-two cases as classified into five major partnership subsector clusters (plus philanthropy, further explored in the next chapter). The various subsector-specific partnerships often have features in common, but also exhibit subsector-specific similarities that we have documented. We believe the lessons drawn from the partnership cases fulfill our promise in the opening passages of this chapter to increase the likelihood partnership success, meaning, and importance; inform the thinking of policy makers, grant makers, and others desiring to stimulate partnership; and raise performance expectations of nonprofit-first partnership.

Among the human and social services subsector cases, for example, nonprofit executives described two common paths for partnership formation. The first was partnerships formed at the prompting of third parties, such as the public sector, through calls or requests for proposals to perform work that meets the purposes of the government funder. These partnerships may be considered examples of principal agent theory, where the heart of the endeavor centers upon contracted work with a service provider outside the public sector. In the second path toward partnership formation, a third-party funder—possibly a private grant-making institution—responds to a proposal devised by the partners, who create their own endeavor.

One way to understand the difference between these two paths is to recognize that the public sector typically relies on nonprofit organizations and businesses to respond to its requests for proposals (RFP). A successful application by the nonprofit actors typically involves a contract with performance stipulations specified by the government agency in the RFP. In partnerships where two nonprofit organizations come together to address a problem, the process of funding may include earned revenue from the endeavor's operations or third-party support in the form of a grant from a philanthropic or business source. As illustrated in table 5.4, partnership characteristics drawn from the eighty-two partnership cases do adhere to a set of partnership performance parameters and outcomes that lend themselves to a grouping of partnership indicators for the subsectors we have described and examined.

As noted in table 5.4, the characteristics of public, societal benefit subsector partnerships present a different emphasis than partnerships in the human and social services subsector. These public, societal benefit subsector partnerships were often described as driven primarily by a desire to promote public good and systemic change. By contrast, health subsector partnerships were seen as endeavors that strengthened the nonprofit actor by raising money that advanced the existing organizational program streams of research, advocacy, and education. Arts and culture subsector partnerships were described as mutually beneficial arrangements heavily aimed toward increasing market share, such as audience and membership. Finally, the education subsector partnerships were best seen as relationships that strengthened existing programs of both partner organizations.

Table 5.4. Subsector Characteristics Drawn from the Eighty-Two Partnership Cases.

Combined Subsector Type	Leading Subsector Characteristics	Measureable Indicators (Specific Characteristics in Bold)
Human and Social Services Partnership Characteristics	Two primary characteristics dominate: those partnerships designed for funding and sustainability of the individual partners, and those partnerships devised for innovation and problem-solving identified by the partner participants, who may then seek supplemental funding.	Resource development or "funding" serves as a catalyst for the partnership actors to come together, frequently involving a competitive grant and contracts process. These partnerships typically include a **formal contract** outlining the rights and performance responsibilities of the actors and the use of **predetermined and measured partnership performance outcomes**. Other indicators are partnerships involving **innovative pairings driven by the program development initiatives** of the partners. Partner actors then **self-fund or propose** their partnership endeavor to a third-party grant maker.
Public, Societal Benefit Partnership Characteristics	Partnerships designed for the creation of public value and the greater good achieved through partnership missions involving systemic change. The contribution of the partnership is to build institutions or improve existing ones that solve a problem or create the conditions for a problem to be solved.	Community-wide **dashboard-type measures** are used to trace changes in society; for example, reduction in poverty, rate of employment, and attainment of education. **"Leveraging"** or the amplification of funding is a feature of these partnerships. Leveraged dollars may be reflected by partnership endeavors that make use of existing revenue streams or stimulate investment or have long-term achievement timeframes.

Health Partnership Characteristics	Partnerships characterized primarily as single-purpose, short-term endeavors devised to fulfill the mission of the nonprofit actor.	Vehicle toward the **organizational sustainability** of the nonprofit actor rather than as an exercise in program innovation. **Fund development** around specific public health priorities or the "cure" of a disease or other health condition requiring advanced research, advocacy, and education.
Arts and Culture Partnership Characteristics	Partnership outcomes typically involve market-share-type development. Partnerships arise from mutuality of interests and individual relationships between leaders of both partnership organizations.	Partnership outcomes typically involve **audience or member development**. Commitment to the partnership endeavor and a desire to solve challenges formally and informally are credited for **documented unanticipated benefits**.
Education Partnership Characteristics	Partnership characteristics typified by mutual program benefits.	Enhancements to existing programs of each partner and **improved program performance**.

Our analysis suggests that partnerships can be divided into five substantive categories based on their missions: human and social services; public, societal benefit; health, arts, and culture; and education. The cases in each of these categories are characterized by common elements concerning partnership formation and mission emphasis. We find that these subsector categories of partnerships constitute a useful way of focusing on the partnering actors' commonalities as well as how to evaluate and achieve them.

Notes

1. Moulton, S., and A. Eckerd. "Preserving the Publicness of the Nonprofit Sector: Resources, Roles, and Public Values." *Nonprofit and Voluntary Sector Quarterly* 41, no. 4 (2012): 656–685; Clotfelter, C. T., ed. *Who Benefits From the Nonprofit Sector?* (University of Chicago Press, 1992).

2. Wodak, Ruth, and Michael Meyer, eds. *Methods for Critical Discourse Analysis* (Thousand Oaks, CA: Sage, 2009); Thach, Elizabeth, and Karen J. Thompson. "Trading Places: Examining Leadership Competencies Between For-Profit vs. Public and Non-Profit Leaders." *Leadership & Organization Development Journal* 28, no. 4 (2007): 356–375, doi:10.1108/01437730710752229; McDonald, Robert E. "An Investigation of Innovation in

Nonprofit Organizations: The Role of Organizational Mission." *Nonprofit and Voluntary Sector Quarterly* 36, no. 2 (2007): 256–281, doi:10.1177/0899764006295996; Hancock, Dawson, and Bob Algozzine. "'Qualitative and Quantitative Research' and 'Setting the Stage'," in *Doing Case Study Research: A Practical Guide for Beginning Researchers* (New York: Teachers College Press, 2006); Dart, Raymond. "Being 'Business-Like' in a Nonprofit Organization: A Grounded and Inductive Typology." *Nonprofit and Voluntary Sector Quarterly* 33, no. 2 (2004): 290–310, doi:10.1177/0899764004263522; McNabb, David E. *Research Methods in Public Administration and Nonprofit Management* (London: ME Sharpe, 2002); Stemler, Steve. "An Overview of Content Analysis." *Practical Assessment, Research & Evaluation* 7, no. 17 (2001): 1–10, http://eric.ed.gov/?id=EJ638505; Gottschalk, Louis Reichenthal. *Understanding History: A Primer of Historical Method* (New York: Knopf, 1961).

3. Hopkins, Bruce R. *The Law of Tax-Exempt Organizations* (Hoboken, NJ: John Wiley and Sons, 2011), 5.

4. National Center on Charitable Statistics (NCCS), http://nccs.urban.org/classification/NTEE.cfm.

5. "About," Foundation Center, www.foundationcenter.org/about.

6. Salamon, Lester M., and Helmut Anheier. *The Johns Hopkins Institute for Policy Studies, Working Papers of the Johns Hopkins Comparative Nonprofit Sector Project* no. 19 (Baltimore, MD: Johns Hopkins University Institute for Policy Studies, ICNPO-Revision 1, 1996); The International Classification of Non-profit Organizations (2017), http://www.statcan.gc.ca/pub/13-015-x/2009000/sect13-eng.htm.

7. Salamon, Lester M., and Helmut Anheier. *Defining the Nonprofit Sector: A Cross-National Analysis* (Manchester, UK: Manchester University Press, 1997).

8. O'Neill, Michael. *Nonprofit Nation: A New Look at the Third America* (Hoboken, NJ: John Wiley and Sons, 2002).

9. Ibid.

10. Salamon, Lester M. "Introduction," in *Explaining Nonprofit Advocacy: An Exploratory Analysis. Center for Civil Society Studies Working Paper Series* 21, no. 1 (Baltimore, MD: John Hopkins University Press, 2002).

11. O'Regan, Katherine M., and Sharon M. Oster. "Nonprofit and For-Profit Partnerships: Rationale and Challenges of Cross-Sector Contracting." *Nonprofit and Voluntary Sector Quarterly* 29, no. suppl. 1 (2000): 120–140, doi:10.1177/089976400773746364; Sherlock, Molly F., and Jane G. Gravelle. *An Overview of the Nonprofit and Charitable Sector: A Report for Congress* (Washington, DC: Congressional Research Service, 2009), 16–19.

12. Isett, Kimberley R., and Keith G. Provan. "The Evolution of Interorganizational Network Relationships Over Time: Does Sector Matter?" *Journal of Public Administration Research and Theory* 15, no. 1 (2005): 149–165, doi:10.5465/APBPP.2002.7519436.

13. Teece, David J. *Managing Intellectual Capital: Organizational, Strategic, and Policy Dimensions: Organizational, Strategic, and Policy Dimensions* (Oxford, UK: Oxford University Press, 2000); Lomas, J. *Improving Research Dissemination and Uptake in the Health Sector: Beyond the Sound of One Hand Clapping* (Ontario, Canada: McMaster University Centre for Health Economics and Policy [Analysis Policy, Commentary C97-1], 1997).

14. Smith, Steven Rathgeb. "Hybridization and Nonprofit Organizations: The Governance Challenge." *Policy and Society* 29, no. 3 (2010): 219–229, doi:10.1177/0002764214534675; McCarthy, J. D. "Franchising Social Change: Logics of Expansion Among National Social Movement Organizations with Local Chapters" (paper presented to the Conference on Social Movements and Organization, University of Michigan, May 2002).

6 Grant Makers' Partnership Practices

Overview

In this chapter, we focus on nonprofit respondents' partnership cases representing grant-making organizations, which offer a unique take on nonprofit partnerships by both entering into and sometimes mandating such arrangements. We examine the cases to see how these grant-making nonprofits conceive and use partnerships to meet community needs. With notable exceptions where the grant maker takes an active operations or other hands-on role in the partnership, the grant maker's perception of partnership is not wholly aligned with those of nonprofit executives in other subsectors. One important conclusion we draw from the research is that in a conceptual continuum of partnership characteristics and performance that perhaps lay between government and nonprofits, grant makers—that is, private and community foundations and nonprofit intermediaries they empower to act in their stead—are weighted toward their own mission fulfillment priorities rather than in stewardship of the three-mission principle of partnership.

Introduction

Among the fifty-two nonprofit organizations contributing their important partnership cases to this study are a subgroup of nine devoted to grant-making, about 20 percent of the sample. These nine organizations contributing the cases show considerable variety. For instance, four are traditional philanthropic institutions with paid professional staff and formal procedures for grant applicants, proposal review, and project monitoring and assessment. These four organizations have the capacity to make grants of up to seven figures, and one is among the more robust community foundations in the United States. A second was formed in the late 1990s from the proceeds of the sale of a nonprofit hospital system to a private health-care corporation. The third and fourth organizations adhere to the model of traditional private philanthropic institutions formed by affluent individuals or their families. One was founded in 1952 and arose from personal wealth generated in the banking industry, while the second was founded in 1967 and traces its origins to business entrepreneurship.

The remaining five grant-making institutions include two federated giving organizations and three not-for-profit intermediary organizations that distribute funds provided to them from private and public funders working individually or through a consortium of grant makers. One of these three intermediary organizations works closely with its public partner to distribute a share of the proceeds from community-wide tax collections for the arts, community development, and economic development purposes. The final three intermediary organizations receive funding through grants and public dollars or other sources, which they in turn allocate to other nonprofit service providers.

Typically, the grant makers in this grouping of nine organizations describe cases that encourage grant seekers to engage in partnerships, and cases that sometimes require partnership. In recounting their cases of partnership, the nine nonprofit executives cast themselves as either serving a catalytic purpose in developing and nurturing a partnership, and hence described the endeavor as "their" partnership, or as an active participant in the partnership operations and functions. In neither model, whether as partnership driver or participant, did the grant makers cite an established method of partnership performance measurement or expectations; nor did they offer elaboration on the nature, boundaries, or limits of their concept of partnership for their partners other than to convey the expectation that partnership take place as a condition of grant-making and grant-receiving.

Altogether the nine grant-making institution executives contributed thirteen cases that they considered important partnerships to this study. Their cases reflect partnership arrangements made typically with nonprofit organizations and occasionally with government. As might be expected, no nonprofit-business partnerships occur among these cases.

With only minor exceptions, the thirteen cases have two primary features in common. First, the funders described important partnership cases between themselves working alone or in coalition with other grant makers and networks of other organizations. In some instances, the funders or their network of funders delegate the coordination of grant-making to a single intermediary nonprofit organization which then provides oversight, compliance, and grants administration to another network of nonprofit organizations providing services that fulfill the purposes of the grant maker (network). As figure 6.1 illustrates, nonprofit executives envisioned many organizations clustered together for a single purpose as a single partner in grant-making roles. This feature of partnership allowed the grant makers to distinguish clusters of both public and private participants as dyadic relationships, a view that offered two advantages. First, they can view and manage their partnerships as between themselves, or a coalition of funders, with one other institutional entity, which is listed as "temporary, intermediary, or third space" in figure 6.1, even though the networks on both sides of the intermediary might represent many participating members. Second,

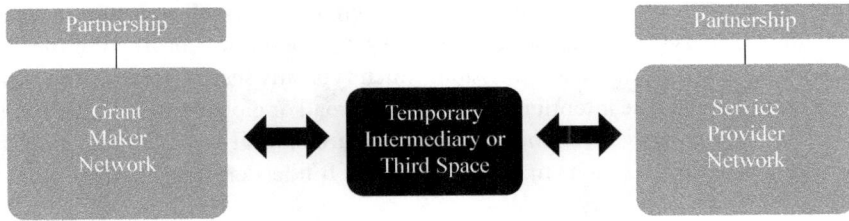

Fig. 6.1 Grant Maker Matrix.

funders can concentrate funding for dedicated purposes in a single project and grant-making operation in a manner that constitutes a "system" drawing on the resources of many organizations. The benefit of this partnership is that grant dollars are amplified through networks of actors that contribute their own resources and expertise to the partnership endeavor directly and indirectly.

The second feature of the grant-making partnership cases is that the lead grant-making institution almost always described partnership as an essential method of mission fulfillment in its engagement with grantees. Although several of the cases include peer-to-peer relationships between grant makers working together to amplify their resources and the impact of those resources, the actual work performed for the partnership endeavors often occurs through the actions of "third-party" nonprofit organizations which we consider "intermediaries." Because of this dynamic, the grant maker nonprofit executives describe their cases with an emphasis on their role as funders and intermediaries who provide funds and additional services to their partners such as technical assistance, training in management best practices, and program problem-solving. The goal is that nonprofit actors can and should be nurtured, guided, and facilitated within this environment created by the grant makers. Instances where grant makers become active participants in partnership with their grantees underlie an important but seldom acknowledged function in the philanthropic and nonprofit scholarship on partnership—that of providing a "third space" for the incubation of the partnership where project conception, planning, and performance assessment take place apart from the pressures of the daily work environment.[1]

Across these grant-making partnership cases, working with networks is a significant distinction from the partnership perspectives described by the forty-three other non–grant maker nonprofit executives who contributed partnership cases to our study. One reason for this difference is that the process of linking complex webs of organizations provides grant makers with the potential for driving societal change faster and on a larger scale rather than through grant contracts with a single organization. For example, testing a concept to address the social conditions contributing to poverty in a community can be devised by a single grant maker—if grants are made through a network of nonprofit service providers. The use of the network presents a single point of coordination that is responsive to the grant maker's mission, which typically seeks to change the way society works with the intention of addressing broad or global problems. Among the partnership cases involving grant makers are several examples of funders using existing organizations in a network and of funders creating their own networks of service providers.

A second distinction is that because grant makers typically do not perform the work or contend with the exigencies of partnership, they do not experience the same challenges of partnership that their grantees might. This situation leads to the dilemma their grantees often note: funders encourage or require partnerships without careful consideration of the challenges inherent in aligning the independent cultures, resources, and capacities of multiple organizations.

This chapter presents the thirteen partnership cases involving grant-making organizations in our sample. These cases offer insight into the work of philanthropic and grant-making institutions in addressing important societal problems. Some of the partnership cases describe horizontal relationships between two grant-making institutions collaborating on a project. Many of the takeaways from these cases of "peerage" institutional relationships will sound familiar because the grant makers tend to act more or less like the nonprofit service organizations we have been describing throughout this book. By contrast, other partnership cases are more hierarchical; that is, they originate as asymmetrical relationships between a grant maker and a grant recipient.

The case descriptions in this chapter follow a similar but not identical pattern. The partnership accounts may include some or all of the following components: a noteworthy quote contributed by the nonprofit executive for the specific case; the partnership definition offered by the executive contributing the case; the partnership purpose; factors that worked toward or against the partnership meeting its goals; and advice to other nonprofit leaders. Each case begins with a quotation that we believe illustrates the anecdotal learning offered by the nonprofit executive describing the grant-making partnership and ends with a "lessons learned" drawn from the case narrative.

The Grant-Making Partnership Cases

Case 1: Community Foundation (CF) Youth Development Partnership

Listening is also vital to a successful partnership.

The Community Foundation (CF) executive defined partnership as two or more organizations with mutually agreed-upon goals, outcomes, and visions coming together to utilize each other's strengths, relationships, fiscal resources, and expertise to accomplish projects. The executive attributed the importance of the partnership to the overarching purpose of influencing public policy for youth development programs and opportunities community-wide.

The CF rated goal attainment satisfaction with this partnership as 7 out of 10 due to the slow progress partners made prior to the direct involvement of the CF. Factors that helped make the partnership successful were each participant's willingness to fulfill its assigned role, while factors that worked against meeting the partnership goals were that the CF did not foresee the difficulties the partners would have in working together without the CF's own active involvement.

In hindsight, the CF noted as lessons learned that the partnership would have become stronger if the participants were more flexible with each other at the beginning of the partnership. The individuals engaged in the back and forth of the endeavor had adopted a "thick-skinned" perspective when the organizational cultures came into conflict, and all participants maintained a good sense of humor throughout, offering a "benefit of the doubt" perspective. Finally, "listening" was a vital performance characteristic that would have made the difference in achieving a stronger, more successful partnership.

Case 2: Quasi-Community Foundation (QCF) Nonprofit Organization Mergers Partnership

Get leadership on board at the beginning of the partnership.

The QCF executive described partnership as a purposeful endeavor leading to a shared goal or outcome based on "give and take" between the partners. Although the QCF recognized collaboration with peer organizations as partnerships, in its grant-making the QCF considered grantees as partners because the organization expected proposals that align with the foundation mission and priorities. The partners included seventeen other funders that pooled $400,000 held by a third-party intermediary to support partnership by nonprofit organizations that would then provide required services to the target populations. Factors that worked toward meeting the goals of the partnership were shared leadership and willingness of the funders to share information. The partnership scored 8 out of 10 because it met most of its goals. Unanticipated benefits include learning about partnership as a function of performing the work and gaining ways to improve programs from operational experiences.

The QCF noted as lessons learned that partnership design required considerable advance planning and active leadership by the QCF to guide project relationships toward effective partnership performance. The executive offered that in addition to serving as funder, their contribution to the partnership success was to do things that strengthened the relationship between the actors rather than focus on the transactional services and output work of the partnership.

Case 3: Quasi-Community Foundation (QCF) Lead-Poisoning Remediation Partnership

Work is more effective when it is done together, but consider partners carefully and ensure that they are trustworthy.

The QCF established this partnership. Although more than eighty organizations participated in the endeavor, the principal actors consisted of the QCF, a nonprofit strategic alliance of service providers devoted to creating lead-safe and healthy home environments in urban settings, two county agencies, and one municipal government. The QCF was the lead funder and provided grant-making advice to the local government, which also provided funding to the endeavor. The project was important to the QCF because the partnership's purpose aligned readily with the foundation mission. The partnership scored 8 out of 10 because a key participant was unable to meet the agreed performance standards. The factors that worked toward meeting the goals of the partnership were strong leadership; transparency about the goals and agendas; open dialogue when goals were not met; and no surprises among the partners. Factors that worked against meeting the goals of the partnership were political turf; competing priorities for public funding; and the limited capacity of the foundation to manage the project.

The QCF noted that its experience in the partnership led to changes in its practices involving collaboration. For example, at the outset of the partnership the QCF had not realized how time-consuming partnerships were, nor did the QCF fully understand the costs associated with collaboration. The QCF concluded that although partnership offers a more effective means to drive institutional investment and involvement, it was not necessarily cheaper for partnering nonprofit organizations to collaborate in delivering services to reach the QCF philanthropic institutional goals.

Case 4: Major Family Foundation (MFF) Regional Economic Development Partnership

Pay attention to what is happening in the partnership and be open to changing goals, because change and transition are necessary.

The MFF executive defined partnership as involving an agreement between two organizations to pursue activities together, with expected benefits agreed to in advance and intended to impact a larger community. The partnership was important because it comprised a major shift in private policy and grant-making by the philanthropic community. Prior to the partnership, grant makers provided support for individual and somewhat isolated initiatives using only their own funding resources. During the partnership, grant makers agreed to concentrate their grant-making resources on priorities devised by their collective deliberations and priorities. The partnership was originally established to determine how to pool funds to engage in three fundamental activities: grant-making, conducting research, and providing community outreach to facilitate economic leadership in the region. The partnership achieved 10 out of 10. Two reasons for this sterling assessment were that the partnership achieved a three-fold increase in the amount of money contributed to the endeavor, and the partnership demonstrated to other local foundations that collaboration between grant makers was possible and could lead to meaningful impact. From the perspective of the nonprofit executive, the partnership affected the way many private foundations in the local community made their decisions.

The MFF noted as lessons learned that partnership goals must be simple to understand, even if they require complexity to achieve. Goals must also be revisited as a project unfolds and new information is obtained from the work of the partnership. Revisiting goals is not an admission of flaws in planning or implementation, but are necessary to inform the work of the partnership and to reinforce the correctness of the goals or the necessity of adjusting the goals to account for changed conditions in the partnership operations.

Case 5: Small Family Foundation (SFF) Entrepreneurship Partnership

> Think carefully about your partner, the dynamics of the relationship, and anticipate as many issues in advance as you can.

The SFF executive defined partnership as a collaborative activity in which two or more initiatives come together for the purpose of achieving a common goal, each bringing different kinds of resources and together using these resources over time to achieve collective goals. The partnership was between the SFF and a large national foundation initiated by the SFF as a pilot project. The SFF's role in the partnership was to provide local matching funds, serve as the project manager for day-to-day oversight and resolution of problems in the partnership, and conduct an evaluation of goal attainment. The partnership rated 9 out of 10 because over time the partners overcame their differences, and the program met its primary goals. Factors that worked toward meeting the goals of the partnership were the expertise of the national funding partner, the high level of accountability of the partners, and the network of strong relationships. Factors that worked against meeting the goals of the partnership were the complexity of managing a multiple-site project involving independent institutions and the inexperience of the SFF, which served as an intermediary for the national partner by engaging in hands-on, field-level project management for the first time. The SFF also stated that foundations typically require grantees to partner—without foundations having to partner themselves. The experience of having to manage the partnership gave the SFF firsthand experience of the difficulties and the possible rewards that accompany partnerships.

One of the lessons learned from this case involves the project-framing emphasis in the SFF's definition of partnership on "two or more initiatives" rather than using the term "participants" or "organizations." Through the framework of partnership occurring between initiatives rather than organizations, SFF sets in place a top-down dynamic of its authority over the performance by the individual partners. The dynamic of a "senior" partner engaging two "junior" partners had several implications: it effectively removed the autonomy of the individual partners performing the work and diminished the importance of their own mission fulfillment as a motivating outcome of the partnership endeavor; it elevated the partnership mission fulfillment and diminished the efficacy of three-mission principle we have described elsewhere; and it recast the endeavor as of principal agency rather than setting the conditions some nonprofit executives in this book ascribe to important and meaningful partnership.

Case 6: Small Family Foundation (SFF) Partnership with a Corporate Charitable Foundation

> Do your homework ahead of time; get to know the leader of the organization you will be working with; make sure the chemistry is right; keep your eyes on the goals; even with preparation there will be surprises, and you have to have flexibility to overcome these challenges.

This partnership was between the SFF and a corporate charitable foundation. The partnership was important because of the SFF's practice of matching national funding sources to leverage its resources whenever possible for maximum program impact. The partnership scored 7 out of 10 because it took a long time to build trust among the participants. The partners' initial enthusiasm for the endeavor was not reflected in their actions or commitment to fulfill their roles in the partnership. The primary factor that worked toward meeting the goals of the partnership was the SFF's determination to succeed in a highly visible program with an ambitious agenda. Factors that worked against meeting the goals of the partnership included the complications of having three partners performing the work products, with two funders each monitoring and requiring progress on slightly different aspects of performance; the fact that each partner had slightly different goals and priorities; the proliferation of intellectual property; and a lack of flexibility in the original partnership design.

Unlike case 5 involving the SFF, this case illustrates and informs us of the difficulties foundations have in shifting between partnerships characterized by hierarchy from those of peers. For the SFF, the experience of crafting and leading a complex partnership premised on a faulty assumption that all foundations behave the same way and will make adjustments for the benefit of their partner was a factor in its perceived lower performance.

Case 7: Faith-Based Federated Giving Institution (FBFG) Partnership

> Partnerships achieve results but require you to recognize the two-way street nature of building relationships.

The FBFG executive defined partnership as occurring when independent organizations formally affiliate with a shared mission and resources to benefit all participating organizations. The partnership was between the FBFG and thirteen member agencies. The FBFG conceived its partnership relationship as residing within two spheres: first as a dyadic partnership with a council of executives representing the thirteen organizations, and second as a partner in relationship with each of the individual organizations. The partnership rated 8 out of 10 because the FBFG was committed to continuous improvement as an organizational value. The FBFG stated that inherent tensions such as lack of reciprocity attend any partnership. Factors that worked toward meeting partnership goals included resources the FBFG brought to the table; the value of the services the agencies offered to the community; and the mutual benefits of exchanges through the partnership. Factors that worked against meeting the goals of the partnership included that the underlying purposes of the partners did not always coincide.

One of the lessons learned from this case is that grant makers do conceive of complex partnerships as multidimensional, where one level of perception is partnership framed as between individual organizations and a grant maker, and the other as a simultaneous condition between the grant maker and a network system of organizations. Both dimensions of partnership adhere to the three-mission fulfillment principle of partnership.

Case 8: Federated Giving Institution (FGI) Public Health Partnership

> Share risks and rewards by carefully considering the mutuality of purpose of a partnership, and make sure the potential reward is distributed fairly equally and the interaction is democratic.... Any suggestion that people are invited to join a partnership after it comes together such as funders who say we should invite people from our target population is a sign of insincere and false equality.... The invite part suggests they have power when they don't really have legitimacy of power to sit as equals.

This partnership was initiated by private foundations to advance public health needs in response to an epidemic of an infectious disease, social stigma associated with the disease, and the opportunity to leverage national and local, public and private resources to combat it. The FGI rated the partnership 9.5 out of 10 because the partnership reached the limit of its ability to leverage supplemental resources below its expectations. Factors that worked toward meeting partnership goals included ongoing shared commitment to the issue of the partnership, peer pressure, and a positive risk/reward ratio. Factors that worked against meeting partnership goals included other funders' perceptions that other actors would take care of the situation, rewards would be limited, and the funding pool would not expand further.

The FGI learned from the partnership experience that the partners themselves define the relationship as a partnership, and that outside third parties (such as funders) cannot confirm a partnership. For the FGI, the only "true" partnerships are among entities that share equally with peers the risks, power, and authority of a partnership and who together comprise a community of purpose. Relationships with grantees are unequal and not partnerships, although they are formed around rational strategies for gaining benefits from participation.

Case 9: Nonprofit Funding Intermediary (NFI) Microenterprise Partnership

> Equality in the partnership is very important; neither organization can "trump" the other; assume both want to grow the pie so that no one partner can achieve the mission without the other; and both partners recognize that the other is contributing to the final product.

The NFI executive defined partnership as occurring between two (or more) organizations when they find mutual benefit from working with each other, and where both find parity in the level of commitment and the mutuality of benefits. The partnership arose between the NFI and a large community foundation, who worked together as equal partners on the project. The NFI rated the partnership as 9 out of 10. Factors that worked toward meeting the goals of the partnership were shared vision and facilitation by organizations that had an interest in the project.

One of the lessons learned from this case was that the executives of both partners had professional experience working together previously and the success of the partnership was derived from that relationship. This view was reflected in the advice to other executives desiring to engage in important, meaningful, and successful partnerships: that partners should have a high regard for and confidence in your partner.

Case 10: Nonprofit Funding Intermediary (NFI) Vacant Land Reuse Initiative

> Being able to anticipate some of the difficulties (that did end up occurring) lessened their impact on the relationship.

The NFI's executive director emphasized slightly different aspects of partnership in this second case he contributed. Rather than focus on mutual benefits, as mentioned in case 9, the second definition emphasizes a theme of two organizations accomplishing an objective that neither were able to achieve on their own. In this second definition, each organization brings something to the partnership, such as skill sets or resources.

The partnership described involved the NFI and the mayor's office, which together served as funding agents, and a third-party nonprofit organization devoted to reuse of vacant urban properties. The partnership supported a centralized effort to manage the available funds and address the issue of vacant land. The NFI rated the partnership as 9 out of 10 as a result of the partners' successful alignment with the partnership mission. Although this achievement was the most difficult and time-consuming to the partnership, other challenges involved external factors beyond the partners' control.

The NFI's advice to other nonprofit leaders was to (1) be clear about the roles and expectations of each member of the partnership, (2) enter into a partnership only with an organization for which the partner has high regard, and (3) nurture and develop mutual respect for all partners.

Case 11: The Nonprofit Intermediary Organization (NIO) Vacant and Abandoned Housing Partnership

> Be clear about the roles and expectations of each member of the partnership; work hard among the partners to build trust when problems arise; [and] communicate quickly with each other when things don't go as expected.

The NIO executive defined partnership as a relationship in which the operations and decision-making between two or more organizations are equitable, open, and honest. The partnership described was a three-year $50 million initiative between the NIO and another nonprofit. The partnership made a program possible that neither participant could perform alone. The NIO rated the partnership as 9 out of 10. Factors that supported goal attainment included the complementary assets of the partners in technical expertise, capacity to perform the work, and financial resources available to support the work of the partnership. Factors that worked against the attainment of the partnership goals were miscommunications early in the endeavor.

One of the lessons learned from this case was that the executives have the most success when there is a realistic view of the partner and together they identify some of the challenges going into the relationship. Anticipating some of the difficulties lessened their impact on the relationship.

Case 12: Arts and Culture (A&C) Community Development Partnership

> Some agencies can adapt and adjust and others cannot due to bureaucracy.

The A&C executive defined partnership as between organizations that have an interest in a shared objective and utilize the complementary talents and skills of the individual partners to achieve it. Partnerships also entail agreement between the partners regarding how they perceive and share the achievements, failures, and risks of the endeavor. The A&C initiated this partnership by issuing an RFP crafted specifically for the partner.

The A&C rated the partnership 7 out of 10 because only the short-term performance goals were met, not the longer-term goals of the partnership. In the A&C's view, among the factors that worked toward meeting the partnership goals was the high visibility of the partnership endeavor, which attracted attention from unanticipated third parties. In addition, partners perceived compatibility in staffing and other resources across organizations and missions and articulated outcomes precisely. Advice to other nonprofit leaders about partnership drawn from lessons learned were that partners should have compatible operating cultures, trust and understanding among partners should deepen over time, partners should start with complementary skill sets and open communications, participants must share the risks and rewards of the endeavor, and each partner should be committed to learning and improving the project.

Case 13: Arts and Culture (A&C) Public Policy and Distributing Funds Partnership

> Make sure the undertaking of each organization is manageable for their abilities and resources; there is compatibility between the organizational cultures; they possess and are aware of complementary skills the other partner may offer; there is a will to develop trust and understanding of each organization; there is a practice for open communication; [and] they are willing to share risks, rewards, and learning.

This partnership concerned the A&C and an appointed county board oversight organization. The partnership was created so that the county had a mechanism to funnel tax funds to private organizations. To do the work effectively, the partnership formed to merge content expertise that would strengthen local private arts and culture institutions in ways that would be accepted by taxpayers as justification for the tax. According to the nonprofit executive, the partnership rated 7.5 out of 10 because it had improved over time but still needed to focus on how both organizations might better understand and utilize outcome measures. Factors that helped the partnership meet its goals included interorganizational openness, honesty, trust, and tolerance; an appreciation of the partnership's organic, dynamic quality; and the partners' flexibility to adapt to changing environments and organizational cultures. Factors that worked against meeting partnership goals consisted of differences in planning and outcome assumptions; lack of communication; entrenched positions; and until overcome, differences across organizational cultures.

In offering advice to other nonprofit leaders, the A&C executive noted that partnerships with public agencies are different than those with nonprofit organizations. The "public" is a stakeholder in these public-private partnerships in a direct manner by merit of the taxpayer origin of the funds with the result that the public actor in the partnership has a fiduciary responsibility to ensure the purposes of the partnership are fulfilled with fiscal transparency. However, not all public actors have the same limitations on flexibility, so it is possible for some to adapt and adjust more readily. Finally, because public agencies can change leadership abruptly, partners of government should be mindful that policies and priorities may change, and that a partnership exit strategy is a wise precaution.

Analysis of Cases

> Our view did change as a result of the partnership. Some of the Foundation's original goals were to get people to collaborate, while we didn't realize how time-consuming this could be. We ask nonprofits to follow our RFP guidelines requiring them to collaborate; they understand there is a cost associated with collaboration, and it is not necessarily cheaper for them to collaborate, but our view is that collaboration is a more effective way to have more institutional investment and involvement.

Philanthropic and grant-making institutions commonly cast their relationships with other parties as a form of "partnership." The thirteen partnership cases described earlier illustrate the diversity of grant-making partnerships. The following analysis considers two types of these partnerships: partnerships established between a grant maker and a service provider, and partnerships between peer grant-making institutions.

Tables 6.1 and 6.2 present data that reflect distinctive characteristics of each of the thirteen case narratives. In table 6.1, a code indicating the partnership participant types was applied to dyads comprised of grant-making nonprofits and their partners. The coding in the third column specifies whether or not the arrangement was institutionalized in writing in the form of a contract agreement, and column 4 displays the executive's satisfaction rating of the partnership.

The thirteen cases constitute examples of important partnerships whose goals were to address a negative condition or other economic or social pathology in the community. The cases illustrate ways in which grant makers enlist nonprofit organizations as partners for the fulfillment of their missions. In seven of the thirteen cases, or 55 percent, nonprofit executives stated that their partnerships were designed to reduce the fragmented delivery of social services and create a stronger, more integrated system of service response. Through partnerships, philanthropic and nonprofit intermediary organizations took on the responsibility of strengthening service-provider networks from a top-down position of authority and provider of resources in the community.

Table 6.1. Grant Maker Matrix.

Case	Partnership Type	Organization	Satisfaction Score
1: Community Foundation youth development partnership	Funder working through an intermediary	Contract	7
2: Quasi-Community Foundation nonprofit organization mergers partnership	Private-public funding policy-making	No Contract	8–8.5
3: Quasi-Community Foundation lead-poisoning remediation partnership	Funder working through an intermediary and intermediary as independent from funder	Contract	8
4: Major Family Foundation regional economic development partnership	Private-public funding policy-making	No Contract	8
5: Small Family Foundation entrepreneurship partnership	Peer-to-peer	Contract	9
6: Small Family Foundation partnership with a corporate charitable foundation	Peer-to-peer	Contract	7
7: Faith-Based Federated Giving Institution partnership	Federated funded network	No Contract	8
8: Federated Giving Institution public health collaboration	Private-public funding policy-making	No Contract	9.5
9: Nonprofit Funding Intermediary microenterprise partnership	Peer-to-peer	No Contract	9

10: Nonprofit Funding Intermediary vacant land reuse initiative	Funder working through an intermediary and intermediary as independent from funder	Contract	9
11: The Nonprofit Intermediary Organization vacant and abandoned housing partnership	Funder working through an intermediary and intermediary as independent from funder and federated funded network	Contract	9
12: Arts & Culture community development partnership	Funder working through an intermediary	Contract	7
13: Arts & Culture public policy and distributing funds partnership	Intermediary as independent from funder	Contract	7.5

In three of the cases, grant makers engaged in partnership to attain specific project outcomes. For example, in cases 9, 10, and 11, programs were created that sought the participation of individuals engaged in microlending for small business development, home health, and affordable housing initiatives. Project opportunities arose from the absence of a market remedy and/or the limited reach of the public sector to perform the tasks necessary to adequately serve individuals and their communities. In the final three cases in the table, grant makers engaged in partnership to address large-scale community housing abandonment, regional economic development, and mergers of social service providers focused on community health issues.

Across the thirteen grant maker partnership cases, we can identify five partnership types. The first type is comprised of arrangements crafted by grant makers as delegation of work to nonprofit organizations with the expertise, capacity, and ability to perform technical functions and provide services. These cases are coded as "funder working through an intermediary" partnerships in table 6.1. These partnerships include the five cases that describe social services provision and community and economic development. In these partnerships, the grant makers viewed the nonprofit participants as a supplement, enabling the funders to project their philanthropic mission into the community. For example, "The partnership is intended to strengthen the region's economic competitive advantage by concentrating the resources of many funding sources that we coordinate and manage, while also allowing us to advocate on the behalf of many funders in a single forum and convening to coordinate services to the community."

From the perspective of the grant maker, the nonprofit partner serves as the arm of the funder to perform the transactional work of service delivery to the community. The arrangement can be viewed as a partnership because it is a channel enabling the grant maker to drive programs into the community and seek and achieve desired outcomes. For example, "The foundation convened funders to develop a program among the funders to help the nonprofits. A neutral intermediary entered into the partnership as a funding recipient and assumed the role as lead agency working with the foundation toward the goal of discovering ways to support the larger community of nonprofits in their efforts to collaborate, raise awareness of the desirability of partnership, and track the progress of partnerships they might form."

The second type of grant maker partnership occurs when the grant maker creates a relationship with a nonprofit intermediary organization that serves the role of the grant maker on the ground. These partnerships delegate the active project management, funding match, and leverage of other funding sources, such as federal or state programs, through formal contractual service arrangements with the other nonprofit actors. These cases, which are the second-most prevalent among the thirteen, are coded as "intermediary as independent from funder" partnerships in table 6.1. They involve considerable complexity in coordination of work and are typically accompanied by a formal contract between the primary actors. As one executive described: "The grant maker approached the intermediary to be their partner because they did not have the in-house capacity to do the rehabilitation of the properties. They set out with the goal of renovating vacant and foreclosed houses to then sell to home buyers, with special attention/interest paid to moderate-income home buyers."

The third partnership type links a grant maker and government and is coded as "private-public funding policy-making" partnership in table 6.1. We note that partnerships in these cases between these two actors are not like some partnerships in which government is the more important actor (public-private partnerships) because of funding resources and a perceived linkage to the fulfillment of public policy. In our cases, grant maker partnerships with government occur at the prompting of the foundation and are characterized by arrangements that are largely informal and noncontractual. But, the work of the partnership occurs through a contractually obligated third party, usually a nonprofit service provider. As two executives noted, "The grant maker has an understanding with the city that the city will match its project funding. The money that the city brings to the initiative is crucial to making the work happen, and we are able to tap it to perform aspects of the work. The partnership allows for the grant maker to claim there is a coordinated and centralized effort that can manage the two streams of funds to address the issue of vacancy."

The fourth partnership pairing, coded as "peer-to-peer" partnership in table 6.1, consists of arrangements between grant makers. The peer-to-peer partnership between the grant makers more closely resembles the partnerships in the non–grant maker cases described earlier in this book. These cases suggest partnerships of considerable scope and potential aligned with philanthropy's transformational aspirations for social innovation.[2] "It is important because two funders were working together as 50/50 partners on a project both have an interest in, but both have a different purpose in, and which neither alone could accomplish, either financially or based on the limits of their own expertise."

The fifth partnership type, coded as "federated funded network" partnerships in table 6.1, comprises partnerships between a federated fundraising organization in the role of grant maker working with a network of organizations, usually nonprofits. The grant-making arms of two federated giving agencies provided these cases, in which partnerships are bound by the funding the agencies provide to the set of nonprofits within their sphere of influence. "The partnership was originally set up to provide funding resources and standards—fiscal, audit, and professional—to minimize duplication and drive agencies to do what they do best. Partnership is the reason for the organization."

In reviewing these five grant maker partnership types, we see that executives of philanthropic institutions emphasize that meaningful partnerships are those that occur between peers, such as two grant makers or two nonprofit organizations, and that something other than partnership occurs between grant makers and their grantees. This sentiment is tied to the hierarchical role many philanthropic actors assume as the provider of financial resources to stimulate a new partnership or enable a partnership to coalesce in the same way a financial or banking institution might "govern" or "hold accountable" a business or an individual to which it provides a loan. Indeed, this sentiment was expressed by one grant maker executive, who made an explicit point in defining "correct" partnerships, as follows: "'Correct' partnerships are with peers that share risks and create a community of purpose. Partnerships cannot exist that are unequal in their distribution of power. In philanthropic partnerships, they can only exist among entities that share equally."

Table 6.2 presents concepts mentioned frequently in the grant maker partnership narratives in answer to the questions posed in the interview questionnaire by the philanthropy/grant maker nonprofit executives contributing their important partnership cases. The concepts listed in the table were determined by a content analysis of all answers under a designated cluster of responses to the same questions asked of each respondent for each case they contributed. The table displays five focus areas of partnership mission fulfillment purposes and characteristics (i.e., policy/goals; strategy; impacts; partnership pros; and partnership cons) of the thirteen philanthropy/grant maker partnerships. The table then lists the sub-themes, which further illuminate noteworthy features of the partnership cases that point to distinctive characteristics of the grant maker partnerships. The corresponding cases are noted in the far-right column of the table.

Table 6.2 suggests two conclusions. Not surprisingly, just over half of the partnership cases (seven of thirteen) provided a function or service in the community

Table 6.2. Grant Maker Partnership Themes, Sub-Themes, and Cases in Which They Appear.

Themes	Sub-Themes	Cases
Policy/Goal	Provide Function or Service	1, 5, 7, 8, 11, 13
	Respond to Market Failure	3, 6, 9, 10
	Create New/Modified Structure	2, 4, 12
Strategy	Coordination of Policy/Resources	1, 2, 3, 4, 7
	Accountability Standards	1, 13
	Build New Relationships/Increase Collaboration	1, 2, 8, 9
	Utilize Best Practices	2
	Conduct Research	4, 13
	Community Outreach	4, 5
	Distribute Risk	8
	Offer New Program	9
Impacts	Cost/Resource Savings	1, 2, 4, 8, 11, 13
	New Knowledge	1, 4, 6, 8
	Increased Collaboration/Capacity	2, 5, 9, 10, 13
	Enhanced Awareness	2, 3, 5, 8
	Increased Efficiency/Time Management	1, 3, 5
	Increased Transparency/Trust	7, 8, 9, 11, 13
	Modified Practices	3, 4, 5, 8
	Delivered New/Enhanced Product	4, 8, 10, 13
	Target Population Impacted	3, 6, 7, 8, 9, 13
Partnership Pros	Strength of Relationships/Leadership	1, 2, 3, 4, 5, 7, 9, 10, 11, 13
	Willingness to Participate/Increase Knowledge	1, 6, 8, 13
	Flexibility and Adjustments to Problems	1, 9, 13
	Shared Leadership, Tasks, Goals, and Visions	2, 5, 7, 8, 10, 12
	Communication and Transparency	2, 3, 5, 12, 13
	Skills/Capacity Within Partnership	5, 7, 11
Partnership Cons	Misaligned or Competing Goals/Priorities	4, 6, 7, 13
	Bureaucracy or Politics	3, 9, 10, 13
	Limited Capacity/Experience	3, 5, 6
	Limited Savings	3, 8
	Lack of Transparency/Flexibility	6, 7, 11, 13

that aligned with the mission of the grant maker. These partnership cases emphasized the grant maker's mission fulfillment by the executives describing them. The grant makers were sought out by civic leaders by virtue of their institutions' capacity, giving ability, professional staff, and technical expertise.

In the remaining 45 percent of the cases (six of thirteen), the grant maker executives attributed the purpose of their partnership arrangements as responses to the lack of services in the community or because of the grant makers' desire to create innovations in services to address various community pathologies. This sentiment of partnership purpose aligns with our assertions earlier in this book about partnerships that aspire to transformational outcomes and impacts in the larger society, such as reduced negative social or economic conditions, rather than simple transactional measures of the partnership project such as dollars spent and clients served. The philanthropic/grant-making executives contributing these six cases described the partnerships as successive service innovations for an entire system of performance, rather than simply as a means of fulfilling the mission of their organization. It is also important to note that the six grant-making organizations in this grouping had fewer staff and human resources committed to performing the work of the partnership than those organizations in the first grouping as an indication that the work of the endeavor was heavily delegated to the grant-funding recipients.

The grant maker cases support two additional themes. First, grant maker strategies work to align the goals and activities of nonprofit organizations to provide useful or improved systems of community-wide service delivery. This theme includes strategies that improve the coordination of community resources to increase the accountability of fund recipients as well as the reach of services. The second theme centers on strategic partnership endeavors designed to create public value. As we discussed earlier in the book, nonprofit organizations create public value through the fulfillment of their missions, by acting as intermediaries in addressing large-scale public undertakings that are typically reflected in public-private partnerships, and by providing a third space where social innovation can take place.[3] Since grant-making institutions follow strategies designed to amplify their philanthropic goals, the sub-themes noted in table 6.2 exemplify ways in which grant maker nonprofit partnerships can strengthen social networks and build social capital.

Impacts

Since the mid- to late 1990s, measures of program outcomes and impact have become important tools for grant makers to evaluate the effectiveness of their mission fulfillment strategies. Awareness of impact is also becoming part of the best practices management toolkit for nonprofit organizations. As Patrice Flynn and Virginia Hodgkinson have noted, "foundations want to know whether the programs they fund are making a difference. Private donors inquire as to how donations serve targeted audiences. Board members ask for detailed information on organizational activities and performance."[4] For mission fulfillment in the area of partnerships, this measurement of outcomes and impacts is also important.

Across the thirteen grant maker cases, nonprofit executives most frequently describe the impact of grant-making partnerships as successful when they observe a demonstrable effect or performance outcome on a target population. They also point to benchmark instances in which the costs of a program or service delivery are reduced or services are made more efficient. These two results are mentioned in nearly all of the cases in table 6.2.

In the view of the grant maker executives, impacts are not solely about the target populations. These executives also feel that partnership can increase understanding of, or knowledge about, a particular problem or issue. Other results noted in table 6.2 include innovations in partnership program designs and the efficiencies and expertise that come with accumulating the partnership work. Over time, learning increases the participants' sophistication and knowledge concerning partnership, their capacity to undertake and fulfill partnerships, and their decision-making acumen regarding partnership. Leaders of nonprofit organizations can translate this knowledge into their own organization's effectiveness and impact.

Partnership Pros and Cons

The productive outcomes to partnership described in these thirteen nonprofit grant maker cases exhibit a narrower band of themes than do the full sample of eighty-two partnership cases undergirding this book. Table 6.2 presents six descriptive aspects that tended to work toward partnership success listed as "pro" and five aspects that tended to work against partnership success, or "con" categories, in these thirteen cases. These characteristics of partnerships offer important lessons for partnership participants and third parties seeking to stimulate the formation of partnerships. One lesson is that the tensions in partnership processes arise in many instances from the limits of each partner participant's capacity to understand the broader context of the work they are performing and the potential ramifications of success or failure on a system of actors of which they may be only vaguely aware.

For example, beyond the necessary outcome of mission fulfillment, the reasons nonprofit executives gave for partnership reflect commitment to affecting systemic change in society through a well-functioning alignment of organizations. In our review of the thirteen grant maker cases, nonprofit executives told us that alignment occurs and sharpens when partners gain greater familiarity with one another through the experience of working together. The grant maker executives consistently stated that partnerships can improve over time, and that organizational actors learn valuable lessons from one another. The "pro" partnership aspects under this theme in table 6.2 reflect features of partnership process that strengthen the relationship as if the relationship itself is the desired outcome and where the endeavor offers the agency necessary to form the partnership.

While it strains credulity that a grant maker would offer funding just to test the viability of partnership as a sole outcome, these cases suggest that one sincere purpose of the partnership to achieve transformation in society—perhaps over a long-term arch of grant-making policy—at least initially, was to establish and eventually learn from the partnership itself, the maturation process that deepened the relationship over time.

Factors that work against the successful achievement of partnership goals are usually the inverse of the factors that support goal attainment. Hence, the "con" descriptive categories reflect challenges that inhibit an organization's ability to serve as a partner or to benefit from partnership. The categories under this theme suggest reasons that alignment between partners or the ability to act as a partner may not be present. The nonprofit grant maker executives offered five principal themes in their case narratives as creating barriers to the partnership meeting its goals which all derive from insufficient communication and lack of organizational capacity.

Conclusion

According to the grant makers, the process of partnership is itself an outcome for both grant maker and grant seeker. These respondents also maintained that well-functioning partnerships are nuanced and complex. The sense that a partnership is successful is strengthened when leaders can point to evidence that the partnership enhanced organizational capacity, strengthened networks between institutions, and fulfilled their goals of creating effective ways to address community needs.

Nonprofit executives engaging in partnership with grant makers are well served to be aware of the grant maker motivation and long-term objectives sustaining the partnership mission. This chapter has elucidated a number of characteristics of nonprofit-first partnership originating with philanthropic and grant-making actors that can easily be recognized by nonprofit executives and leaders as critical to their work in partnership.

Among the most important aspects of partnership for this particular subsector of nonprofit organizations is whether the partnership endeavor is the primary or sole purpose of the partnership or the partnership itself is the intended outcome. The former points to partnership motives and performance outcomes that are transactional, easily recognizable, and likely to be short-term. The latter points to partnership motives and performance outcomes that test the ability of the actors to work together successfully, perhaps forming a system for action toward transformational mission fulfillment over a much longer term.

In researching the general principles of philanthropy, scholars note that grant makers provide intermediation between themselves and the people or societal conditions they seek to address.[5] Intermediation obliges the formation of partnerships to stimulate and guide work performance, operations effectiveness, and outcome achievement. As these executives related, the role of the grant maker as intermediary exposes them to the promise and pitfalls of partnership. The implication is that policy makers and philanthropic institutions desiring to stimulate partnerships will have success in achieving their goals if their emphasis is on strengthening partnerships once they are formed. As a criterion for evaluation, they should consider including partnership, in addition to other outcomes, rather than simply requiring partnerships as a condition for funding.

Notes

1. Mendel, Stuart C., and Jeffrey L. Brudney. "Cross-Sector Collaboration and Public-Private Partnerships: A Perspective on How Nonprofit Organizations Create Public Value in an Archetypical City in the United States," in *Creating Public Value in Practice: Advancing the Common Good in a Multi-Sector, Shared-Power, No-One-Wholly-in-Charge World*, ed. John M. Bryson, Barbara C. Crosby, and Laura Bloomberg (Boca Raton, FL: CRC Press, 2015), 225–244; Mendel, S. C., and J. L. Brudney. "Putting the NP in PPP: The Role of Nonprofit Organizations in Public-Private Partnerships." *Public Performance & Management Review* 35, no. 4 (2012): 617–642, doi:10.2307/23484758.

2. Goldsmith, Stephen. *The Power of Social Innovation: How Civic Entrepreneurs Ignite Community Networks for Good* (Hoboken, NJ: John Wiley and Sons, 2010); Le Ber, Marlene J., and Oana Branzei. "(Re)forming Strategic Cross-Sector Partnerships Relational Processes of Social Innovation." *Business and Society* 49, no. 1 (2010): 140–172.

3. Mendel, Stuart C., and Jeffrey L. Brudney. "Doing Good, Public Good, and Public Value." *Nonprofit Management and Leadership* 25, no. 1 (2014): 23–40, doi:10.1002/nml.21109.

4. Flynn, Patrice, and Virginia A. Hodgkinson, eds. *Measuring the Impact of the Nonprofit Sector* (New York: Springer Science & Business Media, 2013); Ferris, James M., and Nicholas P. O. Williams. "Offices of Strategic Partnerships: Helping Philanthropy and Government Work Better Together." *The Foundation Review* 5, no. 4 (2014), doi:10.9707/1944-5660.1180; Brown, E., and J. M. Ferris. "Social Capital and Philanthropy: An Analysis of the Impact of Social Capital on Individual Giving and Volunteering." *Nonprofit and Voluntary Sector Quarterly* 36, no. 1 (2007): 85–99, doi:10.1177/0899764006293178; Ferris, James, and Elizabeth Graddy. "Contracting Out: For What? With Whom?" *Public Administration Review* 46, no. 4 (1986): 332–344, doi:10.2307/976307.

5. Anheier, Helmut. "Resourcing Nonprofit Organizations," in *Nonprofit Organizations: Theory, Management, Policy* (London: Routledge, 2014), 203–224; Frumkin, Peter. "Introduction," in *Strategic Giving: The Art and Science of Philanthropy* (Chicago: University of Chicago Press, 2006); Boulding, K. "Notes on a Theory of Philanthropy," in *Philanthropy and Public Policy*, ed. Frank G. Dickinson (Cambridge, MA: National Bureau of Economic Research, 1962), 57–72; Mattessich, Paul W., and Barbara R. Monsey. *Collaboration—What Makes It Work: A Review of Research Literature on Factors Influencing Successful Collaboration* (St. Paul, MN: Amherst H. Wilder Foundation, 1992).

7 Toward Nonprofit Theory: Collaboration as a Way of (Work) Life

> The goals of the partnership were to have a high-quality group, conduct meaningful research, and conduct outreach to the community. Trust among the members that were fully engaged, the quality of learning together by everyone for each other, and the mutually agreed-upon successes [that] have stimulated a desire for the partnership to grow have all contributed to the overall success of the partnership. The partnership had an impact on the organization—as the work has proceeded, the partners have worked to change grant-making styles so that grant officers across the program areas try, and get, greater gains. The partnership changed the way foundations make their decisions. The partnership had an impact on the target population because it persuaded the marketplaces to look at the region differently.
>
> —Executive of a grant-making institution in partnership with a coalition of other grant makers.

Overview

In this chapter, we revisit our research methods and the larger implications of our findings. We reiterate the benefits of a nonprofit-first approach to partnership, demonstrating the many advantages that an arrangement prioritizing the nonprofit partner's mission and culture can offer all partnering actors. As we revisit valuable theories of partnership and outline real-world indicators of partnership readiness, we hope to raise the outputs of our research to the level of applicable case-based or case-derived theory by offering nonprofit leaders valuable takeaways that will help them assess and enhance their own partnership readiness and expectations.

In the introduction, we identified the audience for this book as including students learning about the best techniques of practice for the field; nonprofit executives and leaders contemplating partnership endeavors; volunteers engaged in partnership work; scholars dedicated to identifying nonprofit-first-derived pedagogy; and institutions in the nonprofit sector such as grant makers seeking to stimulate effective partnerships. We also made promises to the audience of readers, which we summarize here as:

1.1 Offer a scholarly contribution to fill a gap in the instructional pedagogy for students grappling with the principles of nonprofit-first partnerships.

1.2 Provide nonprofit executives and others better understanding and insight into partnership options, advantages, characteristics, and expectations.

1.3 Focus, sharpen, and articulate a formal set of partnership theories drawn from the nonprofit-first perspective for application by nonprofit executives to increase the performance, effectiveness, and success of important and meaningful partnership arrangements.

1.4 Suggest the implications for nonprofit actors engaged with grant makers and grant makers-seeking (and public policy makers) to stimulate important, successful, and effective partnerships.

1.5 Analyze the sector and subsector dyad differences in partnership features and characteristics to provide insight on how nonprofit executives should expect to perform and contribute in the different combinations of partnerships types.

1.6 Gain insight into the three-mission principle of nonprofit-first partnership and the variations in applicability across the sectors, including philanthropic grant-making institutions.

1.7 Improve the understanding of the role behaviors that promote trust and relationship reciprocity, "soft measures" to which nonprofit executives may stay attuned as they engage in partnerships.

This chapter provides a recap of the general themes of the book that respond to the seven listed promises. We aspire to create theory useful to nonprofit-first scholars and practitioners, and to offer new insight on nonprofit partnership scholarship and practice. Among the outcomes of our research are seven partnership principles derived from nonprofit-first perspectives that are reflected in a dashboard of nonprofit-first partnership measures and indicators.

Introduction

As we also explained in the introduction of this book, one of the most important reasons to write a book on nonprofit-first partnerships is to better understand and explain the qualities that nonprofit actors attribute to the successful workings of their partnership endeavors. The foundation of our inquiry has been our interest in identifying productive means of making nonprofit-first partnership effective, positive, durable, and replicable.

To do so, we used inductive research methods to draw on the partnership experiences of nonprofit executives.[1] In chapter 1, our inquiry also considered and compared the ways in which partnership has been cast in the literature of nonprofit management and other scholarly disciplines. In summarizing our findings, we observed that by their nature, nonprofit organizations seek partnerships in order to maximize both reach and impact: to this end we might even say that partnership is a nonprofit's *raison d'être*. As we also noted in chapters 2 and 4, partnership engagement differs across the institutional sectors. Although we identify many ways in which partnerships differ, an important one has been parsing and making sense of the different language nonprofit, government, and business actors use when forming partnerships with nonprofit organizations. Our research and findings also led us to develop a set of seven principles on nonprofit partnership that we contribute to formal nonprofit sector epistemology and for use in practical applications by nonprofit executives, leaders, and others striving to achieve important, productive, and durable partnerships.

General Concepts of What Partnership Is and Why We Should Care

We have learned from our research interviews that "partnership" may be understood as a "noun," or achievement, and "partner" as a "verb," or set of activities. From one perspective, "partnership" compromises institutional actors' reflection of the same "association" facets of civil society in the United States that Alexis de Tocqueville described in the early 1800s. In this perspective, the actors both achieve and engage in partnership. By another perspective, though, "partnership" arises from all the stewardship actions of nonprofit organizations, grant makers, and their intermediary institutions that enable societal innovation, change, and the creation of public value. In both of these ways, nonprofit executives define and practice partnership as a way to enable mission fulfillment and, in many cases, the amplification of that mission.

From the standpoint of experienced nonprofit executives, partnerships may or may not meet all established goals. Also, partnerships can still rise to the level of "important" and meaningful even if they have met (only) most or some of their goals. We attribute this characteristic of nonprofit-first partnership experience to the experiential and continuous learning that often accompanies the practices of nonprofit executives and decision makers. We also consider it an outcome of the pragmatism required of nonprofit decision makers, who must be able to adjust to the vagaries of policy makers, grant makers, volunteers, and societal factors that lie well beyond their ability to control. The comments of one participant of this study who serves as chief executive officer for a nonprofit membership coalition of institutions illustrated these points when he stated,

> My view of partnership did change as a result of the partnership work. I learned that aggressive communication is essential to sustaining the partnership. Listening to feedback and continuing to change always affects what we are doing.

The maturity of the partner organization is important to establishing our priorities and reaching successes for the partnership. My sense of it is that if the partnership is strong, the services are strong, and the bottom line ROI to members are their reason for staying in the partnership. This includes cost savings, life enrichment for the community, and signs that programs are working.

Another defining note about partnerships was found in the consistent way that nonprofit executives described certain characteristics of important partnerships. These include the presence of dedicated labor and committed resources, self-determination and choice, and mutuality. We also learned that nonprofits often have to assume the transaction costs of partnership, such as meeting/organizing, waiting for payments from funders, making accommodations for insufficient funding, providing space, and so forth. It became clear that the readiness to partner must weigh into nonprofit leaders' and others' calculations, so that wise nonprofits will not normally enter a partnership unless they are prepared to assume the costs of such an engagement.

Because nonprofit organizations or nonprofit executives may not be ready to enter a partnership—and should not enter every partnership opportunity—our research suggests several indicators of partnership readiness. One major indicator encompassed the learning of the interviewees, who shared that they became better at partnership engagements as they gained experience over time. Among these learnings are the appreciation of the prime actors and conditions driving the partnership endeavor; the thoughtfulness and the provision for governance, authority, performance expectations, and approach to problem-solving by the participants; and the ability of the participants to adapt to changed conditions affecting their partners or the partnership endeavor.

Our research led to changes and expansion to several aspects of our initial views regarding nonprofit partnership—views that we often see reflected in the literature as well. For instance, our preliminary notion that a standard for measure of partnership could be devised through a *quid-pro-quo* list of exchange of goods and services between partners did not present a complete picture. Instead, we learned that the benefits drawn from partnership performance goals are the rather blunt, obvious, and less-nuanced outcome benefits that experienced actors seek in important and meaningful partnership endeavors. "Sharing" resources, responsibility, and accountability rather than "exchanging" them was ultimately the more accurate depiction of what transpires in important partnerships. Additionally, we learned that worthy outcomes of important and meaningful partnerships resulted from experiencing the process of partnership, and that the partnering organizations might also influence the nonprofit's own operations or worldview.

We note that institutional theories from other fields of public and private endeavors fit the schema of the nonprofit sector. The literature of organizational theory and development, for example, contains many general treatises on managing nonprofit organizations. But we also note and use as a primary justification for the research underlying this book that little of this "theory" applies to nonprofit organizations as independent institutional forms worthy of their own guiding principles apart from government and business.

A small group of leading scholars have carved out the rough institutional boundaries and principles for nonprofit organizations, which we can point to as seminal nonprofit sector "theory."[2] This book on nonprofit-first partnership adds to nonprofit sector theory through the characteristics of partnership we describe that reflect nonprofit organization governance, operations, and management that scholars point to as core pillars: mission primacy, volunteerism, and collaboration among separate institutional entities.[3]

Surprising Discoveries

As we wrote in chapter 2, funding was important for partnership so long as it enabled the partnership to thrive, but it was less important as a motivator to enter into a partnership, reward for forming the partnership, or reason that a partnership rose to the level of being important.

Nonprofit actors frequently overcome a reticence to form relationships with organizations with which they perceive themselves to be in competition. To many of the nonprofit executive respondents, the decision on whether to engage in a partnership with another nonprofit, government agency, or business was not a self-evident way to create greater opportunity for success than going it alone. This sentiment was reinforced as many nonprofit executive respondents explained their approach as a careful and deliberative weighing of partnership pros and cons prior to engagement in partnership, during the performance of the partnership, and in weighing whether the return on investment rose to the level of partnership success.

Virtually all the nonprofit executive respondents contributing cases to our study placed high value on learning during the experience. As we mentioned in chapters 3 and 4 during our discussions on partnership benefits and performance and satisfaction, learning by the nonprofit executives and hence their organizations occurred in multiple ways and times during the partnership engagement: through the act of partnership engagement as an outcome in and of itself, from their partners, from grant and policy makers, and from third-party stakeholders and constituents.

The sensibility described by executives in chapter 3 and subsequent chapters that the more satisfying and higher-performing partnerships are those that the nonprofits themselves initiate rather than those "encouraged" by third parties was a common thread throughout the cases. One frequently stated indicator of this sentiment was the assertion by the nonprofit executive that involvement of a reciprocal peer leader of sufficient stature from the partner organization—ideally the person at the top of the organization—was a signal that the endeavor was a priority for each organization. The inverse was also described as a truism.

Over the course of our research for this book, we hypothesized that the body of knowledge informing nonprofit-first partnership rose to the level of theory or theories specific to nonprofit sector leaders and others.[4] We believe that our primary research, as grounded in the experiential learning of the nonprofit executives interviewed, offers the foundation for a theory of strategic management of nonprofit organization partnerships. Our analysis of the executives' experiences, their advice to others interested in forming nonprofit partnerships, and their recommendations on important partnerships ultimately rise to the level of nonprofit sector theory for several reasons.

First, we confirmed a growing awareness that theories of public management and business administration do not satisfy the practical needs of leadership and management for the majority of nonprofit organizational leaders.[5] Neither government nor business practices account for nonprofit-specific characteristics, such as volunteerism or mission-based organizations dedicated to making society work better. Similarly, no other sector has acknowledged the same awareness that a nonprofit's understanding and performance of partnership improve over time and with experience. This "learning by doing" is characteristic of the nonprofit sector as a field of practice. Consequently, our documentation of multiple experiential learning cases uses field-based evidence to lead readers toward inductive theory and the practical tools necessary to systematically craft their own effective outcomes.

A second reason that our research on the advice offered by nonprofit executives may rise to the level of theory is the practical need for consistent methods to craft important and meaningful partnerships. This need is felt by a variety of actors, including nonprofits and public managers, policy makers, and executives as well as by many others. To meet this diverse and growing need, we proposed five measures for establishing important and meaningful partnerships in chapter 1, table 1.2 as supported but not dictated by extant scholarship. As depicted in figure 7.1 on next page, these included: (1) balance and equity in the partnership, (2) strength of a partnership bond, (3) longevity of a partnership, (4) formality of the bond between organizations, and (5) evidence of societal transformation. We also posited that these five measures may comprise a conceptual tool kit for creating and measuring the conditions of important and successful nonprofit partnerships.

A third reason that we believe our research on partnership may inform new ways of thinking for the field is the nonprofit-first perspective framing the values and processes that our interviewees described as authentic and essential for important partnerships. Although several aspects of the desired partnership characteristics and outcomes described in previous chapters may

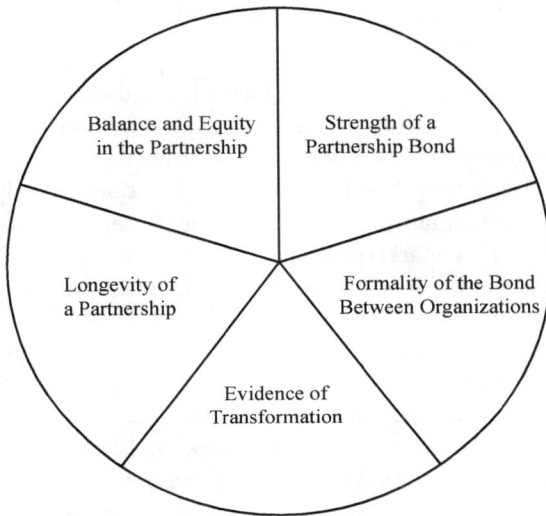

Fig. 7.1 Relationship Measures of Important and Meaningful Partnerships.

seem unremarkable as individual concepts, when taken together they comprise a catalog of distinct perspectives yet to be articulated in nonprofit scholarship.

A fourth reason for our research's value as theory can be found in the way that volunteerism is central to the character and nature of nonprofit organizations. The principles of volunteerism involving governance, operations, work products, advocacy of mission, and enthusiasm for collaborative engagements touch on every aspect of nonprofit partnership.[6] Yet, the social values that volunteers instill in nonprofit organizations and the necessity of emotional intelligence in nonprofit partnership settings are sadly overlooked. Volunteers bring a sense of ownership, a variety of experience, and the tug and pull of multiple personal perspectives to the decision-making and organizational culture of the nonprofit.[7] These effects, which may trend toward intuitive or emotional, must necessarily pervade a nonprofit organization, and will affect partnership performance. Integrating volunteer-driven values reflected by expectations that relationship equality, equity, and fair play were essential characteristics of partnership requires executive actors to be attuned to the nuance, nonverbal cues, and communications perspectives of volunteers. These same skill sets apply to nonprofit partnership endeavors for exactly the same reasons: to engender trust, respect, and reciprocity of action. Consequently, the ability of nonprofit executives to be sensitive to the opportunities, threats, strengths, and weakness of their partner is an essential characteristic of the higher-performing partnerships that is an important contribution of this book to the scholarly literature and theories for nonprofit-first partnership.

Volunteerism and a Theory of Management of Nonprofit Organizations

Fair play is a cornerstone concept for the formation and function of social capital, volunteerism, and nonprofit sector ethics.[8] In practice, fair play is closely tied to the degree of cooperation between two organizations through mutual trust between the partners: trust that is tested through actions of reciprocity, equity, and equality.[9] Although fair play is a significant concept for political economy, business ethics, and the marketplace, it is a surprising and significant weakness of the existing scholarly literature, which seldom links fair play to partnership involving nonprofit actors.

Yet, "fair play" was not explicitly articulated by the nonprofit executives interviewed. None mentioned fair play as a baseline expectation for partnership despite its embedded corollary in their descriptions of partner's intentions, how the governance of the partnership should work, and to what extent each participant was invested in mutual benefits. For example, the supplemental work required to build trust between partners was typically framed in expectations of reciprocity: each participant had an obligation to assume a share of responsibility toward achieving partnership outcomes. Fair play was also encompassed in the definitions of partnership, the descriptions of barriers to successful partnership outcomes, and the expectation of benefits derived from successful partnership described by the nonprofit executives.

Another aspect of volunteerism that contributes to a theory of nonprofit management involves the principle of mission fulfillment. Unlike government, whose legitimacy and functions arise from the rule of law, and business, which is governed by the exigencies of the marketplace, mission fulfillment is the central existential rationale for a nonprofit organization. Mission fulfillment typically occurs through service that will advance the interests of the partners; advocacy with public, private, and nonprofit actors; or engagement in social innovation to help solve a problem and provide for the community's well-being. The mission-fulfillment ethic for nonprofit-first partnerships drives organizations to use the financial resources of their partners in government, business, and elsewhere in the nonprofit sector to improve conditions in society. The "mission fulfillment" rationale for entering into partnership is further distinguished by what might be termed a three mission principle, which fulfills the missions of the partnership participants as well as those of the collaborative endeavor.

Component Theories of Nonprofit Partnerships

In table 7.1, we offer seven component principles of nonprofit-first partnership theory drawn from the experiences of the nonprofit executives we interviewed.

Table 7.1. Nonprofit-First Principles for Partnership.

Components	Description, Rationale, and/or Examples Among the Partnerships
Nonprofit-first	The perception and depiction of events from the point of view, lens, or frame of the nonprofit sector actor is essential to address the practical problems created for nonprofit executives who must look to nonprofit pedagogy as separate and distinct from that of public management and business administration. In the absence of nonprofit-first pedagogy, the field of nonprofit practice has depended upon experiential learning and anecdotal models that lead to nonprofit partnerships improving with experience and time. This practice has led to the atomization of partnership practices and inefficiency of partnership replication and performance.
Nonprofits must form partnerships to fulfill their missions.	As a result of their role in civil society—creating public value, building the "commons," serving as intermediaries, and facilitating institutions—nonprofits must form partnerships to fulfill their missions. The act of forming a partnership builds networks of problem-solving actors and strengthens civil society by bonding people of differing interests together.
The principle of a third mission.	The primacy of mission fulfillment in nonprofit-first partnerships occurs when the actors align three missions: those of each actor and of the partnership endeavor.
The partnership process is a desired outcome and rationale for engaging in partnership endeavors.	The process of forming a partnership is considered a worthy outcome of nonprofit partnership because it generates public value or contributes to the greater good of society. The notion of the greater good is a justification nonprofit executives point to as an influence on their decision to enter into a partnership.
Mutuality of rights and responsibilities lead to the validation of each partner by the other.	The perception of each participant that their partner contributes to the success of the partnership is a sought-after benefit beyond mission fulfillment of the partnership. This aspect of nonprofit partnership builds upon the social capital of a community and creates a system of performance among independent organizations that can be engaged to solve the problems of society.
Benefits of partnership accrue over time.	Nonprofit executives make the case that the benefits of partnership are direct outcomes, much like the stated performance goals of the partnership endeavor. Benefits are also indirect in the respect that as a partnership progresses through its work and endures over time, positive feelings among the participants and partner stakeholders produce more opportunity and increase its effectiveness.
Volunteerism and fairness are central to the partnership dynamic.	The values of volunteerism cascade throughout partnership governance, labor, commitment, and effectiveness, contributing to the complexity of bringing differing organizational forms and cultures together. Fairness is a framing aspect of the partnership design and performance.

Engaging in partnership is a fundamental principle of the field of nonprofit organizations and a core concept driving our proposed additions to nonprofit theory, yet this principle is not well understood by government, business, and even the nonprofits themselves. Conceptually, partnership is complex because the institutional form of partnership—that of at least two separate organizations coming together to accomplish an agreed-upon purpose—comprises a system of action where, through direct and indirect outcomes, the nonprofit actors commit to fulfilling three missions simultaneously: their own, their partner's, and the partnership's. Nonprofit actors derive certain benefits from the processes of forming and fulfilling their partnership obligations, and these benefits include strengthening nonprofit networks and providing information to policy makers, grant makers, and others based on their work as facilitators and intermediary institutions.

Throughout the interviews, the nonprofit executives outlined a principle of autonomy that was crucial to their sense of whether a partnership was worthy of their investment and participation. Choosing when to engage in partnership, with whom, and for what purpose were important features of this principle. In our understanding, mandated collaboration and partnerships typically generated conditions that were less than ideal and that frequently resulted in misaligned expectations between the sponsors of the partnership and the participants. In partnerships where two organizations were brought together by a third party, participants were less inclined to embrace their partners beyond the mechanical, transactional roles required to perform the work of the partnership endeavor. The nonprofit executives stated repeatedly that such induced partnership arrangements had more to do with political expedience or the desire of the funder or other third party to model partnership than with actual partnership processes and results. These partnership relationships were often framed by written contracts where the performance capacity of the actors served to dominate the relationship. Organizations participated in these so-called partnerships for a variety of reasons, including loyalty to a third-party funder, a deliberate strategy for revenue generation, or some other strategic advantage.

Through our interviews with nonprofit leaders, we learned that the benefits of partnership arise through incremental and time-consuming processes. Nonprofit executives revealed that important partnerships may be planned deliberately, but frequently unfold in ways that are gradual, typically aspirational, and often unknown at the outset of the partnership endeavor.

We also found that partnerships benefited nonprofit actors by conferring on them legitimacy among counterparts perceived as peer institutions. Legitimacy arises from actions and expectations of mutuality and commitment between partners, so successful partnership experiences are reflected in the validation one partner bestows upon the other in terms of advocacy or promotion on their behalf, of partnership longevity, and/or of a track record of successful and successive partnership endeavors. Nonprofit executives recognized mutuality in the reciprocity, predictability, and flexibility of their partners, which suggested opportunities for trust.

Signs of Partnership Readiness Necessary for Forming Important and Meaningful Partnerships

Nonprofit executives contemplating nonprofit partnership can gain valuable takeaways from our research.

Timing

From the perspective of the nonprofit organization, the timing of partnership is important in at least two ways. First, as we have discussed, many nonprofit actors may not be ready for a partnership and the investment of labor and resources necessary to achieve its success. Second, public and private policy makers and funders must be patient with the nonprofits engaged in collaboration due to the time-consuming process of developing trust over time through multiple interactions. In complex initiatives, these time-consuming processes are not well served by short project horizons. Policy makers and grant makers hoping to stimulate meaningful partnerships should consider phasing their investments over time and establishing progress benchmarks and adaptive timetables.

Shared Values

Meaningful partnerships endure because of shared values and functions between the participants. Shared values, which may or may not be strictly mission-based, drive each member to take on the duties of stewardship for the partnership and transcend the isolated, self-interested transactions often contrived by funders. Shared values characterize partnership just as much as mutual benefits, yet can be more difficult to discover or nurture. This dilemma can be attributed to several concurrent requirements: trust-building by the leaders of both partner organizations, leadership actions at the beginning of a joint venture, and removal of risks during the collaboration. According to this point of view, meaningful partnership would be based on familiarity between organizations, and trust would be nurtured at all relevant levels of staff in both partnering organizations.

Adaptive Nature

A sub-theme common to many of the case narratives was the notion that executives typically attributed open-ended, flexible, and adaptive processes as leading to more intense connections between partners. One illustration of these points is offered by the one executive who noted,

> Unexpected successes happened! One is that professional musicians became committed to the cause through their interactions with the children in our after-school program and [this] changed the relationship with our partner ... and this required openness to changes with our partner due to circumstances. In the end, this strengthened our relationship [as] the scope of the program had to change. There were time challenges in the beginning. More and different types of parent involvement was necessary and encouraged us to seek other collaboration work with them.

We also noted that many nonprofit executives opined that flexibility was not part of the undergirding ethos of all partnership arrangements. One executive suggested that "policy makers, funders, and nonprofits frequently talk past one another due to their different understandings of the requirements of collaboration and partnership. The people charged with making policy and allocating funding tend not to credit the views of the nonprofit recipients as credible for changing their policy and funding implementation models and expectations for partnership."

A tool to address miscommunications that actors might use is an adaptation of the "logic model" processes commonly applied to project outcomes in grant and contracted work.[10] Policy and grant makers typically frame their logic model processes with their own mission and purpose, rather than on the outcomes that are important to the nonprofit actor. Nonprofit actors, by contrast, seek mission-based partnership benefits that include outcomes contributing to the public good; for example, the good feelings, familiarity, and experience a nonprofit gains from an act of partnering that may produce no direct, measurable outcomes. Using a strict logic model format can dissuade actors from innovating or reaching unanticipated, yet beneficial results. Hence, partnership processes and outcome logic models should allow for emergent, shifting needs and partnership-mission outcome logic models as well as unanticipated benefits of partnership.[11]

Toward a Nonprofit-First Approach

Despite the strides that we have made in advancing nonprofit-first partnership as a distinction of the field of nonprofit sector study and knowledge, questions remain for the practice of partnerships that involve at least one nonprofit participant for not only nonprofits but also government, business, and philanthropic leaders desiring to encourage effective partnership processes, performance outcomes, and mission impact. As we have pointed out earlier, while government and business, which derive their legitimacy from the rule of law and the marketplace, the legitimacy of the nonprofit sector arises principally from people voluntarily coming together for the purpose of shared values. Put another way: for nonprofit-first partnership arrangements, the partner actors' voluntary participation serves to validate the collaboration endeavor and confer greater good and the creation of public value upon the larger society. Examples of greater good and public value are partnership outcomes that stimulate and encourage collaboration, create the "third space" necessary to incubate ideas to transform society, and leverage resources to increase the return on their investments toward systemwide change. These outcomes are framed by expectations of fair play and equality of participation, which are bound within the nonprofit sector as some of its most distinctive characteristics.

Therefore, it should come as no surprise that volunteer-driven nonprofit actors in collaborative endeavors would look for reciprocal fair play and equity from their partnership counterparts—whether or not their partners are driven by, or even recognize, these same principles. In practice, many partnership endeavors fail to achieve the nonprofit's perceived ideals in terms of the partnership's costs and risks. Because of the role they play in nonprofit partnership, the central values of volunteerism on partnership culture and values, emotional intelligence required of nonprofit executives and their partnership counterparts, and the concept of fair play in the partnership deserve much more scrutiny in the study and practice of partnership.

Since nonprofit grant makers need partners to perform their own mission fulfillment and frequently require partner arrangements of their grantees, it is ironic that they often create the conditions for contrived and superficial partnership arrangements. More study is needed to understand the tendencies that grant makers and other philanthropic actors follow in funding partnership, which may lead to functional or dysfunctional partnerships for nonprofit organizations.

In addition, few scholars have compared the implications of the fact that public, private, and nonprofit actors use, understand, and refer to interorganizational relationships in different ways. Without a nuanced understanding of partnership purpose, authority, and accountability, partnerships may fail to reach their goals because they are poorly conceived, led, and designed; in addition, they are often slow to adjust to changes in the partnership's actors or environment and take time to initiate, develop, and mature. Many of the nonprofit executives we interviewed emphasized the time and resources needed for network development, leverage, or amplification that public and philanthropic funding seldom acknowledge or appreciate. They also emphasized sponsors' common expectations that nonprofits will contribute their own resources, uncompensated, to accomplish the partnership mission.

Despite the many obstacles our research has uncovered for the study and practice of nonprofit-first partnerships, we are confident that the benefits of this approach outweigh the challenges. Moreover, we would assert that just as partnerships typify nonprofits, so nonprofit-first partnerships are themselves the optimal means of highlighting the nonprofit's own stakes and aspirations in such a relationship.

Toward a Nonprofit-First Partnership Dashboard

We close this book with an effort to offer nonprofit managers, leaders, and others a useful tool drawn from the experiences their peers have shared with us on non-profit-first partnerships. "Data dashboards" are visual displays that feature the most important information needed to achieve specific goals. The origins of the digital dashboards are traceable to 1970s and 1980s-era business management and decision-making theory, and today dashboards are regularly used in business performance management.[12] Since scholars tell us that effective dashboards should be designed as monitoring tools that are understood at a glance to gauge exactly how well an organization is performing,[13] nonprofit executives, such as those who participated in this study, can use this dashboard to process the complexities of partnership potential and performance information clearly and concisely.

We are adapting the concept of a "data dashboard" to organize the key bits of information drawn from our interviews with nonprofit executives underlying the primary research of this book. Our nonprofit-first partnership dashboard is depicted in table 7.2. The column headers offer dashboard users an at-a-glance assessment through a simple "yes/no" test of performance on a collection of partnership characteristics and other criteria drawn from nonprofit-first partnership. Our view is that a more detailed and involved assessment mechanism for performance is possible, but in this treatment would unnecessarily distract dashboard users from the purpose of the tool. Since the yes/no assessment in the dashboard column offers the opportunity for a "scoring" on partnership performance based on the presence or absence of a particular condition of partnership that is observable by the participants or an interested third party, we devised a simple system to allow for a rating of partnership components and the overall partnership for the purposes of future comparison. We offer an additional weighted score option of 2 for instances where a partnership may have a characteristic that is stronger in performance than the yes/no response and scoring might accommodate and thus merits a slightly higher weighting. This type of allowance is made for cases in which partnership satisfaction was extremely high, as was reflected in the view of nonprofit executives who had rated their partnerships as 10 on our scale where a score of 1 meant that the partnership met none of its goals while a score of 10 indicated that the partnership met all of its goals.

The row headers for table 7.2 were devised based on the themes introduced and subsequently reinforced in the progression of chapter narratives in this book. Another way to look at the themes is as indicators we have identified whose presence or absence offer a means of comparing and forecasting partnership character, viability, and performance.

Table 7.2. Nonprofit-First Partnership Performance Dashboard.

Partner Design Parameter, Performance, or Outcome Indicator	Descriptor		Yes/No 0 = No; 1 = Yes; 2 = Strong Yes
I. Nonprofit-First Partnership	Is this partnership prompted by a nonprofit actor?		
II. Preferred Partnership Characteristics	Evidence of:	Operational mutual benefits	
		Relationship (governance and authority) equity	
		Relationship reciprocity	
		Relationship trust-building	
	Fulfills the mission of each of the partnering participants		
	Evidence of shared financial/nonfinancial resources		
	Evidence of strengthening the larger community		
	Presence of a formal contract		
III. Organization Mission Fulfillment	Are the partnership outcomes fulfilling the mission by merit of transactional measures such as people served?		
	Are the partnership outcomes fulfilling the mission by merit of societal transformation through systems or networks?		
IV. Partnership Mission Fulfilled (Third Mission)	To fulfill the mission of the partnership endeavor, does the work of the required partner:	Complement the partner mission?	
		Supplement the partner mission?	
		Converge with the partner mission?	
V. Partnership Readiness Indicators	Evidence of partnership preparedness:	Are the partners ready for partnership?	
		Are the partners willing (voluntarily) for partnership?	
		Is the timing for partnership appropriate?	
		Can the partners cope with ambiguities of partnership?	
		Is there interest in renewing or continuing a partnership?	

VI. Balance of Partnership Authority & Governance	In the practice of the partnership:	If there is a lead partner, does the subordinate partner have shared governance and veto authority?
		Do both partners perceive a relationship equality?
		Is there a mutual validation of the partners by the partners?
	Do the partnership participants make decisions and resolve problems together?	
VII. Greater Good & Public Value	Evidence of the impact of partnership outcomes or transformations for the larger society:	Stronger social networks and social capital?
		Greater trust between organizations and with the larger community
		Validation of organizations as valued institutions
		Reduction of negative community pathologies (crime, poverty, illiteracy, truancy)
VIII. Commitment to Partnership Excellence	Evidence of partnership process improvement:	Did the partnership benefit from experiential learning, or did the leaders learn ways to improve the partnership from experience?
		Does the partnership involve the active leadership of both partners?
		Did the partners adapt to changes in conditions, needs, and circumstances for the benefit of the partnership?
		Did the partners' organizational administration and priorities align to support partnership success?

The dashboard indicators may apply to planning stages of partnership and inform the decision-making on partnership viability, partnership design, and partnership performance benchmarks; during the operations stages of partnership as way to predict outcome trajectory; or as an end-stage assessment of partnership performance.

The origins of the row header themes or indicators of nonprofit-first partnership performance are traceable to repeated and consistent references nonprofit executive respondents gave of their important partnership cases between a nonprofit and a nonprofit, a nonprofit and government, and a nonprofit and business.

The Indicators

Since our dashboard concept is conceived as a tool for nonprofit executives, leaders, policy makers, philanthropic institutions, and others to judge or map a single partnership, the lead indicator establishes the partnership as anchored from a nonprofit-first perspective. This starting point for monitoring partnership performance is consistent with the context we have established in the book and is important to synchronize the remaining seven categories as executives and others completing the form use the perspective of the nonprofit actor.

The second indicator concerns partnership characteristics that nonprofit executives tell us are important at an early or planning stage of relationship-building. The preferred partnership indicator tests whether partnership operations have potential for mutuality and equity between participants; a mechanism for resolving conflict or unanticipated conditions; agreement on whether or not a partnership fulfills the independent missions of the two partners; and insight to inform on the partnership efficacy for the community.

The next indicator considers whether the individual partner missions align, offering a predictor of the mutual commitment behaviors of each partner to the success of the other over a joint agreement to achieve a third mission, that of the partnership. Differing degrees of alignment are a signal of the limit in commitment of one partner toward the other.

The fourth indicator considers the partnership mission, or the third mission, and the commitment behaviors required of each partner to fulfill that third mission. This indicator offers insight into the scope and scale of the partnership, providing a sense to the participants of the commitment potential for performance complexity and the added costs and risks that complex conditions might add to the endeavor. As has been discussed throughout this book, the difference between partnerships whose outcomes are derived through transactional outputs, such as clients served and funds expended, and transformational outcomes, such as systemic change in the organization or society, is an important characteristic of important and meaningful nonprofit-first partnership.

The fifth indicator considers an organization's self-assessment of its readiness and willingness to enter into a partnership and how the partnership timing aligns the partners' abilities for overcoming barriers, ambiguous conditions, and societal circumstances.

The sixth indicator considers the perception of the nonprofit-first partner of mutuality in equity in the operational workings of the partnership. Since most nonprofit executives asserted that their sense of fairness and of a "level playing field" was essential to their view of successful, meaningful, and important partnership, this indicator offers insight into the relationship dynamic and perceived respect between the partners.

The seventh indicator considers the potential for impactful change and suggests a partnership committed for a longer duration and high performance. Although the nonprofit-first partnership cases stimulated by grant makers and the funding of nonprofit intermediary organizations may readily make use of this indicator as a tool for partnership mission fulfillment, partnerships stimulated by a single nonprofit actor engaged with other nonprofits and government will point to successful mission fulfillment and institutional validity and credibility from a "yes" performance rating.

The eighth and last indicator will convey to third parties the sense of the nonprofit-first partners' status as "learning organizations" committed to process improvements, partnership quality, and high performance.

Interpreting Dashboard Scores

Although future research is necessary to establish a refined scorecard and performance ratio for nonprofit-first partnership as proposed in this closing chapter, readers of this book are asked to consider the dashboard as a tool to plan and design partnerships based upon the research, findings, analysis, and conclusions of this study. The dashboard might also provide an opportunity for comparison of operating partnership performance across sector partnerships and subsector partnerships, and as a recap of completed partnership endeavors.

Notes

1. Glaser, Barney G., and Anselm L. Strauss. *The Discovery of Grounded Theory: Strategies for Qualitative Research* (Piscataway, NJ: Transaction Publishers, 2009).

2. Powell, W. W., and R. Steinberg. *The Nonprofit Sector: A Research Handbook* (New Haven, CT: Yale University Press, 2006); Selsky, J. W., and B. Parker. "Cross-sector partnerships to address social issues: Challenges to theory and practice." *Journal of Management* 31, no. 6 (2005): 849–873.

3. Van Til, J. *Growing Civil Society: From Nonprofit Sector to Third Space* (Bloomington: Indiana University Press, 2000); Hall, P. D. *"Inventing the Nonprofit Sector" and Other Essays on Philanthropy, Voluntarism, and Nonprofit Organizations* (Baltimore: JHU Press, 2001).

4. Anheier, Helmut. "Resourcing Nonprofit Organizations," in *Nonprofit Organizations: Theory, Management, Policy* (London: Routledge, 2014), 203–224; Toepler, Stefan, and Helmut K. Anheier. "Organizational Theory and Nonprofit Management: An Overview," in *Future of Civil Society: Making Central European Nonprofit-Organizations Work*, ed. Annette Zimmer and Eckhard Priller (Wiesbaden, Germany: Verlag für Sozialwissenschaften, 2004), 253–270; Herman, Robert D., and David O. Renz. "Advancing Nonprofit Organizational Effectiveness Research and Theory: Nine Theses." *Nonprofit Management and Leadership* 18, no. 4 (2008): 399–415, doi:10.1002/nml.195.

5. Bryson, John M. "Introduction," in *Strategic planning for Public and Nonprofit Organizations: A Guide to Strengthening and Sustaining Organizational Achievement*, vol. 1 (San Francisco, CA: John Wiley and Sons, 2011), xi–xx; Denhardt, Robert B., and

Janet Vinzant Denhardt. "The New Public Service: Serving rather than steering." *Public Administration Review* 60, no. 6 (2000): 549–559, doi:10.1111/0033-3352.00117; Toepler, Stefan, and Helmut K. Anheier. "Organizational Theory and Nonprofit Management: An Overview," in *Future of Civil Society: Making Central European Nonprofit-Organizations Work*, ed. Annette Zimmer and Eckhard Priller (Wiesbaden, Germany: Verlag für Sozialwissenschaften, 2004), 253–270; Ospina, Sonia, William Diaz, and James F. O'Sullivan. "Negotiating Accountability: Managerial lessons from identity-based nonprofit organizations." *Nonprofit and Voluntary Sector Quarterly* 31, no. 1 (2002): 5–31, doi:10.1177/0899764002311001.

6. Brudney, Jeffrey L. *Emerging areas of Volunteering* (Association for Research on Nonprofit Organizations and Voluntary Action (ARNOVA), 2009).

7. Austin, J. E. *The Collaboration Challenge: How Nonprofits and Businesses Succeed Through Strategic Alliances*, vol. 109 (San Francisco, CA: John Wiley and Sons, 2010); Anheier, H. K. *Nonprofit Organizations: an Introduction* (London: Routledge, 2006).

8. Ostrom, Elinor, and James Walker. Trust and Reciprocity: Interdisciplinary Lessons for Experimental Research (New York: Russell Sage Foundation, 2003), 49, 51–52, 154–155; Solomon, Robert C., and Fernando Flores. *Building Trust in Business, Politics, Relationships and Life* (Oxford: Oxford University Press, 2003).

9. McCabe, Kevin. "A Cognitive Theory of Reciprocal Exchange," in *Trust and Reciprocity*, ed. Elinor Ostrom and James Walker (New York: Russell Sage Foundation, 2003), 147–169.

10. Frumkin, P. *Strategic Giving: The Art and Science of Philanthropy* (Chicago: University of Chicago Press, 2006).

11. Bedsworth, William, Ann Goggins-Gregory, and Don Howard. *Non-Profit Overhead Costs: Breaking the Vicious Cycle of Misleading Reporting, Unrealistic Expectations, and Pressure to Conform* (Boston: Bridgespan Group, 2008); Granovetter, Mark. "The Strength of Weak Ties: A Network Theory Revisited." *Sociological Theory* 1, no. 1 (1983): 201–233, doi:10.2307/202051.

12. Few, Stephen. *Information Dashboard Design* (Sebastopol, CA: O'Reilly Media Inc., 2006); Wayne W. *Performance Dashboards: Measuring, Monitoring, and Managing Your Business* (San Francisco, CA: John Wiley and Sons, 2006).

13. Smith, V. S. "Data Dashboard as Evaluation and Research Communication Tool," in *Data Visualization, Part 2. New Directions for Evaluation*, no. 140, ed. T. Azzam and S. Evergreen (San Francisco, CA: John Wiley & Sons, 2013), 21–45.

Index

STUART C. MENDEL is the first Fellow appointed by the Nonprofit Academic Centers Council, co-editor of the *Journal of Ideology*, and associate editor for acquisitions for the *Journal of Nonprofit Education and Leadership*. He is the Executive Director of the National Center on Nonprofit Enterprise. Previously he served for twenty years as assistant dean and director of the Center for Nonprofit Policy and Practice at Cleveland State University. He is author of *Mediating Organizations, Private Government, and Civil Society: Disinvestment Through the Preservation of Wealth in Cleveland, Ohio (1950–1990)* and *The Essential Fundraising Guide for Deans and Directors in Higher Education.*

JEFFERY L. BRUDNEY is the Betty and Dan Cameron Family Distinguished Professor of Innovation in the Nonprofit Sector at the University of North Carolina–Wilmington. His publications include *Fostering Volunteer Programs in the Public Sector: Planning, Initiating, and Managing Voluntary Activities.* He directed the film *Building a Better Wilmington: Giving and Volunteering in the Port City,* which was screened at the Cucalorus Film Festival.

www.ingramcontent.com/pod-product-compliance
Lightning Source LLC
Chambersburg PA
CBHW071023280326
41935CB00011B/1465